Contemporary Indian Criminology

About the Author

James Vadackumchery, formerly Criminologist, Police Training College, Thiruvananthapuram; Author of 60 books and nearly 1000 articles published; a name listed in Limca Book of Records 2006 for authoring most books in the special area of crime, police and justice; Recipient of the Distinguished International Scholar Award for Life Time Achievements in Criminology of the American Society of Criminology 2003; honoured by the University of Calcutta for insightful writings in Criminology by awarding the prestigious Supreba Deb Gold Medal 2007, recipient of the Award of Excellence by the Archdiocese of Changanassery, 2007 and a PROFILE viewed by 5 per cent of the 200 million people in LinkedIn during 2012; and an Advocate in Thiruvananthapuram Bar. Dr. James Vadackumchery, M.A. (Crim.), D.Ph., LL.B., Ph.D., First rank holder for B.A. (Crim.) of Karnatak University and M.A. (Crim.) of Saugor University, second rank holder for LL.B. (Law) and D.Ph. examinations; Ph.D. in Criminal Justice (Kerala University), Gold Medalist and National Merit Scholarship Winner/twice.

Member of many professional organizations; Visiting Professor in universities and institutions of higher learning, research and training including Reserve Bank of India; National Judicial Academy etc.; Member, Board of Studies in Criminology of Karnatak and Saugor Universities and State Advisory Board on Correctional Administration; Member, State Prison Review Committee (Kerala), Consultant to Police Welfare Commission; Public Speaker and Human Rights Activist; Broadcaster over AIR and Telecaster in Indian and International T.V. networks and a constant Consultant to the media (print and electronic) on criminological and human rights issues.

Examiner in Universities, Service Commissions and Public Undertakings; Evaluator of research works and theses and supervising teacher for Ph.D. degree in Kerala and Mahatma Gandhi Universities; and a name listed in the International Dictionary of Biographies of the IBC, Cambridge.

Contemporary Indian Criminology

Dr. JAMES VADACKUMCHERY
Criminologist & Advocate

CONCEPT PUBLISHING COMPANY PVT. LTD.
NEW DELHI-110059

ISBN-13 : 978-93-5125-100-2

First Published 2015

Published and Printed by

Concept Since 1974

Concept Publishing Company Pvt. Ltd.
A/15-16, Commercial Block, Mohan Garden
New Delhi-110059 (India)
T: 25351460, 25351794, *F*: 091-11-25357109
E: publishing@conceptpub.com, W: www.conceptpub.com
Editorial Office: H-13, Bali Nagar, New Delhi-110 015, India.

Cataloging in Publication Data—*Courtesy:* D.K. Agencies (P) Ltd. <docinfo@dkagencies.com>

Vadackumchery, James, author.
Contemporary Indian criminology / Dr. James Vadackumchery.
pages cm
Includes bibliographical references (pages) and index.
ISBN 9789351251002

1. Criminology—India. 2. Criminal justice, Administration of—India. I. Title.

DDC 364.954 23

Dedicated to

CHAKKAPPEN [Jacob]
MARIAMMA [Mary]
—My parents

and

Anna, George, Ammu
Maria & Ann
—My grand children

and

Abhilash, Martin
—My sons-in-law

and

Neethu, Neethie
—My daughters

and

MARY
—My Wife

Preface

I spent about six months in U.S.A. during 2010-11 and then I got an opportunity to directly watch and study the crimes committed in United States of America. I could see the Americans exactly like the Indians in many aspects and respects. Both Indians and Americans commit crimes and many studies and researches about the etiology of crimes have been conducted in America. Perhaps—or better, certainly—criminology has its development in U.S.A. While I was staying there, I got ample opportunities to hold discussions with criminologists there and had recourses to very good libraries which contained a lot of authentic books in criminology, justice and allied subjects. I made a survey of literature to study the development of criminological thoughts from demonology to victimology. My objective has been to study: "What is the true etiology (cause) of crime and criminal behaviour?" Criminologists have been holding different views about the etiology of crime. My more than four decades of study and researches in the special and specific areas of crime and criminal behaviour have proved that the cause-effect relationship has nothing much to do with crime-doers and the crimes they commit. Crime may be an effect of a person's act, yet one cannot say what makes him to commit that act. Yes, the crime is a human act and very much a social fact.

A few years ago, I formulated a theory about the causation of crime and the theory was called the **Push-Pull-Ego Factor** theory. I got it published in scientific journals of criminology, in newspapers of repute, in periodicals and finally in two of my books titled (1) *Police Criminology and Crimes,* **(2)** *Indian Police and Nexus*

Crimes. I felt that I was able to explain the etiology of crime in a scientific way. In America, I wanted to develop the theory already formed or formulated by me. I think that I have been successful in my venture and, therefore, the title *Contemporary Indian Criminology*. I got my observations published in a *Blog*– [http://james_vadackumchery.blogspot.com] in English.

Proudly I say that I received many feedbacks, criticisms (*Pro and Contra*), appreciations and adherents incredibly. The theory of causality has been a topic of study for my Ph.D. course and, therefore, my attempt was not at all to find out a cause-effect relationship between a crime-doer and the crime he committed. An approach to identify the cause-effect relationship in every crime detected will be an exercise in futility. Hence, my attempt has been to explain why people commit crimes and I have been attempting to answer the question from my own theory of crime causation, say the *Push-Pull-Ego Factor* theory.

Why human beings behave the way they do? There may not be any fool-proof or perfect answer to that question. Psychologists, criminologists, spiritual men, moralists, theologians, sociologists, politicians, priests and so on answer the question in their own way—most favourable or palatable to them. Commission of crimes is not a noble act. It is mean to be a criminal. Lombroso, the Italian anthropologist and prison-doctor said that every criminal was atavistic (reversion to an earlier type). Of course, his theory today is a rejected one; yet the fact remains that he observed in criminals some features which were found in apes. Forget about him and his theory of atavism (Positive School). What about Goddard who said that the criminals were mentally retarded? Did he mean that the people committed crimes as they were more influenced by instincts (not intelligence) seen in animals? This theory too is a rejected one now as there are intelligent, very intelligent and super-intelligent criminals amidst us. In Classical School of Criminology, the pleasure-pain principle (hedonism) was brought by Bentham and Beccaria to explain why people committed crimes. Animals, being activated by instinctual forces, go after pleasure (avoiding pain) and man too sought after pleasure when he committed the crime. Was it the thinking of the Classical School of Criminology? Of course, the Classical School's approach (theory) is not fully rejected till now as many Penal Codes, Codes of Procedure and

Evidence Acts were framed under the pleasure-pain theory and punishments awarded employing the hedonistic calculus. St. Paul, the Apostle, St. Thomas Aquinas and many other theologians spoke about animal instincts and their impad on human behaviour (criminal behaviour). Were they wrong in their observations and interpretations? 'Animal–men' is an expression in many languages to show that some people behave just like animals. Every man has an animal in him and sometimes, that animal comes out. Some police officials were (are) nicknamed once upon a time in India as *'Lion, Leopard, Vulture, Tiger'* showing that their behaviour resembled (resembles) the behaviour of wild animals. The Penal Code in any country contains traditional crimes (crimes seen from the birth of a man or from time immemorial) which include murder, rape, hurt, grievous hurt, theft, robbery, etc. Animals too commit the same acts (such as murder, hurt, grievous hurt, rape, theft, etc.) and, therefore, such crimes will continue till the man is on earth. Darwin's theory of evolution emphatically asserts that man is an evolution from apes and precisely, therefore, he cannot be completely devoid of animal behaviour. No doubt, the animals behave in a particular way because of the instincts in them. In simple language, an instinct is a natural or innate impulse, inclination or aptitude. In psychology and also in layman's understanding, it is an inborn pattern of activity or tendency to action common to a given biological species. In animals, instincts are the *Activating Forces* to do something or *Activators*. Of course, animals can do anything as per their instincts whereas man, as a social being with intelligence, reason and morality cannot do things as simply activated by the instincts. Hence, the *Instincts* in man is called *Drives*. In other words, Instincts+ Intelligence and reasoning power is what is called *Drive* in a man. This is to say that a *Drive* is an instinct guided or controlled by intelligence, reason and morality. In psychology a *Drive* means an inner urge that stimulates a response, inciting or repressing action; a basic or instinctive need (see The Random House College Dictionary). In this book, I name the *Instincts as Push Factors*. *'Push'* here means an urge to some action or course.

William Adrien Bonger (1876-1940) spoke about (1) Criminal motivations [i.e., animal instincts] and (2) Stimulating situations through which the criminal motivations were executed. He observed that "it is possible for the environment to create a great egoist, but it does not mean that an egoist must necessarily become a criminal". I think that Bonger was talking about **Pull Factors** when he said about '**Environment**'. Accordingly, in order that the crime must be committed, he believed that there must be facilitating environmental conditions. Criminologists in Europe and especially in America recognized Bonger's concept of 'Facilitating Environmental Conditions' for committing crimes when they spoke about the etiology of crime. Many, therefore, conducted researches in that line. As a result, a number of sociological theories came into existence. The prominent theories were of the Chicago School (Ecological Theories) and of Edwin H. Sutherland (Differential Association Theory). In explaining the etiology of crime and delinquency, social structural theories were very helpful [Anomie theory, sub-culture theories, culture conflict theory, cultural lag theory, etc.] and influential. Quatlet (1885) said once: "Everybody is guilty in crime...except the criminal". Is it true to think so? Anyway, social structural theories attempted to explain why crimes took place in society. Till then, the assumption was that a man committed crimes because he had some physiological defects. This assumption was questioned by social structural theorists. In America, the social scientists turned their attention from the individual criminals to the social structure, environments, etc., which they thought were important factors to cause crime. In other words, they gave a lot of importance to **Pull Factors**. The emphasis was shifted to the characteristics of the social melieu [**Pull Factors**] from the characteristics of the individual law breaker (**Push Factors**]. Nevertheless, two questions remained to be answered and they were–

1. Why didn't all people exposed to the same type of **Pull Factors** [Social Structure] become criminals?
2. Why did many people who were not exposed to the same **Pull Factors** [Social Structure] become criminals?

I am of the firm view that neither the **Push Factors** alone nor the **Pull Factors** alone can or will make someone a criminal. In my view, the personality (**Ego**) is developed by and only through an interaction between the **Push** and the **Pull Factors**. This will be further elaborated in the first chapter. The American sociologists argued that there were some processes involved and those processes would explain the differential reaction of people to their environments **[Pull Factors]**. Gabriel Tarde's (1843-1904) and Sutherlands' contributions in that area were quite noteworthy. The 'imitation' of Tarde and the 'differential association' coupled with the process of learning of Sutherland made attempts to explain why people committed crimes. Nevertheless, further researches proved that the sociological factors could only work at best as indirect causes of criminal behaviour. Psychological theories started to explain criminal behaviour by acknowledging the working of human 'Psyche' and Psychodynamic factors within the internal system. Psychologists thought that their explanation was an answer to the question: Why did an individual involve in the commission of crimes? One doubts very much how far or how much the psychological interpretation of the causes of crime from the angle of human 'Psyche' acceptable? In my view neither the sociological approaches nor the psychological interpretations of the causes of crime and criminal behaviour satisfy a true seeker of "**cause-effect**" relationship in criminology. I prefer to say of "Related Factors" rather than "Causal Factors". The sociological, psychological, hereditary, endocrinological, cultural, political, economic, etc., factors are crime-related factors and not at all causal factors in criminology. The fact that crime related factors exist does not mean that a crime should take place. At the most, we may say that a crime is likely to take place and nothing more or nothing less. For, one cannot find a "**Cause-Effect**" relationship in criminology. Hence, the study of the Etiology of crime means a study of the **"Related Factors"** of crime and not the **"Causal Factors"** of crime.

In my approach of **Push-Pull-Ego Factor** theory, I do not say that it is a theory explaining the "Etiology of Crime"—rather a theory which speaks about 'guilt feelings' accompanying a criminal act. Of course, the "Feeling of Guilt" may work as a powerful source in some to stop the commission of crimes. More about this approach is discussed in Chapter I of this book.

My theory in nutshell is –

1. The **Push Factors** is the root cause of all sorts of crime. They activate the individuals to commit a crime. The higher one goes (namely, writing of research books, doing scientific researches) in his activities, the instincts give way

to intelligence. Crimes are the violations of law and precisely, therefore, they are of a low type of human activities.

2. The **Pull Factors** are plenty in society. There are positive factors as well as negative factors. The **Push Factors** are pulled by positive or negative pull factors. The **Push** and **Pull Factors** interact to form an **Ego** (personality) in a growing child. This interaction is in a socio-cultural melieu which accepts or rejects certain values. The development of **Ego** depends upon the values accepted/rejected by the socio-cultural melieu. This is the reason why I say that the **Ego** should be developed in an upright way in the right direction. How to decide the uprightness of the **Ego** development? There are some scales/criteria for the same to decide the uprightness of **Ego** development in the right direction. This is discussed in Chapter 1 elaborately.
3. The infrastructure or the foundation of the **Ego** is built up by the time a child becomes 13-14 years of age. If his **Ego** is uprightly formed in the right direction, certainly he will refrain himself from the commission of crimes. Or, if at all he commits a crime, he will have the **feeling of guilt** in him. This will be further elaborated in the 1st chapter of this book.

India has a variety of crimes which America does not have. Why? The reason is that the **Pull Factors** in India are certainly different from the same in U.S.A. Naxalism is seen in India. Visa/ N.O.C. rackets are plenty. Employment Frauds, Investment Frauds, Corruption money-fixing are seen in India. What about the situation in U.S.A? There too, various types of crimes almost similar to what are seen in India can be found out but they will be the products of the socio-cultural environments prevailing there. Nevertheless, the **Push Factors** are the same in India and in America. An American may have a guilt feeling when he commits an act which causes no guilt feelings among Indians? This depends upon the inculcation of the values in U.S.A. and the same in India. What may cause guilt feelings in Americans need not necessarily cause the same in Indians. There may be absolute values and they may be same in U.S.A. and in India. There are relative values as well. Hence, one cannot say that there will be guilt feelings in

Americans as well as Indians when they commit one and same act. If there is a guilt feeling when an act is committed/omitted, certainly it will stop the commission of crimes in India as well as in America. Or alternatively, both Indians and Americans will experience guilt feelings after the commission of a crime. Hence, my theory is: The interaction between the **Push Factors** and **Pull Factors** results in the formation of an **Ego** in a given socio-cultural melieu. One will have guilt feelings depending upon the formation of his/her **Ego**. If the **Ego** is formed in an upright way in the right direction, the person will refrain from the commission of a crime or alternatively, he will experience intense **guilt feelings** during or after the commission of crimes.

This book gives a number of crimes seen in India and I have tried to interpret them in the background of the theory I have formulated. Any suggestions to improve the theory/approach will be gratefully appreciated and acknowledged. I thank everyone especially my wife, MARY and my daughter, Neethie who helped me to bring out this title.

DALLAS, TEXAS
U.S.A.

Dr. James Vadackumchery
Criminologist & Advocate

Contents

Part – I

A New Approach in the Cause-Effect Relations in Criminology

A Scientific Theory on the Causation of Crime—that has been my aim for the last four decades. And, I have a theory now and in simple terms, it is nothing but *there is or there can be no cause for any crime.* There exists no **cause–effect** relationship between a crime-doer and the crime he commits. When a crime is committed, the crime-doer is made the sole cause and he is punished for the same without probing into the *why* of the crime.

During my career as a criminologist in police, I had any number of opportunities to interact with known, declared and convicted crime-doers of various kinds and descriptions. As a child born and brought up in traditional Catholic faith by ardently religious parents, I had many occasions to participate in spiritual retreats organized by the Holy Church and there, one whole day would be devoted to meditate over the *sins* committed by those who participated in the retreat. *Sins are nothing but the violation of the divine laws* or religious rules and thereby the sinners move away from the love of God. At the end of the retreat, people go to the *confessional* to get their sins absolved by the annointed priest. Confession is a Sacrament for the Catholics and the penitents get some penitential discipline imposed by the priest (i.e., the penance) for getting forgiveness from God. There too, the penitent is considered as the cause of the sins he committed and no one asks the "**Why**" of his sins. The presumption has been that the penitents have "**guilt feelings**".

In our daily life and common interaction with people, many use the expressions *"Excuse me, pardon me, sorry"* etc. and they say so because they have a feeling that they did something wrong. Mistakes are common and, therefore, correction becomes essential. *Errare humanum est, parcere divinum est*—in other words, *to err is human and to forgive is divine*. It means that a man is not always wholly responsible for the errors–mistakes–sins-crimes he commits. Accordingly, correction, forgiveness, absolution etc. get more and more acceptance to the extent of reforming, resocializing, rehabilitating and reintegrating crime-doers to society. The crime-doer alone is not wholly responsible for the crimes he commits.

Etiology of Crime

The quest for locating the etiology of crime away from the crime-doer has its roots in demonology. Adam and Eve in Holy *Bible* committed the original sin violating God's commandment. Really, the Satan was the villain in the story. Nevertheless, Adam and Eve were punished along with Satan (who was the serpent). People believed that the demons caused crimes and criminal behaviour. No one has seen demons, although many talk about them, their invisible powers, spirits' nature etc. In cultural programmes, dramas, cinemas, literature and prayers, the demons are shown but in a very abhorring manner. The artists paint demons in pitch black with horns, protruded teeth etc. in a detesting way. Exorcism is practiced to expel evil spirits. They were blamed for causing sins and crimes. Honestly speaking, I have not seen any demons in my life and I have no factual or empirical data or evidence to show that there exist demons to cause crimes or sins.

My researches to find out a causative theory has landed me to **Push-Pull-Ego Factor** approach. In my earlier writings for about 2 decades and in my book ***Police Criminology and Crime,*** I have exposed my **Push-Pull-Ego Factor** approach. But, now I want to expose my views more vividly, elaborately and perfectly. The first part of this book *"Contemporary Indian Criminology"* contains my **Push-Pull-Ego Factor** approach in a detailed way.

Push-Pull-Ego Factor Approach

According to the demonological approach, as said above, the demons caused sins/crimes and exorcism was the only remedy then and now. Why did the demons cause crimes/sins? What was/is their vested interests in doing so? No one had any answer. Whether or not the Biblical interpreters agreed or theologians accepted or practitioners of exorcism approved, the fact remained/remains that there worked/work some **Push Factors** in man to violate the laws. In my view, they are the *instincts* (in animals) or *drives* (in man) which come up spontaneously or automatically (i.e., without any external force) whenever a *stimulus* is available to them. For example, whenever food is seen by a hungry man, the *food-seeking* instinct (drive) with an accompanying emotion called *appetite* comes up. The pre-scientific men who were unaware of the working of instincts (drives) called this *Food-Seeking* instinct (drive) to be a ***demon***. Another example is about *lust*. When a man/woman is seen by a person of his/her complementary sex, then the instinct (drive) of *sex* with an accompanying emotion called *lust* comes into being. The primitive man called it '**demon**'. Many a time, the people find it difficult to fight against the instinctual (drive) forces and more often than not they yield to them. Therefore, the early man said that the innate depravity of man to fight against the demonological instigation was the cause of crime and criminal behaviour.

According to many theologians, the work of the devil/demon had a negativity and every religion made attempts to strengthen people to fight against those negative forces. A close scrutiny and a deep study of those 'so-called' negative forces would show that they were instincts in animals and drives in man. Certainly, they were not negative forces—negative energy—rather, they are the motivating or activating forces. Those activating forces were necessary for insects, fishes, animals and men to live and survive on this planet. Every instinct (drive) has a purpose. For example, *pugnacity* (combat) is an instinct (drive) and it is necessary to save oneself from danger to self/others.

The satisfaction of the instincts in animals or satiation of drives in man is essential and inevitable for the animals and men to live and survive without tension and conflicts. It is seen that the homeostasis of man is established only when his drives are satiated. In the case of man, his drive-satiation is possible through legal or illegal way, moral or immoral way, social or anti-social manner, legitimate or illegitimate way, etc. If it is satiated *via* illegal, antisocial, immoral etc. way, he violates the law and thus he commits an offence, antisocial act, vice respectively. In order to explain this negativity, the early prescientific men brought negative (evil) spirit, i.e., demon. They could explain the etiology of crime thus in an easy way. No one then questioned them.

Today, the instincts (drives) and their role as an activating force in man (and animals) are fairly well established and accepted. It is proved that an instinct has *need, means* and *goal*. The means to reach the goal can be illegal, immoral, irreligious, asocial, etc., and if so, it becomes a violation of the law, i.e., a crime.

Hedonism and Classical School of Criminology

When St. Thomas Aquinas [1225–'74] explained the concept of sin from the Scholastic (philosophical) points of view, he had recourse to the *freedom of will*. According to him, man had the freedom of will and he thought that people committed sins because they had the *freedom of will*. Man had the *freedom of will* and, therefore, he could choose between good and the evil. When he exercised his freedom in favour of the evil, he committed a sin. He did not explain why did the people exercise the freedom of the will in favour of the evil. Perhaps, demenological thinking was in vogue even when Thomist interpretation was given. Being influenced by St. Thomas Aquinas (an Italian theologian) later, Cessare Beccaria (1735–1795) from Italy further elaborated the Thomist Freedom of Will by giving an explanation for '**Why**' did the people opt to the evil when they exercised the *freedom of will*. Thus, he brought the concept of *hedonism* which meant a doctrine that pleasure or happiness was the motivating or activating force for opting the evil. Concurrently with Cessare Beccaria's explanation, Jeremy Bentham [1748-1832], an English jurist and philosopher proposed the theory of *rationalism* based upon the concept of *free will and pleasure–pain theory*. Thus, they, namely St. Thomas Aquinas, Cessare Beccaria and Jeremy Bentham contributed a lot to understand sin/crime. All of them knew little or very little about instincts (drives) and, therefore, the demons/pleasure/happiness continued to dominate the etiology of crimes. As a result, religious practices to get away from the instigation of devils and infliction of punishment on the basis of a hedonistic calculus (i.e., more pleasure, more severe punishment) continued to rule the theological (religious) and legal world. Still the Penal

Codes and Procedural Codes in many countries work on the basis of Bentham–Beccaria interpretation of crimes. Resultingly, punishments are awarded on the basis of the hedonistic calculus brought out by Bentham–Beccaria. Penal laws today accept the *freedom of will* although criminology is presently more concerned with the **Why** of the crimes and criminal behaviour more than the **What** of the same.

An indepth research into the **Push Factors** of human behaviour including criminal behaviour will take us to the working of instincts (drive). It shows that the satisfaction/satiation of the instincts/drives will ensure pleasure or happiness to people. If the satisfaction is derived from the commission of a crime, it is nothing but the expression of an instinct (drive). Bentham and Beccaria put everything in a single factor which they called hedonism. My researches prove that the single factor approach is faulty as the pleasure or happiness is just only one of the many instincts/drives a man has. Happiness or pleasure is just an accompanying emotion of the instinct (drive) called *Laughter*. I do not and cannot blame Bentham–Beccaria for their observations and study. For they were not well informed of the activating effects of instincts in animals and drives in men at a time when little or very little was known about the working of instincts/drives.

William McDougal (1871-1938) was an American Psychologist and Psychiatrist and it was he who contributed enviable literature on the development of elaborate systems of instincts (drives) which were thought to be basic to all forms of animal and human activities. We cannot expect Bentham–Beccaria for their ignorance of instincts (drive) as motivating– activating force in animals and men. The **Push-Pull Factor** approach accepts hedonism or pleasure–pain (amusement) as one of the many emotions which accompany instincts (drives).

A Village Story of a Lion

In children's literature, one sees animal police, animal lawyer, animal judge and animal courts. There was a lion in a forest. It used to eat other animals in the forest. Hence, the animals lived in the forest in fear or terror.

One day, a deer was the victim. It came to the lion in terror. It explained its difficulty to come to the lion at the appointed time.

Its argument was that there was another lion in the same forest and it wanted to eat it. The deer in tears explained to the lion that it was not possible for it to leave the lion and come in time. After listening to the explanation in tears, the lion got infuriated. In anger, the lion asked the deer to show the other lion which pounced upon the poor deer.

The deer walked with the lion and took it to a well which had clear water. The lion was made to believe that the problem-created lion was hiding in the well. When the lion looked into the well, it saw its own reflection in the water. Seeing it, the lion became angry and jumped into the well to catch it. Thus, the lion was confined. It was an imprisonment. The lion in the story was a "*goonda*" in the forest and see how the *goonda* was imprisoned.

Look at the way the lion was activated to behave. Pugnacity (combat) is an instinct in animals and anger is the accompanying emotion. Self-assertion is another instinct and the feeling of superiority is an accompanying emotion. In other words, the lion behaved the way it did as it was activated by two instincts, namely pugnacity and self-assertion. In my studies, I could find that animals would commit almost all types of crimes which human beings might commit. My mother had some pigs which brought income to our family. There was a man near to my home and he had a number of male pigs. He used to come to our house with his male pigs. As soon as they saw the female pigs, their sexual instinct would be activated and they had sexual relations with the female pigs 'against their will, without their consent, with their consent when the consent is obtained by .... (section 375, I.P.C. 1860)'. Animals, birds, fishes and insects commit theft, murder, rape, extortion, criminal force, affray, etc. What are the activating forces in their commission of crimes – or prohibited acts? In simple terms, they are nothing but the **instincts**.

Researches so far conducted give me plenty of evidence and proof to show that the behaviour of non-human beings are instinctual in nature. The survival of the fittest, as Charles (Robert) Darwin (1809-1882) said in his theory of evolution [Darwinian theory is that the origin of species is derived by descent, with variation, from parent forms, through the natural selection of those best adapted to survive in the struggle for existence] works well and it is, to some extent because of the crimes (if it can be called so) committed by them. Small fishes are eaten by the big (This is as good/bad as human rights violations among the people] and thus the bigger fishes deny the right to live for the smaller ones. Vulchers take off the chicks, zebras are killed by cheetas and eaten. The cocks have numberless sex-contacts with hens and they do not have any restrictions in such matters. If such violations are seen among human beings, they are violations of the social, cultural, moral and penal codes. People have no objection in animals and birds violating the laws although we do not allow such violations amidst the people. Why?

The Norway rats (the common brown rat) kills mices and studies show that the mice-killing nature of Norway rats is seen only in some. In human kingdom too, some people only become killers/murderers. What about theft? Some insects are thieves of their own associates' food. Birds are the thieves of man's grains. The rats are a national problem and the Food Corporation of India invests crores of rupees for pesticides. Pests are plenty everywhere. If non-human beings commit crimes as they are seen in nature owing to their instincts, one may say emphatically with assertion that human beings too commit crimes owing to instincts (drives). I do not find any difference in animals' behaviour different from the behaviour of man. Animals behave in the animals' way whereas the humans behave in the man's way—that is all!

McDougal and Sigmund Freud

Instincts have been described by many psychiatrists among whom McDougal is one of the pioneers. According to him, an instinct is an "innate or inherited psychophysical disposition which (determines) makes the organism to attend to certain kinds of objects rather than others, to experience an emotional excitement of a particular quality upon perceiving such an object and to act in regard to it in a particular manner or at least to experience an impulse to such action".

In the Dictionary of Psychology (1934), Warren H.C. says that an instinct is "an organized and relatively complex mode of response, characteristic of a given species, that has been phylogenetically adapted to a specific type of environmental situation."

According to Sigmund Freud, an instinct is a primal trend or urge that cannot be further resolved. From the Freudian view, there are only two primal instincts and they are those of life and of death.

There are criticisms against the descriptions of instincts given by all authors including McDougal, Freud and so on. Whatever, may be the appreciation/criticisms for or against instincts, the fact remains that instincts do exist or instincts are realities and they do activate living organisms to behave. About the aim of instinct, Robert J. Cambell says that its aim is "the reestablishment of that state of relative total organizational balance that existed before the instinct was aroused, through either external or internal stimulation. The state of instinct arousal in an organism is a state of tension or unpleasure in that organism driving the organism, as a whole, in the direction of finding and applying the appropriate means for releaving the arousal of tension or dissatisfaction through gratification." [*Psychiatric Dictionary*, 1981]

Of course, Sigmund Freud's (1856-1939) psycho-analytic theories conceived that the major motivating forces in behaviour were man's (instinctual) drives. In his introductory lectures on Psychoanalysis (1933) he said: "An instinct may be described as having a source, an object, and an aim. The source is a state of excitation within the body, and its aim is to remove that excitation, in the course of its path from its source to the attainment of its aim the instinct becomes operative mentally. We picture it as a certain sum of energy forcing its way in a certain direction." Of course, he was a psychotherapist and precisely therefore, he was not speaking as a criminologist. Psychoanalytic school subscribes to the doctrines that—

(1) behaviour is largely determined by unconscious psychological forces or drives.
(2) the functional behaviour disorders arise primarily because of conflicts related to the unconscious drives which interfere with the normal or required activities of the individual.
(3) that the treatment is to help the patient to gain insights into his unconscious drives.

According to psychoanalysis, an *over-effect* of the **id** is a cause of criminal behaviour. **'Id'** is a content of human personality. It is the deep reservoir of instinctual forces (drives). The **Push-Pull-Ego Factor** approach does not subscribe to the Freudian view that an *over-effect of* the 'id' in people causes crimes. In patients, it may be true. But, in criminals, particularly among the white collar criminals, nexus criminals, bureaucratic criminals, political criminals, JEL criminals, corporate criminals and so on, the explanation of the over-effect of the 'id' is unacceptable. At the same time, there is no difficulty to accept the view that instincts (drives) become the activating source (**Push Factors**) in criminality or in commission of crimes. More about this will be discussed later.

McDougal and his Classification of Instincts

McDougal classified instincts and identified 14 such instincts. Today, some schools of psychology, as pointed out earlier, use the term "**Drive**" instead of "**Instincts**" when they speak about man. According to them, an **instinct** is considered to be an innate capacity or necessity to react in a stereotyped way to a particular set of stimuli; it is a lower level, automatic response (such as reflexes). The term **drive** on the other hand ordinarily does not refer to the organism's response but instead emphasizes the state of central excitation; unlike the instinct, the response to the drive is not automatic but requires the functioning of the **Ego** and depends on learning and experience (Robert J. Campell, 1981). Whatever, may be the explanations or interpretations of instincts and drive, McDougal's classification of instincts are as under—

Instincts	*Accompanying Emotions*
1. Escape	Fear
2. Repulsion	Disgust
3. Curiosity	Wonder
4. Pugnacity (Combat)	Anger
5. Sex	Lust
6. Parental	Tender emotions
7. Appeal	Distress
8. Submission	Humility
9. Self-assertion	Feeling of superiority
10. Gregariousness	Feeling of lonliness
11. Food Seeking	Appetite
12. Acquisitiveness	Feeling of ownership
13. Constructiveness	Feeling of creativeness
14. Laughter	Amusement

Critics to McDougal's classification of instincts and his explanation of them argue that instincts are innate or unmodifiable and, therefore, man does not behave instinctively. They argue further that man too has some inherited tendencies (fear, sex, etc.), but they cannot be called instincts. Why does the man behave the way he does? They explain it by the help of drives and motives and not by instincts. —**Push-Pull-Ego Factor Approach** does not enter into such explanations, controversies and criticisms. At the same time, it admits that men and animals have (1) Pugnacity (combat), (2) Sex, (3) Parental, (4) Food–seeking, (5) Escape, (6) Repulsion, (7) Submission, etc., and all other instincts McDougal has brought out.

In my view, animal behaviour is instinct-originated. What about man's behaviour? Man's behaviour too is instinct–originated, but they have intelligence and rationality added to the instincts. Hence, I have no objection to say that man's behaviour is instinct originated but intelligence and rationality added. If this is what is meant by drive-activated– 'yes', I have no objection to accept such an explanation. For, a man is a rational animal.

An Illustration

Being moved by the instinct of food-seeking, all animals/birds search for food. They consume food and not bothered about the ownership, possession, etc. Why? There is no rationality or intelligence for animals. Therefore, there exist no laws or controls for animal behaviour.

The man too is activated by food-seeking instincts (here, **drive**). He searches for food and gets it either in a legal/moral way or in an illegal/immoral way. If it is in the illegal/immoral way, he commits a crime/vice. As the animals are not rational, the above view/logic is not applicable to them.

The animals/birds trespass into another's land and eat the food belonging to others. In such instances, they do not commit crimes. This way one can bring all instincts and give similar illustrations to show that man alone can or will violate the legal/moral laws and the logic or rationale is not applicable to animals and birds.

Why Push Factors?

PUSH—I mean a vigorous 'onset'. 'Onset' means a *beginning* or *start*. Whenever, a mother sees her child, her maternal instinct has a sudden and vigorous onset. Self-assertion is an instinct (drive) which everyone has and resultingly, the one who has self-assertion does have a feeling of superiority. I do not and cannot find any other forces other than instincts in animals/birds/insects and drives in man activating them—activate them to behave and in the case of a man to behave in a particular way including in a criminal way. If one cannot notice the instinct/drive directly in one's behaviour, he may see them operating in an indirect way provided he goes deeper as the forces activating him or as the origin of his behaviour.

Man and Rationality

'Rational'—means (1) agreeable to or in accord with reason; (2) having or exercising reason, sound judgement or good sense; and (3) being in full possession of one's reason, sane, etc. Man belongs to the animal kingdom and certainly, therefore, he has animality. Basically, man is an animal and the specific difference (s.d.) which makes a man different from animal is his **Rationality**. Rationality has some logical consequences which animality does not have. The logical consequences of rationality are—

1. Man is social.
2. Man is cultural and lives in a cultural environment.
3. Man is tradition-bound and custom chained.
4. Socio-cultural-politico-economical environment influences man's behaviour.
5. Man is religious or moral.
6. Rules, laws, regulations, traditions and customs are important in a man's life.

Rationality is different from intelligence. Intelligence, psychologists say, comprises of such capacities as comprehension, inventiveness, memory, persistence and critical analysis. Intelligence plays a vital role in the commission of crimes. There was a time some scientists thought that criminals were not intelligent and criminal activities do not require intellectual programming and execution. Now, that belief is no longer valid as many of the nexus criminals, corporate criminals, bureaucratic criminals, organized criminals, consensus criminals, white-collar criminals, cyber criminals international racketeers, terrorists, hijackers, spies and so on are found to be exceptionally intelligent. Many crimes require extensive conceptualization, preparation and planning.

Intelligent people need not necessarily be rational. For, rationality consists of doing things in an upright way in the right direction. Intelligence does not mean that one must execute his work in a moral, socially acceptable, legal manner. For example, an intelligent terrorist may not be moral. He violates the law to satisfy his vested interests.

Satisfaction of Push Factors and Rationality

The **Push Factors** in man can be satisfied in two ways, namely, in the right way or in the wrong way. How to decide the **Right** and the **Wrong**? There are many scales to decide the right and the wrong ways. One such scale is the socio-cultural scale. The socio-cultural scale includes the laws, rules, customs, regulations, traditions, morality, religion, etc. If one's behaviour is agreeable to the socio-cultural scale, one may say that he is rational. Otherwise, it is not rational whatever may be the role of intelligence.

Illustrations

(1) A terrorist causes the death of ten people by a bomb blast. He has executed his plan very intelligently. Nevertheless, he is considered as "**Not Rational**" as the death of 10 people in the bomb blast cannot be justified under the moral laws.

(2) An intelligent bureaucrat commits nexus crimes and thereby amasses a lot of wealth. His act is not rational, though intelligent, as it is a patent violation of the penal laws.

A man is said to be rightly rational if and only if he performs his act in an upright way in the right direction.

Rationality and Guilt Feelings

Guilt, the Dictionary meaning is the 'fact or state of having committed an offence, crime, etc., especially against moral or penal law! Guilt feeling, the Psychiatric Dictionary meaning is the 'realization that one has done wrong by violating some ethical, moral or religious principle'. The Dictionary continues: "Associated with such realization typically are lowered self-esteem and a feeling that one should expiate or make retribution for the wrong that has been committed." Rationality, in the words of Jung, is the reasonable—that which accords with reason. I conceive reason as an attitude whose principle is to shape thought, feeling, and action in accordance with objective values.

What are these objective values? They are the **Dos** and **Donts** inculcated to human mind from its birth. Sociologists may call it *socialization* process, i.e., making a neonate a socially acceptable person with desirable personality traits and values. The moralists may call it *conscience formation* in an upright way in the right direction. Upright way in the right direction means with an objective value. Psychotherapists—particularly those in psychoanalytic school—may call it *super-ego forr ˀtion.* Psychologists may call it *Ego Formation* with correct values.

Conscience Formation: What Is It?

Conscience formation in the right way means "without guilt feelings" when an act is done. Yes, in matters of conscience, there is no compromise. If compromise is done, the guilt feeling will follow a man like a shadow. I have seen, talked and interviewed several convicts (in prisons) who suffered guilt feelings. While treating patients afflicted by psychoneurotic disorders, I have observed many affected by guilt feelings. Many go for pilgrimage with their sins and guilt feelings and some of them wash away their evil doings in holy rivers and come back refreshed. People take penance and have recourse to various kinds of religious practices like fasting, alms giving, making offerings, etc., to get a relief from their guilt feelings. Some people compensate the victims of their evil acts and such people are restless until they get relieved from the burden of having the guilt feelings. It is said that the crimes committed by a man may stay in him as a snake in his mind. Such people do not have peace of mind. As a pious seminarian, I had closely watched dying people suffering from the fear of death. It may be a phobic reaction or irrational fear, yet people have it. Praying to God for pardoning sins, craving for mercy for absolving of the wrongs committed, confession to priests, fear of hell, purgatory, rebirth, saying excuse me, pardon me—there are many such things and practices in daily life and all of them indicate the existence of guilt feelings. In the development of penology and prison system, an objective of punishment was said to be atonement, expiation in prisons. The presumption was that the crime-doers had a conscience and consequent feeling of guilt.

Conscience in an Upright Way: How?

When an infant is born, the neonate has a mind where nothing is written. It is a *Tabula Rasa* which means a mind not yet affected by any experiences, impressions, etc. It is a plain blackboard where nothing is written. No doubt, a blackboard is for writing or drawing on it with pencil or chalk. Here, everything is written or drawn by many and the most important person at the birth and immediately after the birth of an infant is the **mother**. The **home** is the first conscience formation centre and the **mother** is the first teacher there.

Conscience formation means the act or process of forming the conscience and there is a formative period for every new born. Formative period means a period during which the conscience is given a form or shape. It is a period of moulding human conscience and the conscience must be formed in an upright way in the right direction.

Yes, the mother writes, the father writes—the family writes—the neighbourhood writes—the community writes—the school writes—the society writes—the media writes—the literature writes—the friends write—the religion writes and thus those who form the conscience of a developing child are many and various. Broken homes, lack of love, alcohol at home, lack of intelligent parental control, easy money making at home, defective moral and family conditioning at home, slum life, life in affluence, obscene literature, family disorganization, divorce and separation, desertion, orphanhood, overcrowding at home, quarrels at home, undesirable conditions at home like immorality, lack of care and concern, deviant family relationship, quality of parent–child, sibling–sibling, husband–wife interaction, unhappy home, too harsh or too lax father, an authoritarian or permissive parent, lack of family solidarity, parental inconsistency, parental discrimination for a favourite child, etc., are seen powerfully functioning in the formation of a developing child's conscience.

What is right and what is wrong? The conscience (of a person) rightly formed in an upright way in the right direction rebels against the wrongs. Whenever, a wrong is committed, he/she has guilt feelings. How does a person internalizes the right and wrong while he/she develops his/her conscience? In my view, every neonate, infant, child, adolescent has drives (instincts). The drives and the stimulating situations (facilitating environments) are important here. Whenever, there exist stimulating situations, the drives (instincts) get developed resulting in the conscience formation. Facilitating environmental conditions for developing a conscience in an upright way in the right direction—and the same for developing a conscience in the wrong direction cannot be ignored. Think about the (criminal) tribes in India. They are not called criminal tribes today as calling them criminal tribes today is found to be unconstitutional. Nevertheless, children born and brought up in such tribes do not develop a guilt conscience even when they indulge in the commission of crimes as defined by law in society. In the situations prevailing in such a tribal culture, the developing children form a conscience which makes them to think that commission of crime is a desirable act, a noble function, a heroic behaviour, etc.

Formation of Conscience: How?

A child forms its conscience by learning and he learns the right and wrong just like he learns to do a job by reading, studying, training or by association with others. By learning, he internalizes the values to which he is exposed. Earlier I said that I was born and brought up in Catholic Faith and I learnt that witnessing or participating in the religious rituals or functions of non-catholic faith was sinful. One day, I witnessed a religious function of a religious group different from the Catholics. That day I could not sleep owing to a guilt feeling that I committed a grave mortal sin.

On the next morning, I made a confession and got the guilt feelings washed away. I am taught the values and I learn the values and thus my conscience is formed. Case studies conducted on the convicts in prisons show that those who had a conscience rightly formed had guilt feelings and correction, reformation and rehabilitation of such people may be easy.

Learning and teaching are the two principal methods by which the values are internalized and the conscience is formed. Once the right values are internalized, the **Push Factors** can be controlled. Self-control is the best control. One can take a horse to a pond, but can never make it drink water. Likewise, the police or any authority can enforce strictly the laws and thereby control crimes or reduce criminal activities. Yet, they do not have the effect or impact which a rightly formed conscience can exert on individuals. Hence, the formation of a right conscience is the best method to reduce and control crimes in society.

So far, we saw the drives (instincts) in man and the formation of a conscience by learning and teaching. In **Push-Pull-Ego Factor** approach, we may have to discuss more about the **Pull Factors**. What are these **Pull Factors**?

Pull Factors: What are They?

In television advertisements, human instincts (drives) are instigated. In films and T.V. serials, the formula for commercial marketing may be (1) violence, (2) sex, (3) eating of food, and (4) showing of various kinds of emotions accompanying human instincts, etc. In village tea-shops and restaurants, the food items are shown in glass almirahs to attract people. Fashion girls wear erotic dresses to capture the attention. Curiosity is an instinct and wonder is the accompanying emotion. In exhibition stalls, novels, literature, conversation, etc., and many other curious matters are brought. People have the instinct (drive) for acquisitiveness followed by the feeling of ownership. How many different types of investment schemes, insurance plans, flat construction companies, employment bureaus, academic, educational and professional courses with an intention to help or cheat are seen in the environment around? Self-assertion instinct (drive) is promoted by many opportunities provided in the market. In my observations and studies, I notice that human instincts (drives) and emotions have a greater working sphere in human transactions. Intelligence has a lesser area than instincts (drives) and emotions have.

For instincts to be expressed, there should be appropriate environments for the same. Every society provides such environments and they are included in the **Pull Factors**. **Pull** means "to take hold of and cause to move toward or after oneself or itself or to take hold of and attempt to bring toward or after oneself or itself". In **Push-Pull-Ego Factor** approach, **Pull Factors** mean all those factors which take hold of and cause to move toward or after themselves and they do so with human instincts (drives). There are hundreds of **Pull Factors** about which an individual, sometimes, will not be aware of. Hence, it may be drawn—

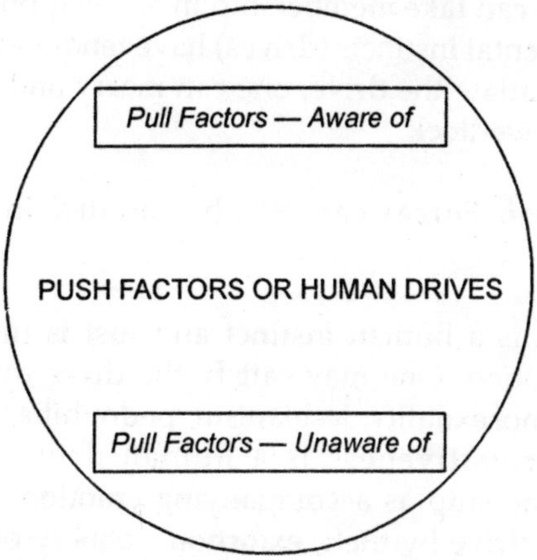

Fig. 1.1

Illustrations

1. In my village, a son killed his father who created family tensions and problems. He was a menace and a nuisance to his son. One day, there took place a verbal dispute between him and his father. Being activated by the human instinct (drive) of combat-aggression, he took a knife and stabbed his father. On questioning, he admitted that the anger he had towards his father culminated in his murder. He was quite aware of the instinctual force.
2. In a rape case of a juvenile girl, her father was caught as

the culprit. On questioning, he confessed his guilt, but was unable to explain why did the sexual instinct in him took him to the extent of raping his own daughter. He was unaware of the driving force behind his offence.

Every driving force in man has a corresponding pulling force. The **Pull Factors** drag the **Push Factors** and the society provides opportunities to satiate the **Push Forces** in a legal way. For example—

1. Gregariousness is a human instinct. It is nothing but "fond of the company of others, sociable". Feeling of loneliness is the accompanying emotions. In order to satisfy the drive, one can take membership in associations, clubs, etc.
2. Parental instincts (drives) have tender emotions. In order to satiate the drive, one can marry and have children in the wedlock.

The **Push Forces** can also be satiated in an illegal way. Examples:

1. Sex is a human instinct and lust is the accompanying emotion. One may satisfy the drive by rape, bestiality, homosexuality, lesbianism, pedophilia, prostitution, etc.
2. Acquisitiveness is a human drive with feeling of ownership as accompanying emotion. One may satisfy the drive by theft, extortion, robbery or other nefarious activities.

People do not resort to such illegal acts if they possess an upright conscience rightly formed. If they do it against such a conscience, they suffer from *guilt feelings*.

Pull Factors and Social Structure

If there is no instinctual drive for man, then the world would have been dead or not dynamic. Every society has a structure. Society means a "highly structured system of human organization for large scale community-living that normally furnishes protection, continuity, security and a national identity". Such a society will have an economic structure, a religious structure, a political structure, a labour structure, a cultural structure, etc. A large society will have sub-societies. Xenophon, Plato and Aristotle made attempts to explain human behaviour in terms of economic structure of a society. Karl Marx believed that the economic structure was the sole determinant of human behaviour including criminal behaviour and, therefore, he advocated that crime could be prevented only if a change in the economic system is effected. In India, economic crimes are plenty. I am not talking about the crimes of poverty such as petty theft or burglary. There is a view that a fight against poverty is a fight against crimes. In a country of the poor economically, the human drive of *Food Seeking* with an accompanying emotion called *Appetite* will be there. Naturally the crimes of the poor will be very many. Studies show that the crime-barometer in India goes up and down depending upon the harvest and food supply. Yes, structurally one sees economically poor class, middle class, upper middle class, high class, highly affluent class. In every class, the human instinct (drive) of *Acquisitiveness* with an accompanying emotion called the *feeling of ownership* is seen. The highly affluent people amass wealth by various methods including organized racketeering, crime syndicates, *Mafia* and other Nexus transactions. It is not the need that works in them. It is not the simple greed that pushes them. It is the **Avarice**—i.e., an excessively insatiable greed for riches or inordinately huge desire to gain and hoard wealth—that pushes them. They are pulled by many forces (like Syndicates, *Mafia*, Nexus Transactions) to find expression to their drives without any conscience.

What do the sub-cultural theories teach? Every infant is born to a society and culture which have different layers—economically and in many other ways. Sub-cultural theories emphasize the fact that human behaviour (including criminal behaviour) is sanctioned by the subculture which prevails in that group (see, Frederic M. Thrasher, *The Gang*, University of Chicago Press, Chicago, 1927). For example, children of poor economic strata and the same of the affluent economic strata have the same (instinctual) drives. Both of them express their drives in their own way. As they have separate behavioural norms, their behaviour is sanctioned by the subculture prevailing in each group. For example, in police service I have noted that drinking chilled toddy by the senior levels of police is considered to be a healthy drink by their subculture whereas the same by the constables (lowest level) is an offence warranting departmental action.

Albert K. Cohen was of the opinion that the boys from the lower class accepted the goals of the middle class. They had a (instinctual) drive to go up; nevertheless, they could not reach there by socially approved means. They violated laws and thereby they went up. In my view, one and the same person is moved by more than one (instinctual) drive concurrently or simultaneously. For example the drives of *Self Assertion* and *Acquisitiveness* will work at the same time as **Push Factors**.

Illustrations

1. A Syndicate or nexus criminal is moved by *'self-assertion'* (accompanying emotion is feeling of superiority) and *'acquisitiveness'* (accompanying emotion is feeling of ownership)
2. A rapist may be moved by *'sex'*, *self-assertion, laughter*, etc. as his (instinctual) drives.

Hence, instead of a multiple causation approach, I propose **Multiple Drives [Push Factors]** approach. There are **Pull Factors** in society and the subculture is a pull factor. Like the economic sub-structure in a given society, there will be the political sub-structure. There are political riots and crimes and they occur so because each one in every political party is activated by the same instinctual drives (**Push Factors**) and the **Pull Factors** in each political party approve them. In spite of the structure of the society with different sub-cultural norms (**Pull Factors**), there exists a dominant culture which may not or cannot accept the sub-cultural norms. Although each political party may approve of the behaviour of their political supporters, the dominant culture will not or cannot accept their behavioural patterns as normal. There is a dominant culture-conscience which may be different from the sub-cultural conscience. Statistical or majority scale is acceptable to decide the normality of behaviour and, therefore, the dictum *"All are equal before law"* is followed.

The labour structure, the religious structure, the ethnic structure, the caste/sub-caste structure, the linguistic structure, and the regional structure– all these become **Pull Factors** in society. Gang rivalry is an often discussed topic among the *goondas*. Why? Every *Goonda* has the same instinctual forces/drives not controlled by an upright conscience rightly formed.

The Chicago School [i.e., Ecological School developed by a group of sociologists known collectively as Chicago School] demarcated five different zones in Chicago city such as—(1) Central Business Zone, (2) Industrial Zone, (3) Zone of working men's houses, (4) A better Residential Zone, and (5) A Commuters' Zone. They found that each zone had crimes and there were marked variations in the rate of truancy, delinquency and adult criminality in different zones. Why? The **Push Factors** in everyone in different zones were the same whereas the **Pull Factors** in different zones were different. We have no information about the *conscience formation* and the feeling of *guilt* among those who involved in the commission of crimes in different zones from the study of Chicago School.

Some Thoughts about Pull Factors

The following are the observations I have made from my studies on the working of the **Push** and **Pull Factors**.

1. The more the **Pull Factors**, the more will be the opportunities for the **Push Factors** to interact.
2. The **Push Factors** are constant and the **Pull Factors** are unlimited and extensive. The **Pull Factors** may be numerous—from negativity to positivity. For example, the **Pull Factors** of the drive *'sex'* (accompanying emotion is lust) may have a range from sex-work to celibacy.
3. The more are the good laws, rules, norms, regulations, etc., controlling the interaction between the **Push** and **Pull Factors**—the more are the implementation/enforcement strategies of those laws, rules, etc.—the more will be the formation of an upright conscience in the right direction. The conscience formation takes place more in infancy and childhood than in adulthood or old age—say Psychologists.
4. The **Pull Factors** may change in due course/during a period of time whereas the **Push Factors** remain to be the same in people. Economic growth, political change,

educational programmes, physical development, etc., are **Pull Factors** and they may change. As there takes place the change, there will be change in the interaction between the **Push** and the **Pull Factors**. Psychologists accept the fact that behavioural modification is possible and they say so because there will be changes in the interaction between the **Push** and **Pull Factors.** Aftercare services for the released inmates from correctional institutions (presently, I prefer to call them Centres for Personality Development) insist that a change in the surroundings and environments of the released will ensure behavioural modification.

5. **Pull Factors** may allow the expression of the **Push Factors** in a particular way and there can be justification for it. For example, the retributive approach in penology was an expression of man's (instinctual) drives. Yet, it was accepted. Today, many countries are inclined to throw away such an inhuman approach. Whenever, the **Pull Factors** give approval for the expression of the **Push Factors** in an inhuman way, still an upright conscience rightly formed will fight against such an approach. That is the reason why a change takes place to one's attitude and approach to criminals. An utter unconcern towards the criminal in the retributive approach has now come to a positive approach accepting the personality of the crime-doers.
6. The more the people, the more will be the crimes. For, everybody has the drives and everybody expresses them. No one is a criminal always although everybody commits crimes. People cannot live without violating the law as everyone has the instinctual forces/drives.
7. The more the law enforcers, the more will be the number of detected law violators—the more will be the law violators among the law enforcers. For, there is a criminal trying to get out in every law enforcer and the criminal is the '*instinctual forces/drives*' in them. The **Pull Factors** allow them to express their animal instincts and they do so. Presently, the crimes of the law enforcement, of the prosecution, of the adjudication, of the correctional machinery are under hot discussion. There is a feeling now that the crimes committed by the various law enforcement/ prosecuting agencies are perhaps more than those

committed by people outside. It is so because the **Pull Factors** are many and the *conscience formation* is defective.

No one can give the real or all causes of crimes although everyone may point out the *Factors* in the causation of crimes. **Push and Pull Factors** plus the *conscience* which make the **Ego** of an individual, that is, what is important and it will be discussed later. Before that, let us see what is meant by **Cause-Effect** approach in criminology.

Cause-Effect Relationship

What is called the **Cause-Effect** relationship? Etiology studies the causes, causation or causality and there is a branch in criminology known as the ***Etiology*** of crime. Cause means the producer of an effect and effect means something that is produced by a cause. In short, where there is a cause, there should be an effect. Reversingly, where there is an effect, there must be a cause. As an illustration, we may quote the cause-effect relationship between a father and the child or better, a mother and the child. One does not have an existence or meaning without the other.

Illustrations

(a) A shoots Z with the intention of killing him. Z dies in consequence. [see the illustration given against (a) under Section 299, Indian Penal Code 1860]. Here, A is the murderer of Z and the question is–

(1) Is *A* the cause of the death of Z. There exists no cause–effect relation between *A*'s shooting and *Z's* death. If there should be a cause-effect relationship, it is necessary to prove that the one cannot be there without the other. Shooting might be a means by which Z was murdered and the means might not be the cause.

(2) Will any theory in criminology answer the question "what is the cause of *A* becoming a murderer? Can **Push-Pull-Ego-Factor** Approach answer the question? That will be discussed later.

(b) *A* is a Cabinet Minister of the Union Government. He is caught for corruption and malpractices. A search in his *pooja*-room brought out more than 4 crores of Indian rupees. Doubtlessly, it is a crime of the affluent. Why does a person of his affluence commit crimes? How does the **Push-Pull-Ego-Factor** approach answer the question?

(c) The terrorists, insurgents, fanatics, fundamentalists, extremists, white collar criminals, crime syndicates, JEL offenders, consensus criminals and so on commit a variety of crimes. Why do they commit crimes? The simple answer to the question is that all of them have drives and they cannot but express their drives. Man has all drives which animals have as instincts. Nothing more and nothing less. I have a survey of literature about the cause of crime. Thus I found—

1. Demons as the cause of crime and I, for one, think that the so-named ***Demons*** were the instincts (drives) in man. These instincts (drives) are not for the purpose of violating laws (committing crimes) but for doing many positive things in a positive way. But some do not do so Why? **Push-Pull-Ego** approach has an answer to it.
2. *Freedom of will and hedonism* were the contributions of Bentham and Beccaria of the Classical School of Criminology and it has its roots in St. Thomas Aquinas. At a time when the concepts of instincts in animals and drives in human beings were not fully known, they spoke of hedonism as an activating factor. In my view, by bringing hedonism as the activating force, they introduced "*instincts/drives*" in the area of crimes and criminal behaviour. The satisfaction or satiation of any instinct/drive ensures pleasure-happiness (hedonism). Hence, instead of the activating forces, they brought out the effect (happiness-pleasure) as the activating force. This view was wrong and the **Push-Pull-Ego Factor** theory has an explanation in this regard.
3. *Crackpot approaches* were crackpot in content. As the word meaning is, they were eccentric or impractical ideas expressed by vested interests without conducting any scientific researches. Reformers,

religious men, theologians, spiritual men and some well meaning people put forward their favourite ideas/concepts to explain the cause of crime. To a community of 100 people, one may ask the causes of crime and from the responses they give, he can come to a decision as to the area from where each one of them comes. I have done so. I have asked such questions to *pujarees*, policemen, professors, politicians, priests, prayer-men, postmen, poor people, businessmen, labourers and so on and I have any number of responses indicating each one's interest. They are not worth discussing here.

4. At one time in the early nineteenth century, geographers in Europe attached climatic variations to criminal behaviour. Their approach was known as *"thermal theory"* according to which people committed crimes against human body owing to hotter climate and the same against property owing to colder climate. Later it was studied and found that people had more human transactions/interactions/face to face contacts during hotter seasons compared to colder seasons. This paved the way for creating many stimuli which activated the people and their human instincts to commit, sometimes, crimes. **Push-Pull-Ego Factor** approach will explain this further.
5. By 1830, statisticians in the west interpreted crimes on the basis of socio-economic conditions. They did so looking at the statistics relating to reported crimes. According to them socio-economic conditions were responsible for the high or low crime rates. They failed to understand that the socio-economic conditions were **Pull Factors** which pulled the human drives to commit crimes under certain conditions. The **Push-Pull-Ego Factor** approach explains the statisticians' argument better here.
6. Cesare Lombroso (1836-1909, Italy), a prison doctor and a criminologist, the Father of Modern Criminology (Positivism in Criminology) found *atavism* (a revision to the primitive or sub-human type of man) as the cause of crime. He found the atavistic

characteristics morphologically as well as psychologically. According to him, because of the physiological and psychological *"throw backs"* to an early stage of evolution, people committed crimes. I think that he understood the importance of *instincts* in animals (drives in human beings) and their activating power to behaviour when he spoke about atavism as the cause of crime. While he noted the importance of **Push Factors**, he failed to see the role of **Pull Factors** in the causation of crime. He brought the concept of *"Born Criminals"* and when he spoke about the *'Born Criminals'*, he was stressing the importance of human instincts—say, the **Push Factors**.

7. Charles Goring (1870-1919) found the *"Weak mindedness"* as the most important single cause in criminality. *"Weak-mindedness"* shows lack of intelligence and thus he was pointing to human drives or instincts as the cause of crime. While he accepted the **Push Factors** in criminality, he seemed to have ignored the importance of **Pull Factors**. For, according to him, social conditions had very little to do with crime and criminality.
8. Gabriel Tarde (1843-1904) refuted Lombrosian views about atavism and physical anomalies. According to him, many criminals were found to be logical in their acts. His views gave strength to the argument that **Push Factors** would work in all human beings—no matter, they were intelligent (logical in their acts) or otherwise. Earnest Albert Hooton (1887-1954), a U.S. Anthropologist supported Lombrosian view of *atavism*. Although he was rejected owing to the unscientific nature of his approach and theory later, the fact cannot be denied that he gave a lot of importance to the **Push Factors** in the causation of crimes. Raffaele Garofalo (Italy, *c.*1852) differed from Lombroso in certain aspects. Nevertheless, he agreed that criminals were abnormal people (not out of physiological factors). Anyway, criminologists in the Positive School of Criminology, with a few exceptions, agreed the importance of **Push Factors**

in the causation of crimes although they did not say specially or specifically that the **Push Factors**, i.e., human drives (instincts) were responsible for crime and criminality.

9. Coming to Enrico Ferri (1856-1929), one notices the significance of society in the causation of crime. According to him, crime was primarily produced by the society from which the criminal hailed. He believed that crime could be reduced in the society if a change in the society was effected. In other words, he admitted the **Pull Factors** as the cause of crime and criminality.
10. By 1920, neo-Lombrosian thoughts dominated criminological theories. Resultingly, school of criminal biology came into existence. Accordingly, constitutional, physical and mental aspects of the crime-doers along with an inherited predisposition toward repetitive criminality got importance to explain the etiology crime and criminal behaviour. Johannes Lange studied identical twins and attempted to show the inheritance of criminality by making comparisons of one-egged twins with two-egged or fraternal twins. From his studies, he concluded that criminality was inherited. Family studies (Jukes and Kallikak– here, Jukes—i.e., the fictitious name of an actual New York family and Kallikak, i.e., the fictitious name of an actual New Jersey family whose history over several generations showed a high incidence of disease, delinquency and poverty) further made attempts to demonstrate that crime and criminality were inherited. Though studies and researches conducted later on the inheritance of criminality *via* twin studies and family studies established that the findings were wrong and not established in a scientific way, the fact remained that they accepted the role of **Push Factors** (human instincts) in the causation of crime. Adolf Lenz contended that the presence of mental diseases and ailments in the familial and ancestral background led to crimes. According to him, it was the predisposition to crime that was inherited. The predisposition to crime

means to give an inclination or tendency to commit crimes before hand. Precisely, therefore, the role of **Push Factors** could not be ignored. When Louis Vervaeck brought the importance and role of hereditary tendencies, temperament, congenital conditions and glandular functioning as the cause of crime, he emphasized the role and importance of **Push Factors**. For, one could not think of heredity, inheritance, congenital conditions, etc. without the role and importance of instincts/drives. They are there at birth and that is the reason why the neonate sucks the mother's breast immediately after its birth. Of course, later studies proved that heredity and environment together were responsible for the development of human personality, including criminal personality. According to later studies, it has been established that people inherited criminal potentialities and their development depended upon the environment. **Push Factors** mean these criminal potentialities and **Pull Factors** mean the environment.

In current parlance and in Malayalam language, there is a saying—i.e. "if the mother has jumped the fence, the daughter will jump the wall." It emphasizes the importance of heredity and environment. "As is the father, so is the son; tell me your mother I shall tell you who you are"—all these sayings are there in the common man's dialogues. This is what Franz Exner, a biologist of the School of Criminal Biology meant when he said that criminality in the family line was very high in offenders– more among repeaters than the first offenders.

11. After 1920, studies were conducted and some such studies did not give any importance to the **Push** or **Pull Factors**. One such area was the study of crime as a result of endocrine malfunctioning. Max Schlapp and Edward Smith were prominent in that line. Nevertheless, their generalizations that crimes and criminality were owing to endocrine malfunctioning

were subsequently rejected by endocrinologists themselves. Later researches in endocrinology and crime causation could not connect endocrine malfunctioning to criminal behaviour.

12. Kretschmer's classification of criminals basing on body-mind type as *asthenic, athletic* and *pyknic* and William H. Sheldon's classification of problem youths as *'endomorphous, mesomorphous* and *ectomorphous* did not pay much attention to the **Push** and **Pull Factors** in the causation of crime. The type approaches have today become a part of the history of the development of criminological thoughts. Everyone, irrespective of his body type has all the human instincts (drives) and, therefore, all types of crimes will be committed by all people irrespective of their body types.
13. Sociology of Crime or School of Criminal Sociology had a start with Enrico Ferri who said that social conditioning like the density of population, family environments and conditions, economic and political situations, etc., were the social factors which had something to do with the causation or prevention and control of crimes. How did they cause crimes was of importance. It was there the **Push Factors** and their interaction with **Pull Factors** (Here, sociological factors) became important. Gastav Aschaftenburg divided criminogenic causes into sccial and individual. Under social causes, he put race, religion, city, economic conditions, etc. Yes, they are the **Pull Factors** and under individual factors come the **Push Factors**.

William Bonger (1876-1940) explained criminal behaviour on the basis of criminal motivations and stimulating situations. Motivations include human instincts (**Push Factors**) and stimulating situations consist of **Pull Factors.** Emile Durkheim (1858-1917) said that crime was normal. Why did he say so? I think that he believed that no one could escape the commission of crimes. Since everyone has the **Push Factors,** and every society has the **Pull Factors,** there will be interaction between them. If there take place interactions between the **Push** and **Pull Factors,** there will be violations of law. That was the reason why Durkheim said emphatically that a society without crime and delinquency never existed. According to him, crime was not due to any imperfection of human nature or society. To it, I add that a human nature without **Push Factors** and a society without **Pull Factors** are imperfect. Hence, crime is natural, normal, necessary and inevitable in any society. **Push-Pull-Ego Factor** approach will explain how people commit crimes and the after-effects of crimes in society.

Durkheim's anomie and Robert Merton's anomie explained the causation of crimes and criminal behaviour further. Merton said that criminal behaviour represented impulses of individuals breaking through social controls. He also said that there were socially induced deviations—deviations which the culture and the social organization conjoined to produce. Merton spoke of conformity, innovation, ritualism, retritism and rebellion as the five modes of adaptation to the situation of disjunction. In my view, they are the five modes expressing the **Push Factors** to the situation of disjunction. Richard A. Cloward developed the '*anomie*' theory further and to cut short, he said that a person became a criminal and it depended upon his contact with people who induced him into criminal behaviour. There too, the interactions between **Push** and **Pull Factors** were aimed at.

Mable A. Elliot and Francis E. Merril spoke about the *Multiple Causation Theory* to explain criminal behaviour. Yes, there is no single predisposing factor leading inevitably to delinquent behaviour. There are multiple causes behind the commission of every crime. **Push Factors** are many and **Pull Factors** are numerous. The **Ego** formed thus comes into being as a result of the interaction between the **Push** and **Pull Factors**. **Push-Pull-Ego Factor** approach has no difficulty to accept and approve of the multiple causation explanation. William Healy did not favour the single factor theories of crime causation. Case studies are needed to bring out the many factors behind one's criminal activities. Cyril Burt studied delinquents and non-delinquents and subscribed to the view that multiple causation approach was the best to explain the etiology of crime and criminal behaviour. Further, Sheldon and Eleanor Glueck compared delinquents and non-delinquents. They found that the delinquent group differed from the non-delinquent group in several counts. Likewise, when a comparison is made between students who involved in student riots in Kerala and those who did not, I could learn that the **Pull Factors** in those who involved in student agitations were many and they differed very much from those who did not involve in student agitations. Many who were active in student riots did not have any guilt-feelings and their ***Ego*** was devoid of any remourse at all. They damaged public property or attacked students who propagated another political philosophy. The ***Ego*** of those who involved in student riots were found to be more assertive, more defiant, more resentful, more vivacious, more extroverted, etc. They wanted to project their ***Ego*** and desired to show their ***'Leadership Qualities'***. Those who did not involve in student riots were less emotional, less suggestive, less stubborn and certainly the families they were born (**Pull Factors**) and reared were adequate and better disciplined than those who involved in student riots grew up. The attitudinal (parents to children), psychological and family differences were very much visible.

XYY chromosomal pattern and criminal behaviour assumed some importance in the study of the etiology of crimes. This approach, in a way, admitted the importance of chromosomes and their abnormality in the causation of crimes. Scientists could unearth numerous chromosomal abnormalities (For example, the *XXY* or Klinefelter Syndrome is one in which the individual is found to be externally or outwardly male, but sterile, somewhat mentally retarded and suffering from some breast enlargement. This abnormality has been linked with crime and anti-social activities—especially alcoholism and homosexuality). The *XYY, XXY* Chromosomal pattern and criminal behaviour did not receive acceptance as there was lack of research evidence to prove the theory. It has been estimated that approximately one out of every 400-500 male births have chromosomal abnormality. If that is a truth, then the picture of criminality will be or should be altogether different. Researches have proved that *XYY* Chromosomal pattern was rare in the population. How did the chromosomal abnormality cause criminal behaviour has been unclear to many scientists even today. There has been no **cause-effect** relationship between chromosomal abnormality and crime/criminal behaviour. There are scientists (Theodore Sarbin, Jeffrey Miller, Fox and so on) who contended that the explanation of the advocates of Chromosomal abnormality and crimes was a modern version of demonism. My view is that the approach totally ignores the importance of **Pull Factors** which might be the social and cultural factors. Again, the importance of chromosomes and the **Push Factors** is not explained or researched into. There are any number of convicted criminals who do not have any chromosomal abnormality.

Recently, an engineering student was brutally murdered by some fellow associates who studied in the same institute of technology. My studies about the criminal activities in educational institutions especially in self-financing colleges in India, gave me evidence to say that there were *gang activities* in such educational institutions. Some students who came to the self–financing colleges were found to be not well motivated. They were forced by their parents, kith and kin to go for professional education. The banks provided loans and financial assistance to students who wanted to study. Thus many (who were undeserved) entered into professional colleges in India. What about the sub-culture of the students who entered in the professional colleges? Thrasher in the west found that gangs developed as a result of social disorganization in the zone of transition. In the self-financing colleges in India, I could notice the development of a subculture in a social class which were economically weaker and they involved in making easy money by various criminal behaviours which were sanctioned by their sub-culture. I could also learn that the managements of such self financing colleges directly or indirectly promoted the gang culture to make education a lucrative business. The **Pull Factors** were found to be powerfully operating in the subculture of the gangs.

Albert Cohen found that the boys from the lower classes accepted the goals of the middle class. Often, they could not attain the middle class goals by socially approved means. This was what could be seen in self-financing professional colleges as well. In order to obtain the financial status of the middle class, upper class, the lower class boys developed a culture of their own. Within the sub-culture of the economically weaker/ educationally weaker/socially weaker, the activities of the gangs were malicious, negativistic, destructive and characterized by short run hedonism and group autonomy. They made easy money by attacking people physically in the name of *'Ragging"* them and the law too took a lenient attitude. It means that the **Pull Factors** were of a questionable nature. Here the **Pull Factors** explain the development of a criminal subculture in the college campuses.

Mention has been made about the ecological approaches in criminology and Chicago School contributed a lot in explaining crimes as a function of social change (**Pull Factors**) that occurred along with environmental change. Thorsten Sellin analyzed crimes in terms of conflicts among the norms. The criminals and the non-criminals respond to different conduct norms. The responses to the conduct norms depend heavily on the formation of ***Ego*** from the interactions of **Push** and **Pull** Factors. The ***Ego*** of the criminal does not have a guilt feeling if at all he commits an offence. But, the ***Ego*** of the non-criminal does have a feeling of guilt when he involves in the commission of a crime. There is a sort of *"Culture Conflict"* in the ***Egos*** of the criminals and non-criminals.

What about the cultural-lag theory? According to them, there are two cultures—material and non-material. The material culture contains tools, inventions, innovations and discoveries whereas the non-material culture contains the values, customs, regulations, traditions and rules or norms of the society/culture. Certainly, there will be a conflict between the two cultures in society. In India, presently one finds a rapid progress in the material culture. The traditional Indians find it difficult to adapt themselves to the changes in the non-material culture. The western values come to India owing to the development in the visual and print media and resultingly, the custom-bound Indians cannot adopt or adapt to the new values in the non-material culture. The **Push Factors** in the changing cultural milieu make many infants, children and adults to adopt and accept the western values which are not sometimes acceptable to the Indian culture.

Tarde's imitation theory and Edwin H. Sutherland's Differential Association theory are two important social process approaches to explain criminal behaviour. Tarde's theory has been that man learns crime just as others learn a trade through training and association with others. Laws of imitation were the basis of Tardian explanation. Things to be imitated come under the **Pull Factors**. According to Sutherland, criminal behaviour is learnt. It is learnt in an interaction with other persons in a process of communication. In other words, criminal behaviour is learnt *via* an interaction with the **Pull Factors**. The ***Ego*** accepts delinquent behaviour because of an excess of definitions favourable to the violation of law. According to W.C. Reckless, People live in a society of alternatives (**Pull Factors**). The ***Ego*** in such a situation has more and more opportunities for acceptance and rejection of available confrontations. He introduced the idea of '*Self-Concept*' as the key factor to explain this phenomenon. In my view, Reckless's self-concept and containment theory is acceptable to some extent as the theory holds the view that if an individual possesses a *favourable self-concept*, then he is directed toward law abiding behaviour, otherwise, i.e., *unfavourable self-concept*, he is directed towards criminal or delinquent behaviour. Reckless does not say anything about the interaction of **Push** and **Pull Factors** in the formation of the ***Ego*** (*Self-concept* in his view). A value contained ***Ego*** will act as an inner buffer against deviance and criminality.

What is the *Labelling Theory*? According to them 'Criminal was only a label and nothing more!' According to Kai Erikson, the '*Social audience*' decides whether or not any particular action should be made a visible cause of deviance. For Howard Becker, a person was a deviant because he was labelled as deviant by the society. The theory was not talking about the causation or causality of crime and criminal behaviour. Precisely, therefore, the question of **Pull–Push–Ego Factors** does not arise here.

Goddard spoke about the I.Q. level of an individual as the cause of crime. In other words, he was saying that people having a higher I.Q. were better organized. Yes, Goddard accepted the role of intelligence in the causation of crime. People having a low I.Q. indulged in the commission of crimes partly as a result of their mental retardation (**Push Factors** may be important here). They may be quarrelsome and are led by chance impulses and instincts. In the mentally retarded people, ***Ego*** cannot be rightly formed in the right direction. However, Goddads' approach was rejected by later researchers—particularly the Post World War-I researchers who introduced intelligence tests to measure the I.Q. level of the people. It was found that many criminals were having high or very high I.Q. and what they lacked was an ***Ego*** rightly formed in the right direction.

Allport's definition of personality and his trait approaches, of course, explained how a man would behave if he committed a crime. However, it did not say anything about whether or not a man would become a criminal if he possessed a particular trait. It showed that the personality traits were not the **Push Factors** in man. Cattels' argument that the personality traits influencing man to involve in criminal activities was found to be unacceptable because the factual evidence showed that a man's behaviour varied markedly from situation to situation (**Pull Factors**), from problem to problem and from role to role. A man has to adjust with the changing reality (*Ego* adjustment) and, therefore, the theory could not explain the causation of crime. Schuessler and Cressey conducted extensive researches and came to the conclusion that criminality and personality traits were not causally associated. Waldo and Dinitz were of the view that there was no clear psychological factors associated with criminality. Social Scientists made attempts to develop a theoretical framework of **'Self-Other'** relationship to relate crime to personality traits. They were not talking about **'Push–Pull–Ego Factors'** in the causation of crime. They failed to isolate a single psychological factor in criminals. Hans Eysenck spoke about extroversion and criminality. According to him, the propensity to crime (**Push Factors**) is universal, but is held in check in most cases by a given person's *conscience* [i.e., an *Ego* formed uprightly in the right direction]. He also said that the *'conscience'* was essentially a generalized set of conditioned responses (**Pull Factors**) built up during childhood and adolescence according to the rules of Pavlovian conditioning. Researchers could not agree with his ideas of Pavlovian conditioning although they accepted his 'Propensity to crime, conscience', etc. According to Eysenck, the *'conscience'* in some will be underdeveloped either through a failure of social and family conditions to provide the proper means of developing it or through innate weakness in the person concerned of the mechanism involved in the elaboration of conditioned responses. Of course, there were research objections to his explanation of innate weakness, conditioned responses, etc. Hans Eysenck postulated that extroverted people tended, under certain conditions, to condition less well than introverted ones. This made them *ceteris paribus* more likely to behave in an antisocial or delinquent fashion. However, there was no research support for his postulation of extroversion and introversion, etc. According to Eysenck, a high degree of anxiety or neuroticism tended to act as a drive strongly reinforcing the extroverted or introverted tendencies favouring or disfavouring criminal behaviour or anti-social conduct. In a nutshell, it may be stated that crime and criminal behaviour would be found more often than not in people whose personality placed them in the high extraversion, high neuroticism quadrant. Thus, his argument pointed to the fact that individuals involved in the commission of crimes because they were not adequately conditioned or they have not acquired an internalized conscience. I cannot agree with his theory as I find that his explanations of "adequately conditioned and internalized conscience", etc. are good only to understand a part of one's criminal or delinquent behaviour. Not only conditioning, but also the teaching, learning, imitating, understanding, absorbing the values of society are important in the formation of an upright *Ego* rightly formed in the right direction. What is this *"Internalized Conscience"*? What is needed is an upright conscience rightly formed in the right direction.

Psychologists bring out Psychopathic personality as the cause of criminal behaviour. It is wrong. Why? According to Hervey Cleckley's description, a psychopath is a person who is free from neurosis, psychosis or mental defectiveness; who knows the consequence of his behaviour but seems to have no inner feeling for what he verbalizes so rationally; who is habitually unable to adjust his social relations satisfactorily; who is not deterred by punishment (instead he seeks it out); who lacks motivation; if motivated the motivation is not congruent with his behaviour; who expresses normal affective responses (but shows a total lack of concern and callous indifference to others); who has poor judgement and who does not learn from experience (This is evident from his pathological lying, repeated commission of crimes and other antisocial acts). Of course, the description is fine and elaborate but, I do not agree with his views in the following points–

1. Some criminals suffer from neurosis, psychosis or other mental defectiveness.
2. Some criminals do have inner feelings of guilt.
3. Some are habitually able to adjust their social relations.
4. Some are deterred by punishment.
5. Some do have motivation.
6. Some do show concern.
7. Some have sound judgment.
8. Some do learn from experience and thus the argument that all crime-doers are psychopaths is fully wrong.

Sutherland and Cressy were of my view as they did not agree with the proposition that all criminals were psychopaths. There might be psychopaths among the crime-doers. Many psychiatrists like Lee Robins were of this opinion. What is the *cause-effect* relationship between Psychopathy and criminal behaviour? My studies show that a psychopath commits crimes because his ***Ego*** is not uprightly formed in the right direction. It is not necessary that a psychopath must always commit crimes. Nevertheless, if he commits a crime, he may not have any guilt feelings. It means that his ***Ego*** is not formed uprightly in the right direction. Why? **Push-Pull-Ego Factor** Approach will explain it in detail in the pages that follow.

Psychiatry is the medical speciality that deals with mental disorders. In psychiatry and criminal behaviour, one may see two schools of thought, namely (1) Psychiatric Contributions and (2) Contributions of Psychiatry unrelated to Psychoanalytic School. The latter may include neuropsychiatrists, clinicians and psychiatrists whose theories are relatively less stigmatizeu than those of psychoanalysis.

Sigmund Freud and his followers explained how the *'id'* and *'inadequate formation'* of **super-ego** caused criminal behaviour. Vold agreed with Freud when he said that the conflict in the unconscious mind gave rise to feelings of guilt and anxiety, etc. August Aichhorn applied Freudian concepts to analyse the criminal behaviour of institutionalized boys and found that some of the boys lacked proper **super-ego** development. Kate Friedlander agreed with Aichhorn when he said that the delinquents were people who expressed anti-social impulses repressed in normal person. David Abrahamsen thought that environmental and social factors had a role to play in crime causation. I agree with Freud to some extent, to Aichhorn to some extent and add further that the upright formation of the ***Ego*** in the right direction should be there to explain the cause of criminal behaviour.

Contributions of psychiatry unrelated to psychoanalytic school have created a lot of confusion about the cause of crime. No, a person affected by psychic disorders cannot commit a crime as he is unaware of what he is doing or what he is doing is contrary to law. They may commit antisocial acts, but one cannot call their acts to be criminal. Hence, in my explanations, the mental patients have no place or scope. There is no meaning in studying the *cause-effect* relationship between mental disorders and crimes as the mental patients cannot or do not commit crimes as described in the penal laws.

In 1948, victimologists started to argue that the victim of crime might become a cause of crime. In other words, the victims might become a **pull factor**. They might provoke, instigate, encourage, entice, etc. a crime-doer and as such the etiology of crime moved to another direction. Thus the quest for locating the causes of crime travelled a long way from demonology (**Push Factor**) to victimology (**Pull Factor**)—from the primitive criminal to the most modern criminal. Crimes too got multiplied and thus various types of crimes from the traditional to the cyber category came into existence. Political crimes, economic crimes, white collar crimes, JEL crimes, *Nexus* crimes, consensus crimes, bureaucratic crimes, sweet-heart crimes, grass-eater crimes, meat-eater crimes, slum crimes, suite crimes, enforcement crimes, international trafficking, network crimes, *mafia*, organized crimes, crime-syndicates, corporate crimes, war crimes, corruption and malpractices, terrorism, insurgency, terror-causing 'isms', fundamentalism, extremism, fanaticism, religious bigotry, crimes by human-gods (so-claimed incarnations of god), business crimes, money chain and multimarketing, internet crimes, financing and investment crimes, media crimes, politicians' crimes, criminalization of politics and politicization of criminals, administration of less justice and miscarriage of justice, flesh trade and pornography, waste justice delivery, etc., are just a few seen on the tip of the iceberg in the sea of crimes today Why do the people involve in the commission of all these or similar crimes? Researches show that crimes are, perhaps, one of the few things which need not be taught to people. For, they learn themselves to commit various types of crimes if they get opportunities. According to me, there is something in man and it makes him to commit crimes. This "*something*" cannot be different from what the animals have. They too have "*something*" which activates them to do thing. Hence, the "*something*" seen common in man and animals may be the ***instincts*** in animals and ***drives*** in man. If philosophers define a man as a "**Rational Animal**" they see animality in man plus rationality (specific difference) in him.

Listen to my explanation of the **Push-Pull-Ego Factor** Theory of crime causation. As I said earlier, the **Push Factors** are nothing but the ***instincts*** (in animals) or ***drives*** (in man). We know that:

1. An instinct is an innate or inherited psychophysical disposition.
2. It determines (makes) the organism to attend to certain kinds of objects rather than others.
3. Man/animal experiences an emotional excitement of a particular quality upon perceiving such an object (**Pull Factors**) and he/it acts to it in a particular manner or experience an impulse to such an action [McDowel].

Remember always that there is no **Push Factor** which does not have at least one **Pull Factor**. This is God's plan and creation. The instincts-drives push the organism to some objects and the organism is pulled by **Pull Factors**. Men and animals have the same activating force, i.e., the instincts (drives). Whatever may be the crime, the root cause will be one or more instincts. As man is rational and intelligent he may make his instincts, sometimes, to look rational and intelligent. Take for instance:

1. ***Money Chain or Multilevel Marketing***: The crime-doer makes his scheme very attractive and he applies intelligence and rationality. People become prey to such schemes. What is the root cause? The activating root cause will be 'Acquisitiveness'—an instinct having the emotion of the feeling of ownership. This is the **Push Factor**.
2. ***Rapes, Relay Rapes, Mobile Rapes, Sex-works or similar Sex-crimes:*** What is the root cause? *Sex* is an instinct and *lust* is the accompanying emotion.
3. ***Political Crimes***: What is the root cause? Self-assertion is an instinct and feeling of superiority as the accompanying emotion.
4. ***Economic Crimes***: Several instincts such as, (1) self-assertion (emotion: feeling of superiority), (2) Acquisitiveness (emotion: feeling of ownership), and (3) Laughter (emotion: amusement) or a combination of them can be the root cause. Thus, in any sort of crimes, one may see a drive (instinct) or a combination of more drives (instincts) as the root cause/s. The root cause/s is/are the **Push Factors**.

What about the **Pull Factors**? The **Pull Factors** are the facilitating environments. They can be, as said partly elsewhere, social, cultural, economic, political or similar environments. *Inter alia*, broken homes, slum-life, motion pictures, T.V. and serial shows, obscene literature, family disorganization, blue films, internet sex, divorced/deserted homes, unemployed and/or overcrowded families, illegitimacy, orphanhood, quarrels at home, intoxication, immorality, poverty, overcrowding, lack of sanitation and care, deviant family relationship, unemployment, under-employment, political chaos, mass-media, low income, delinquent subculture, alcoholism and drug addiction, generation of new set of values, delinquent-gangs, underprivileged environment, caste/sub-caste system, ethnic conflicts, agrarian unrest, student-riots, religious bigotry, decline in moral standards, physical deterioration of areas, anomie, economic system, political fights, lack of recreational facilities, failure of the criminal justice system, poor law enforcement, crime-wave, too much of affluence, defective educational system, lack of human values, *goonda* culture, doctrine of easy money-making, corruption and corrupt practices, bureaucratic crimes, nexus transactions among the politicians, businessmen and bureaucrats, syndicate crimes and organized rackets, adulteration of religious values, sale of gods, promise of fortune and thus the **Pull Factors** are incredibly long in the modern society.

Development of Human Personality [Ego]

An infant born with all drives (instincts) develops his personality in the society to which he is born. This may be drawn as:

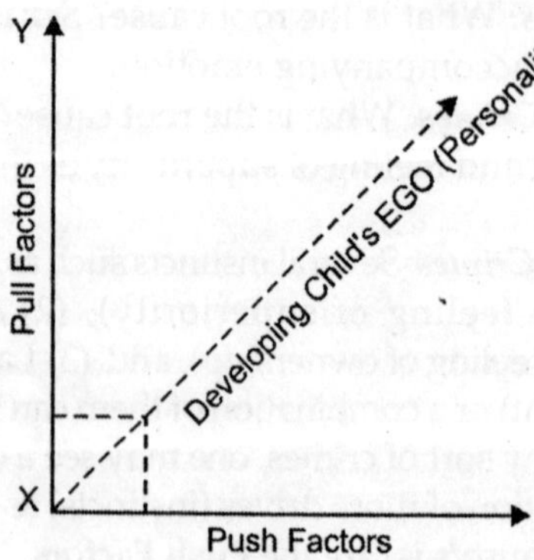

Graph - 1.1

Push Factors are in the *X*-axis and they are the instincts (drives)

Pull Factors are in the *Y*-axis and they are the environmental realities.

The child develops his ***Ego*** (personality)—How? This takes place in a socio-cultural milieu which accepts certain values and they are the socio-cultural values of the society. Hence, the Graph 1.1 may be redrawn as under:

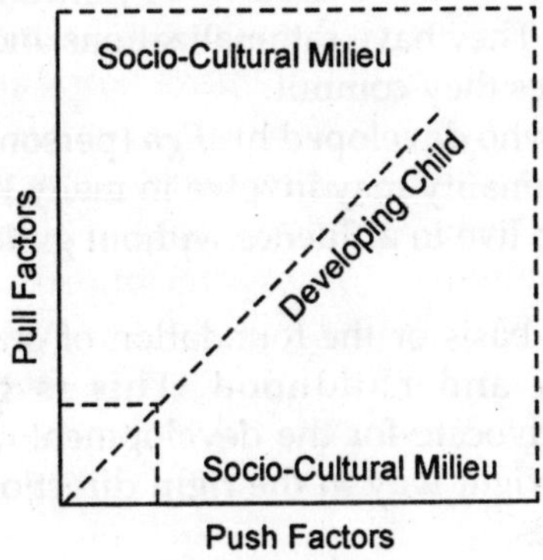

Graph - 1.2

This shows the socio-cultural melieu containing the values and the child develops his/her personality in that melieu. He/she internalizes the values and by the time he/she becomes 13-14 years of age, the foundation of the values is fully constructed. Further development of his/her personality is on this infrastructure of values in him/her.

Examples

1. A child born in a family having high religious values will have an infrastructure having strong religious values. If he commits an act against his religious values (faith), it is likely that he experiences guilt feelings.
2. A girl born and brought up in a family of a hereditary prostitute where the mother hands over the work of prostitution to her daughters without any shame of a life of immorality is likely to have no guilt feelings if at all she becomes a hereditary prostitute.

3. A child born and brought up in a poverty-stricken home where he lives in a culture which accepts the value that the poor can misbehave to others to make money for livelihood. He may not have a guilt feeling even when he commits a theft or robbery or chain snatching, etc. Interviews with the recidivists in prisons for the repeated offences like pocket–picking, burglary, theft, etc., they commit one after the other do not have often any guilt feelings. They have rationalizations and justifications for the crimes they commit.
4. A child who developed his ***Ego*** (personality) in affluence and criminality may involve in many kinds of economic crimes to live in affluence without guilt feelings.

In short, the basis or the foundation of one's ***Ego*** is the life during infancy and childhood. This is the reason why criminologists advocate for the development of one's ***Ego*** from infancy in an upright way in the right direction for reducing or preventing crimes.

Whenever, a person with an ***Ego*** uprightly formed in the right direction commits a crime, he certainly experiences guilt feelings. Otherwise, he may not have any feelings of guilt. The feeling of guilt before, during and/or after the commission of a crime is the index or proof of one's ***Ego formation*** in an upright way in the right direction. Crimes committed during the period of adolescence, adulthood or old age may be interpreted in the following way—

1. The individual has an ***Ego*** as his foundation with values, perverted values or no values.
2. If the facilitating situations (**Pull Factors**) at the time of committing the crime are excessively very strong, he may involve in the commission of crimes owing to the lack of strength or the surcharged energy or force of the **Push Factors.** Sigmund Freud said that an over-effect of the 'id-complexes' caused crime. Yes, it is true. **Push-Pull-Ego Factor** says that the crime-doer will feel guilty before doing and/or after the commission of a crime if the ***Ego*** has been uprightly formed in the right direction. I have seen many patients coming to psychotherapist's clinics suffering from

guilt feelings and expressing neurotic behaviour to get out of the guilt conscience.

3. **Push-Pull-Ego Factor** theory proposes that an *Ego* uprightly formed in the right direction is a powerful force ***not to commit crimes***. In spite of it, if he commits crimes he will experience guilt-feelings.

Push-Pull-Ego Factor theory says that an inadequate formation of the *Ego* in an upright way in the right direction will become a cause of crime. It does not mean that everyone with an inadequate *Ego* will commit a crime. But, if he commits a crime with an *Ego* uprightly formed in the right direction, he will certainly have guilt feelings over the crime he has committed; otherwise he will not.

Questions that Need Answers

1. What are the causes behind traditional and modern crimes?
   Ans: The root causes of any kind of crimes will be a drive/s (or instinct/s) either alone or along with others. The source drive must be identified when the surface causes are unearthed.
2. What are the **Pull Factors**?
   Ans: They can be anything: social, cultural, environmental, economic, political or a combination of two or more. They are very powerful and they interact with the **Push Factors**.
3. How is the *Ego* formed?
   Ans: The *Ego* is formed out of an interaction between the **Push Factors** and the **Pull Factors** during the early infancy/childhood upto 13-14 years of age. This is called the ***"Foundation EGO"*** or ***'Basic Ego'*** or ***'Infrastructure EGO'***.
4. What is called an *Ego* formed uprightly in the right direction?
   Ans: The *Ego* formation uprightly in the right direction means an *Ego* with right values, motives, vision and a feeling of guilt when the values are violated or a crime is committed and/or afterwards.

5. Who/What inculcates values, right motives and vision in a developing *Ego*?

   Ans: The agencies are the homes, schools, religious institutions, media, literature, neighbourhood, community, society, etc. If they are rotten then the *Ego formation* too will be rotten

6. How do you decide the uprightness of the values?

   Ans: There are scales to decide the uprightness of an individual. They can be (1) the normative scale, (2) the subjective scale, (3) the majority scale, (4) the socio-cultural scale, and (5) the clinical scale. They are used to measure the uprightness of *Ego formation* in the right direction.

7. What do the sociologists say when they speak of the social factors like 'family, social disorganization, unemployment, slum life, etc.', as the cause of crime?

   Ans: They speak of the "**Pull Factors**" and their impact on the commission of crimes. They can never become the causes of crime. They may become only factors in the causation of crime. Any social factor or combination of social factors do not have the importance of ***Cause-Effect*** relationship. For example, the slum-life, deviant–family, unemployment either alone or along with other social factors cannot have an effect called *Crimes*. For, there are any number of such social factors which do not cause crimes.

8. What do the psychologists say when they speak of psychological factors like intelligence, mental disorders, mental retardation, personality traits as the cause of crime?

   Ans: Again, they mean that they can be the **Push Factors** in the causation of crime. A psychological factor either alone or along with other psychological factors cannot have the ***Cause-Effect*** Relationship. There are many who have the above psychological factors do not commit crimes.

9. What is meant by an interaction between **Push** and **Pull Factors**?

   Ans: It means that man can survive only by fighting and/or interacting with his environments. In other words, it is algebraically put—

$$CB = \frac{\text{Pull Factor}}{\text{Push Factor}} \quad (1)$$

$$\mathbf{CB = Pull\ Factor \times Push\ Factor} \quad (2)$$

Where **CB** = criminal behaviour. Whenever, the **Pull Factors** and **Push Factors** interact either by fighting [as shown in (1)] or by cooperating [as shown in (2)] a value is obtained. The personality with this value is called the ***Ego***.

10. What is meant by inculcation of values to form an *Ego* in an upright way in the right direction?
Ans: The interactions (1) and (2) above take place in a socio-cultural melieu which contains many values, norms, rules, traditions, customs, practices, laws, etc. Thus the ***Ego***, contains the socio-cultural 'Dos and Don'ts'. Hence, the result of the interaction is a personality with an *Ego* having values (fair or foul) inculcated.
11. What happens when the *Ego* commits a crime?
Ans: If the ***Ego*** is formed uprightly in the right direction, the crime-doer experiences guilt feelings before, during and/or after the commission of a crime. If it is not, he may not have any guilt feelings.
12. How does the ***Ego*** become a cause of crime?
Ans: An ***Ego*** uprightly formed in the right direction will experience guilt before, during and/or after the commission of a crime. Hence, such an *Ego* may not involve in the commission of crimes or if at all involved, it will have guilt feelings. It is in this sense, the **Push-Pull Ego Factor** says that the EGO is the cause of crime.
13. Can we explain the ***Cause-Effect*** relationship from the point of view of *Ego and crime*?
Ans: An *Ego* uprightly formed in the right direction will not commit a crime. This is a wrong proposition and as such one may emphatically say that there is no *cause-effect relationship* between an *Ego and Crime*. At the same time, one may say that an upright *Ego* rightly formed will have guilt feelings before, during and/or after the commission of crimes. If so, it is unlikely that an upright *Ego* commits a crime. At the same time, an *Ego* inadequately formed

will commit a crime without guilt feelings. Hence, the *cause-effect relationship* is limited between *Ego* and *crime*.

What is the conclusion formed? The search for locating the etiology of crime in criminology is a futile exercise. To conclude, I may quote from my own book *Criminology and Penology* published in 1983 and there I said:

> "From Demenology and innate depravity, the quest for locating the etiological factors in crime has come to victimology". Now, I have a different view and in simple words, I may say that there is nothing called the etiology of crime. Many and different people commit crimes owing to many and different factors. One cause (single cause) approach or multiple causation approach will not answer the question why people commit crimes. For, there is no *cause-effect* relationship between any etiological factors and crimes in criminology. A man commits crimes and he does so because of several factors known or unknown to him—known or unknown to others. But, the society and the law make the man solely responsible for the commission of crimes. For, the society and the law want to punish him for the violation of crime. No one asks the **Push Factors** in him—the **Pull Factors** in and around him—the *Ego* and its formation– the feeling of guilt before, during and/or after the commission of crime. Everyone wants to have a crime-free society and speak loudly "Punish the guilty, punish the guilty", but no one comes forward to study the **Push Factors, Pull Factors and the Formation of the Ego** in a crime-doer. The chapters that follow expose the various kinds of crimes seen in India and I am making an attempt to analyse them with the help and in consultation with a few American Criminologists in the light of my theory the **Push-Pull-Ego Factor Theory**. This is only the tip of the iceberg of crimes in India and as such it has limitations as well.

PART – II

Issues in Criminology and Justice in India

PART PROHIBITION AND REDUCTION OF LIQUOR

That was a Saturday afternoon and Martin, my son-in-law, told me that he would very much love to take me to Branson city in Missouri State—only two hours' drive from Bentonville and that too through a rural road. Rural roads here are as good as city roads in India and, therefore, we could not make out the difference very well. Any way it was a cold day and there was fog on the way to Branson city where people go during their weekends to spend time and leisure. **The Titanic Museum** was a real attraction there for the tourists to Branson and we were issued with boarding passes to get into the ship. **Titanic's** crashing in the Atlantic Sea was known to all and we could see how it was. The Guide who took us through the cabins, halls, decks, etc., of the ship told us about the intensity of coldness of the water at the time Titanic crashed. He asked us to put our index finger in the water and a stop watch was there to show us the duration of the time we could put our index finger in the chilled water. Maximum time was three minutes and I pulled my finger after 50 seconds or so. There was benumbing and according to him, no one could survive the coldness of the water more than three minutes. We saw the signalling system, Mores Code, dining hall, sleeping arrangements, food storage, indoor games hall, etc., and they were superb. We were not allowed to carry our camera and, therefore, we could not take a photograph of visit and left Branson city at about 4 O'clock in the evening.

On our way back through the rural roads, I asked Martin to tell me whether or not liquor was available on the way. Why did I ask him so? Once I was travelling from Thodupuzha to a nearby town in Kerala State (India)—about 20 kilometres distance—and I could count nearly a dozen toddy shops and I was shocked to hear that the rural folk there enjoyed drinking toddy either alone or toddy mixed with alcohol/spirit. Martin told me that liquor was prohibited in that county and he could get one for me from the nearby county where the sale of liquor was permitted. Honestly, I did not want liquor and, therefore, my discussion turned to an academic direction. For, X'mas was just over and I did listen to the Malayalam T.V. telecast about the liquor sale during the X'mas season 2010 and the incredible rise in the sale followed by the routine channel discussions taking us nowhere about the causes, control and prevention of liquor sale in the beautiful State of Kerala, God's own country in India.

In Kerala, there is a long queue in front of every liquor shop and liquor shops are seen throughout the State. If I remember correctly, it was Mr. A.K. Antony's Government which enforced a total prohibition of the sale of *arrack* in the State and permitted the sale of toddy alone. Even at that time, there were strong criticisms against his Government's not well-studied and thought-out decision. Many were of the view that the total prohibition was no solution—rather creating awareness about the evil effects of drinking was a better solution. I too wrote articles in the vernacular dailies and I remember to have written an American decision to impose prohibition and later their decision to lift the total prohibition as found to be an utter failure. No one heard about it or if at all heard, did not attend to it seriously.

Now in U.S.A., there are counties where the sale of liquor is permitted and there are counties where there is prohibition. People who want to drink liquor go to counties where the sale is permitted and purchase bottles. Of course, side by side, there is strict and serious law enforcement in counties where prohibition prevails. ***Certainty*** of punishment is ensured for the violation of law so much so that I did not or I could not find hooch anywhere there. I do not think that liquor addiction is a police problem here, rather is a psychiatric problem. Of course there is drunken driving and the law takes its course, if caught.

In Kerala (India), my question is: 'Why don't we allow the

sale of *arrack* in selected talukas and impose prohibition in other talukas?' People who want to drink *arrack* will purchase bottles from the talukas where they are available. The non-availability of liquor lavishly everywhere at the beck and call of the people is a sure and proved method of reducing the number of people who drink. It is learnt that the U.S. experiment was a real success and they could considerably reduce the number of people who drink here. As liquor shops are plenty in Kerala, people are tempted to drink. *Hooch is available* and illicit transport of spirit is in vogue. Law enforcement is said to be weak and there is allegation that there exists an unholy *nexus* among the bureaucrats, liquor businessmen, politicians so much so that the sale of poison is in full swing in the State. My humble suggestion is to impose or enforce Part Prohibition (area-wise) for the reduction of the incredible sale of liquor and illicit liquor.

Curiosity is a drive in man with an accompanying emotion of *wonder*. Certainly, curiosity is a push factor, and it is seen from infancy. *Curious* means arousing interest and many including children desire to know what happens if liquor is consumed! Availability of liquor (including hootch) is a social fact in many parts of India. Liquor is a major source of income or revenue for many States in the country. Doubtlessly, it is a **Pull Factor**. Every man has many frustrations and mental conflicts. He expresses distress as an accompanying emotion of his drive 'appeal'. People drink everywhere and any festivity without liquor is no festivity at all. The little children make merry by drinking and the old drink liquor for many other reasons. Girls and women consume liquor and they have their special brands for drinking. The bars and drinking dens are full of youngsters who include girls as well. Social stigma attached to drinking has almost vanished to thin air. The **Ego** formed as a result of the availability of liquor everywhere coupled with one's drive—**curiosity**—will or can be a root factor to become alcohol prone. Everyone including the children of tender ages start drinking alcoholic beverages without any guilt feelings. People do so in many situations for *amusement* (an emotion accompanying a drive called **laughter**), for wiping of *loneliness* (which accompanies the drive *gregariousness*). A lot can be written about the causative factors of drinking. There is no dearth of research studies and literature in that area. Such details are outside the scope of this book.

I notice that the danger is more in the development of an **Ego** favouring or embracing the consumption of alcohol or drinking of liquor without any guilt feelings even when one takes it excessively. Ultimately he becomes sick or is converted to an alcoholic proper. My suggestion is to reduce the availability of liquor everywhere coupled with strict enforcement of liquor laws. I may further recommend the creation of an awareness about the evil effects and damaging impact of liquor on personal, employment, family and social life. Governments must refrain from making and increasing the revenue by making people sick in life and stop the sale of liquor in Governments' sale outlets. Many die of liver diseases and an industry is being developed in making medicines to protect the health of the liver. While the business is in full swing, nobody makes any honest or serious attempts to educate the people about the ill-effects of alcoholism or alcohol consumption. They want to sell curative medicines instead of initiating preventive strategies.

The **Ego** of the people—from early infancy–should absorb the truth that liquor is injurious to health and must experience guilt feelings if they become drunkards. People must abhor drinking and drinking habits. One's **Ego** must develop resentments against people who drink. This is called "Awareness Creation". Accordingly, the **Pull Factors** must be made available and for this, the Governments, civic-minded people, concerned citizens, parents, kith and kin of a developing child, teachers, religious and moral men, medical doctors, N.G.Os and other value developing organizations must invest any effort and money. Reduction of **Pull Factors** in society is the only option. Let the American experiment and experience be a practical guide for Indian administration and people.

WHITE ARKANSAS AND BLACK INDIA

I woke up at 3 O'clock in the morning and saw heavy snowing. Neethie, my daughter told me before I went to sleep that there would be good snowing on the following day. I called Mary and asked her to enjoy the snowing in Arkansas. By morning, there was about 3′ of ice and Neethie did not go to WALL*MART then to work. She had to login from home as her associates did and that was the usual practice, I understand, in WALL*MART when there was the heavy snowing. By 12 O'clock, the entire area was white and I had seen such scenes only in cinemas and never in reality. Mary, Maria and I went out with Neethie during her noon interval and took some photographs and loaded them in our laptop. We decided to email them to some of our friends and relatives in India. We wanted them to feel jealous of us too.

Once Mr. Jacob Punnoose I.P.S, the present Director General of Police, Kerala State (2010) said publicly that the *Hawala* money in the State was more than ₹ 50,000 crores in an year. It was a shock to many and the India Vision, a private T.V. Channel in Kerala in their **'Talk and Vote'** programme (?) called me to their studio to comment on the view of the Director General of Police. They wanted to get a studied view of the then State's only Criminologist on the subject. My observations and researches of the flow of *Hawala* money and its impact on Kerala's economy and crimes gave me enough proof to assert that the view of the Director General of Police was totally wrong—far away from being true. I said so boldly and frankly in the T.V. Channel because the Director General of Police was giving an underestimated figure. What is the real truth? The reality was that the *Hawala* money in Kerala was very much higher than ₹ 50,000 crores. It could cross even ₹ 1,00,000 crores and unmistakably it was proved later that my view was realistic. The real-estate business, the *Mafias* of all descriptions, the crime syndicates, the organized criminals, the nexus criminals, the racketeers, the fake-lottery kings, the political sharks, the flesh traders, the traffickers, the corrupt bureaucrats and their meat-eater criminal partners, the white collar criminals and economic offenders, consensus criminals, the terrorists, insurgents, fundamentalists, fanatics, *goondas* of all types, bandits and unprincipled men, the resort-owners of dubious integrity, the drive-in-bars with other motives, massage centres with flesh trade and thus, thus...the entire Kerala (just like many other parts in India) is seen contaminated with such crimes as Arkansas is seen today with snowing and ice everywhere making the smooth life of the ordinary man/citizenry in real difficulties. The only difference between Arkansas and Kerala (India) is that Arkansas is white whereas Kerala (India) is black-black with black money!

If snowing is seen at Bentonvilla, Arkansas, U.S.A, raining and flowing of black and/or fake money may be seen in Kerala and India. Today's children grow up in such an atmosphere of affluence in many parts of the country. Of course, there is poverty in India, but many children who are seemingly poor lead really a rich life. They have many nefarious activities by which they make money. Youngsters are minting money *via* means and methods known only to them. The emotions seen in many children are found to be (1) amusement, (2) appetite, (3) lust, (4) wonder, (5) feeling of superiority and many a child expresses them in different ways. The *drives* (instinctual) are respectively (1) laughter (2) food seeking, (3) sex, (4) curiosity, (5) self-assertion, etc. Sometimes, **pugnacity** (combat) is seen as a drive followed by **anger** as an accompanying emotion. These *drives* work as **Push Factors**. What are the **Pull Factors**? People want to satisfy their drives and many of them desire to enjoy an *adipoly* (*Adipoly* in Malayalam language means a very pleasant and pleasurable life) life style. In order to live an **adipoly** life and to satisfy the human drives, one must have money. There is no substitute for money. Hence, they say that a substitute for *Money is Money* alone and nothing else. Therefore, make *Money and Easy Money by any means*– seems to be the motto or only aim of many—is the value in most of the people. Thus, one observes *Hawala* Money, *Pipe* Money, False Employment Bureaus, Employment Rackets, Visa Syndicates, *Nexus* Dealings, Corruption, *Mafia*, Adulteration of all kinds, Economic Crimes and Money Laundering, Crimes by the Affluent, White Collar crimes, Bureaucratic crimes, Foreign Bank Accounts, Money Chains and Multi-marketing, Corporate crimes and thus the list for making of or minting money is indeed very long.

People go to amusement centres, flesh trade, pilgrimage, gold markets, *goondaism*, five-star prostitution, massage spots, resorts and thus their **Push Factors** find naked expressions in many and various ways. Corresponding to the **Push Factors**, there should be **Pull Factors**. If there exist no **Pull Factors**, then people will create them. Hotel business, Reality shows, Acting in Films, T.V. Serial acting, Fashion Shows and Modelling, Blue-Album productions and production of blue films, weekly picnics and stay in tourists resorts, House-boats and 7 star stay in costly hotels, etc., are **Pull Factors**. The impact of the **Push** and **Pull factors** clubbing together in the formation of an **Ego** with no guilt feelings if at all they involve in all sorts of pleasure getting and/or giving, erotic, happiness providing activities, etc. Certainly, in such situations, the **Ego** is not or cannot be formed in an upright way in the right direction.

Developing children inculcate values in their personality from the time of their birth and thus must have an **Ego Formation** with upright moral and spiritual values. Epicureanism, hedonism, selfishness, sexuality, erotic satisfaction, drinking, making money by any means including *goondaism* or underworld activities, etc., should not work deeply as **Pull Factors**. Money is important but money is not everything. Ill-earned money goes ill-spent. Too much money is poison. Extreme riches made in an illegal way ensure early death. Nevertheless, those values are to be seen strongly controlling the **Ego**.

Arkansas becomes white by snowing and Kerala (India) becomes black by black and fake money. Wherever one goes out, people come there with plenty of money. Go to a textile shop, a bar, a restaurant, a jewellery, the beach, a grocery shop, a cinema theatre, a liquor shop, a bank, a car selling shop, a casino, a hospital, a pilgrim centre, a club, a boat house, a self–financing college, share-market, a baby shop, a gambling den, a dancing hall, a medical shop, a tailor, a grocery store, a T.V. selling shop…., one finds people with abundance of money. One is always in the queue and everyone spends money without any reservations. From where does the money come? Is it from the container money sent by some foreign nations? Is it the fake money manufactured here or elsewhere? People get counterfeit money from banks' A.T.Ms and they are shocked to listen that the bank accounts of some of "our" leaders, religious men, business sharks and industrialists in foreign banks are incredible. There is, no doubt, a parallel economy in the country and children born into such an economy will develop an **Ego** with little or no guilt consciousness if at all they make easy money by any means, foul or fair. The snow at Bentonville, Arkansas gets melted when the sun becomes hot. But what about the black money in India?

RETIREMENT AS VOTE BANK AND CORRUPTION

"Retirement at the age of 55 is ridiculous. When I was 65, I still had pimples"—said a professor who retired from Michigan University when he heard that I retired from active Government service at the age of 55 on superannuation. He could not believe me and I think that he still does not believe me. Yes, my friend from Rochester, New York, is 73 years of age now and he retired from his active service only about a couple of years back.

In Kerala, India, some people retire at the age of 65, some at the age of 60, some at the age of 58, some at the age of 55, some do not have retirement at all from Government service and some get reemployment after retirement. Is there any place in the entire universe where so much confusion and differences in the age of retirement exists?— There is unreasonableness too in the matter of retirement. People are literally kicked out or forced to retire at the prime of their youth from active Government service for enabling (said to be so) new job seekers to get into the service. I am told that the number of pensioners is going to outnumber the number of employees in Government service. I understand that the fund spent from Government exchequer to give pension to the young pensioners is very huge and the amount of money spent for giving salary to the new entrants to the service is indeed very high. Adding them together, it is easy to understand that the Government service is highly expensive and the people are condemned to get inferior services as the experienced employees are at home as retired people. The inexperienced new entrants render their services and by the time they become mature and experienced, they too are dragged out or kicked out of service. They know their bad fate so much so that an employee who joins the service at the age of 40 gets hardly 15 years to go for his retirement. He must live even after his retirement and corruption becomes the easiest shortcut to amass wealth and live comfortably after his retirement. In my view, the early retirement is a factor for corruption and bribery in Government service.

"Before getting employed in Government service, a man yearns for a job and after getting the employment, the 'Y' is silent"— and this is so because he has to say good-bye to his service at the age of 55 on superannuation. If at all the exchequer has a great loss—if at all the service is rendered by the newly appointed in an inferior way—if at all corruption is multiplied-if at all confusion and unreasonableness persists in the matter of retirement age, one thing is ensured, i.e., the **Vote Bank** is well protected. All is well that ends well. Nevertheless, some remedies are worse than the disease and the decision to pull out the Government employees at the age of 55 on superannuation in the most literate State in India is said to be a 'Remedy' for unemployment, but certainly worse than the **Disease.**

Acquisitiveness is a drive (instinct) in man and it is followed by an emotion of a feeling of ownership. Self-assertion is another drive with an accompanying emotion of feeling of superiority. These two **Push Factors** work strongly in all individuals. In America, I could notice that many Indians working here work hard (not like what they do in India) and one of the driving forces is acquisitiveness and another is 'self-assertion'. People are not satisfied with what they have. Those who are in the low economic strata of the society want to go up vertically to reach the middle strata who in turn make all attempts to reach the high...top... still top strata of the society. Some American studies do show that the drive for the vertical mobility is a cause of crimes. For vertical mobility in finance, politics, status, stability, people are having recourse to fair or foul means. For the actualization of the **Push Factors**, there are any number of **Pull Factors** in India. Take, for example, the corruption in the country. Many people are there to offer corruption money. Criminologists are of the firm view that in a country of corruption, it is only through corruption that wisdom can rule. Allegations are plenty to show that many government services are pregnant with corruption money, corruption money fixing and corruption money splitting, etc. The atmosphere there is such that the government employees are adament in accepting corruption money and the people are graciously willing to offer money/favours. They have no option but to become gracious. When both are put together, we have a corrupt civil service in India. Corruption and malpractices are of many types and varieties and are seen not only among the executive wing of the Government but also amidst some of the personnel working in judicial services. The corruption money is sweetly called "service money" and many involved in giving or accepting corruption money, favours, fortunes, promises, etc., do not have any guilt feelings. They do not develop any guilt consciousness. It is so because many of them are born and brought up in an environment which has been saturated with corruption. Post-independence period in India has been a period of developing bribery (of the British India) into corruption (of the independent India). The **Pull Factors** to become corrupt are indeed very many and, therefore, the contemporary India witnesses corruption getting percolated deeper and spread wider and wider.

In America, the opportunities for employment are brighter than what we have in India. They have well developed social security schemes in which the unemployed are looked after. We do not have any such schemes worth mentioning and precisely, therefore, there is anxiety—*anxiety neurosis*—among the unemployed, underemployed and employed people. An early retirement from the government services makes many to develop an **Ego** which accepts the fact that there is nothing wrong in being or in becoming corrupt. Make money *via* corruption and illegality! Yes, it is the right of the poor man to misbehave and the one in service has little or no time for retirement on superannuation! Hence, hurry please! They have justifications for their corruption and one rationalizes his action by blowing of the anti-corruption laws working as a less powerful force. Resultingly, an **Ego** with no guilt feeling is formed even when one is recruited to the service. He becomes corrupt as years go by. Inculcation of the anti-corruption laws, moral and religious values as forces will work as an internal policeman against one becoming corrupt in service. Concurrently, the retirement age on superannuation must be raised to 60, or 62, or 65 as the case may be to make uniformity. This will make everyone happy and no one will have the feeling of relative deprivation while they are in service. Corruption and malpractices may be in America too, but quickly I may say that it is certainly not as severe as one sees in a developing country or under-developed country or an undeveloped country. Age of retirement on superannuation from government service and the duration of service are twin factors that work behind corruption in Kerala, in India and in other parts of the world.

EX-HUSBANDS AND EX-WIVES IN PLENTY

Ex-MLA, Ex-Minister—such expressions are familiar to Indians because the number of such personalities in the country is really incredible. I do not think that in our culture, we have heard of ex-husbands and ex-wives. But, here in U.S.A., ex-husbands and ex-wives are numerous and I could see an ex-husband and ex-wife smiling (quite naturally) in a birth day party here. Just a couple of days ago, my son-in-law told me about the sad and premature demise of the wife of his associate in the office. He said that his colleague was really very melancholic because he has been living with her for 22 long years—really a long period which, as a general rule, cannot be thought of by many urban Americans.

Delores Bohman from Ohio was known to me for the last 40 years and she has three children—Deb, Dan and Don. Her husband Lowell L. Bohman died of cancer on October 31, 2010. They had a pleasant family life and such pretty families, I am told, are not many here. Amidst the ex-husbands and ex-wives, there are good souls living together for twenty or twenty-five years and the family of the associate of my son-in-law belonged to that rare community.

What about Kerala, India? It has been observed by the sociologists that the family is an institution most disrupted in the State in the entire country today. Divorces are going up, desertions are very high, and separation is in vogue besides the disorganized families everywhere owing to several factors—visible and invisible. Long ago, I wrote a number of articles about the rising trend of divorces in Kerala. At that time, there was only one Family Court in Thiruvananthapuram and it attended to family cases from Thiruvananthapuram and Kollam districts. Now, family courts are established and functioning in many talukas and the work load is really very heavy in every court. Incidentally, I may recollect my experience. After enrolling myself as an Advocate before the Bar Council of Kerala, I was seated in my office in Thiruvananthapuram. A lady and her daughter came to me for legal advice and they wanted immediate divorce. I said that I could not take up the *vakkalat* as divorce cases did not come in my area of practice. Also, I did not want to give legal advice to a divorce case as my first case. Being in police, I had many occasions to interact with couples and I do not exactly remember the number of family disruption cases compromised by me.

The reasons for the incredible increase in family disruption may be many and various and enumerating them here is not my objective. I am very much afraid and am terribly upset and frightened to notice the incredible increase in divorces, desertions and separations in family life in Kerala, India. Are we going to increase the number of ex-husbands and ex-wives amidst us? What about our children then? Yes, when the values are westernized, certainly the family will be westernized. Home, **Sweet Home** may be a home in our dreams and not in reality in the near future!?

Enduring sex relationship is an essential ingredient in family life. Sex is sacred and the relationship in man is not purely instinctual as the animals and birds have. There is the responsibility of upbringing of children born in the wedlock. Marriage is not simply a civil contract as the State laws may say. It is much more and is a sacrament—religiously conceived as a bond till the death of one of the partners in marriage. In America, the values of marriage and family life may be different. Most desperately such values are flowing down to India as well more freely than what it was in the past.

Sex is an instinct with lust which is an emotion that follows. Lust means a sexual desire or appetite, especially when uncontrolled or illicit. It is a passionate yearning, i.e., over-mastering desire. This sort of sex or lust is not the one which must be seen in married life. Marriage is a responsibility and when children are born, it is a responsible parenthood that should come into being. But owing to the infiltration of new values into our culture in India, the instinct of sex becomes no more a responsibility, but remains as an instinct with a following emotion of lust. Man becomes an animal and the animality becomes the **Push Factor**! When the instinct of sex overpowers, many other **Push Factors** like escape (accompanying emotion is *fear*), repulsion (accompanying emotion is *disgust*), etc., come into being. What about the **Pull Factors**? Traditional sanctity given to family and family life is getting vanished. Quarrelling parents, disorganized families, fighting children, male/female superiority, my money–your money attitude, lack of understanding between parents and children, anger causing behaviour, divorces, separation, desertion etc., become the **Pull factors**. Financial independence of the husband and wife, My bank account-Your bank account approaches, lack of love and concern, etc., have accelerated the family disruption. As a result, a perverted **Ego** is formed even in developing children. In America, I hear them telling that everyone expects a divorce even before his/her marriage. In India, still we cannot think of divorces/desertions. A divorce is no surprise to the Americans. It is so because the *Ego* of every growing child has reconciled with the reality.

In India, a woman usually suffers her husband in spite of many problems and difficulties. In India, most husbands tolerate wives and adjust/accommodate with them. For, the social stigma to divorced, separated or deserted wife/husband is unbearable–more in the past than what it is today. Now, Indian children too develop an Ego which may reconcile with the reality of divorces. The law is not in favour of divorces, yet may grant separation/divorces on genuine grounds along with maintenance allowance from husbands to wives—from parents to children. In spite of such strict laws, people go to Family Courts in large numbers. The problems related to the divorced to get married again are getting thinner and thinner and thus, I am to think that we too are nearing to the American attitude and approaches to family life.

Seeing the American family life and paining in the rise of divorces in India, I wrote tweets and got them published *via* internet. Some of them are—

- A house is constructed by bricks and a home by emotions. A family has both.
- A faithful wife and husband, a loving father and mother, a mutually understanding parents and children -they make a sweet home.
- Husband, wife, father, mother, children—all are candles which light for others and consume themselves.
- A sweet home is one where couples-parents-parents and children themselves disagree on many things without being or becoming disagreeable.
- A good wife is a man's best wealth, a good husband is a woman's best health, good children are health and wealth of a sweet home.
- 'Understanding' is a great lubricant in a sweet home.
- Any quarrel between a husband and wife should be like cutting water with a sword.
- Overlooking and overseeing—very effective strategies to make a sweet home. Practise them.
- 'Anger' is only one letter short of 'danger'—true in a family life too. Beware of.
- As the husband, so is the wife or *vice versa*; as the parents, so is the child; as is the yarn, such is the cloth.
- Blessings are not valued till they are gone and so is the sweetness in family life. No divorce or desertion, please!
- Bitter pills may have blessed effects— so are the issues in our family life. No divorce or desertion, please!

- Better is poverty with a sweet family than riches in a troubled family. No divorce or desertion, please!
- Happiness in a home is never experienced until it is shared by all at home. Happiness is a thing to be practiced by all at home.
- A wise husband takes more advice from his wife than what he gives and a wise wife is one who takes more advice from her husband than what she gives.
- Keep your eyes wide open before marriage and half-shut afterwards in a family life.
- He that speaks ill of his wife dishonours himself; she that speaks high of her husband honours herself.
- Husband and wife who want to expand their heart by love, concern and understanding must contract their mouth.
- He who has a pure mind sees everything pure. Suspicion of the life partner is the greatest curse in family life.
- Husband and wife—though two in physique—are one in love. This is the secret of success in family life.
- Don't own anything that won't fit into a happy married life. This is the secret of success in marriage.

Thus were my thoughts when I saw the ex-husbands and ex-wives in U.S.A. Certainly, the **Ego** of the children, marrying partners and married couples must be formed, reformed or shaped or reshaped accepting the sublime principles and values of family life—**a sweet home**!

FROM SMALL ACORNS, GIANT OAKS GROW

A child-boy of 4 years of age has only a 'shuddy' to cover his privates and a girl of 3 years of age too has a 'shuddy' to cover her privates. Both are in a standing position—face to face—and looking curiously something inside the 'shuddy' of the boy. This is an advertisement picture and in it, the girl pulls the 'shuddy' of the boy and both of them with wide mouths and curious eyes look at the privates of the boy and remain there in that position without understanding much. And an advice: **"From Small Acorns, Giant Oaks Grow"**. Everybody driving a vehicle and travelling through that road cannot but see the erotic 'enjoyment' of two innocent children in our country. I saw it and I have the memories of that advertisement coming and going to and from my mind without my permission. Let it be there. No salvation!

My first visit to USA was in 1986 and then I had to drive to McHill University, Montrial, Canada *via* Niagra Falls and Toronto. Dr. Peechatt was driving his car and I closely and keenly looked around and out to find some advertisement boards on the road. I wanted to study how did Americans and Canadians publish their commodities. Then I could not find any advertisement boards on roads, road-sides, foot-paths, etc., both in USA and in Canada. Later, I had been to many other countries, particularly Singapore where my daughter, Neethu works in the Ministry of Education. She stays with Abhilash Varghese Koikara, Senior Vice President, Citi Bank there. They have three kids—Anna, George and Ammu. I have stayed with them for many days and travelled extensively through the roads of Singapore almost everyday. I could not find any commercial advertisement boards on roads or road sides there too. I had been to UAE (Sharjah and Dubai) and my boosom friend Adv. George Varghese Kallummottil drove me to various places. There too, no commercial advertisement boards on roads or road sides. They have only road signs and boards—and again they are only for the safe driving and the safety of the road users. They are not at all to distract the attention of the road users.

How many advertisement boards are seen on our roads, centre of the road, road junctions, road-sides, foot-paths in Kerala/India? God alone knows them! Are our roads intended for commercial advertisements or for safe driving? Sale of bras, panties, jetties, cigarettes, clothes, jewellery, food items, etc., are on roads and they are illuminated throughout the day and night. Beautiful girls dressed in erotic styles with their **Half** in and **Half** out, boys with attractive jetties in semi-nakedness or only with jetties, children in urinating position, old women without any upper clothes tasting food and thus one sees all sorts of undesirable advertisement boards—very colourful and attractive—during their road journey. For what? For the safety and protection of drivers? For the safety and protection of other road users? For the purpose of educating the public on road safety? Oh God! Forgive them. We do not see many road signs, signals, markings, speed regulating devices, lights, etc., on roads there. Posters of politicians, religious speakers, miracle makers, sports stars, cinema 'super stars', models, serial girls, cheese-cake girls, erotic boys, exotic girls, flesh traders and racketeers are plenty to distract the attention of road users in India. Accidents occur every second and everybody is deaf, dumb and blind to these social evils which are nothing but crimes indeed. Even now, I do not see any advertisement boards on roads in the whole of America (2011) and they fail to understand why are there so many advertisements on roads in India!

Acquisitivenss is an instinct which is a **Push Factor** with feeling of ownership as an accompanying emotion. In America, people purchase very costly cars and the types of car which they have really make them superior to others in their culture. The same attitude and approach may be seen in India too in these days. Many luxury cars are on roads now. In America, there is speed restriction which people are expected to observe meticulously. If they violate the speed restriction, they are likely or surely caught. In India too, there is speed restriction, nevertheless people do not observe the rules and certainty of punishment to violators is not ensured there. We do not have many cameras on roads or radar system installed. Hence, the **Pull Factor** is that one may drive the vehicle as he desires. In U.S.A, there are no advertisement boards on the road or road-sides. Hence, their attention is not often distracted while they drive the vehicles. In India, one may see any number of advertisement boards and they do capture the eyes of the drivers. Sex stimulating pictures as advertisement on roads are real distracters so much so that the drivers cannot but see and enjoy such erotic posters on roads. Even after many hours of seeing such eroticism, the emotion of lust, sometimes, continues to control them. Resultingly accidents may occur.

Youngsters who drive the vehicles are having *curiosity* as a push factor followed by the emotion of *wonder*. They drive their vehicles with higher speed as *self-assertion* is a **Push Factor** accompanied by the emotion of a *feeling of superiority* over other drivers. The omnibuses, lorries, trucks, tip-lorries, luxury cars, government vehicles, police jeeps, etc., show their feeling of superiority, perhaps, in violating the rules more than in observing the road laws and ethics. Yes, they *laugh* **(Push Factor)** and have *amusement* (accompanying emotion) on roads.

Little children of tender years of age, girls, youth and so on drive vehicles on roads. Many people make a living by driving in India and they drive their vehicles in a rash and negligent way.

Pugnacity (combat) is seen in them as a **Push Factor** followed by an emotion called *anger*. Road rage is a topic widely discussed in India and many drivers do not adhere to road ethics. They speak foul language and sometimes fight one another. Sometimes, they behave like *goondas* and instances are plenty showing road rage and anger reported in the media. The children born and grown in such an atmosphere develop an **Ego** which justifies every fair and foul doings on road. If the **Pull Factors** are such that the **Ego** of the developing child is not formed in an upright way in the right direction, then vehicles may become a powerful killer of people on roads. Vehicle accidents result in causing serious injuries to road users.

The suggestions to develop an upright **Ego** formed in the right direction may be—

- No safety distractors on road; No commercial advertisement boards; no erotic pictures on the way or road-sides!
- Strict enforcement of speed rules, lane traffic system, certainty of punishment for violators of law.
- Clear road markings in the correct way, road signs and signals at all places.
- Perfect maintenance of road, proper licensing system and procedure and enforcement of traffic regulations.
- Educating children about observance of traffic laws, rules, regulations and ethics to form an upright **Ego** in the right direction.

In Victoria State, Australia, I am told that little children studying in schools were taught traffic laws, rules, regulations and ethics for 10 years at the end of which they could reduce the number of traffic accidents on roads to a considerable extent. **The Push Factors** and **Pull Factors** together formed an **Ego** that accepted traffic law violations as undesirable acts or offences under law.

WALL*MART AND GOD'S OWN COUNTRY

'You purchase anything from **Wall*Mart**, you can return it if not satisfied and it must be within a specified period'. Once you take back the purchased item, they return your money with pleasure, without any questions and with a smiling face. 'Smile deliberately whether one feels like it or not, for it is almost impossible to have miserable thoughts when one turns the corners of his mouth upwards'—This is **Wall*Mart** approach. **Wall*Mart** family believes that smile is a commodity which must be sold in their stores. This philosophy makes many to go to **Wall*Mart** and purchase as much as they want. For, the people know that the purchased items can be returned if they are qualitatively inferior or not up to the mark or their expectations. **Wall*Mart** feels that it is their success in business and they are the biggest retail-business people in the world—I am told.

Adulteration is not a new thing in Kerala/India. It is seen there in A to Z and people die of food poisoning, hooch, fake medicines, inferior treatment and what not? Duplicate articles are plenty and genuine parts of many things may be a rare commodity for purchase. False employment bureaus, fake companies, false N.O.C./Visa, *blade* companies and cheating enterprises, adulterated preachers, prayers, *poojaries* and politicians, false promises and programmes, fake advertisements for flesh trade, modelling, production of song albums, acting in cinema and T.V. serials and what not? Are the Governments aware of these nefarious activities? If they are aware of, what does the machinery do to prevent them? **Wall*Mart** philosophy, i.e., returning of purchased items if found to be inferior or duplicate is not possible or unheard of. Nevertheless, proper vigilance and control may be possible. Flourishing of these crimes in India and particularly in the most literate State in the country indicates that the administration is weak and far away from being satisfactory. The never ending **'False and Fake'** is and should be an eye-opener for the administration to believe that all is not well in the **God's Own Country**! No doubt, the situation may be worse in other States.

How many people cheated by various persons and agencies get proper remuneration or compensation and victim justice? Hardly any. When anything unpleasant happens, immediately there come false Government promises: "Strict action", "Law will take its course", "The criminals will not be allowed to escape" and thus the people are given the vain hope that they will be taken to the promised land or the ***Yahweh*** will come at last. Like the

Jews, the Keralites/Indians live under a hope—a helpless hope for the better and the 'better' never comes. Many States in India produce duplicate items and send them to other parts of the country. Many States have fake companies and production centres. 'Duplicates' of everything available everywhere are in the Country.

Coming to **Wall*Mart** back, we too have retail shops in the Country. People are cheated and the bills they receive after purchase contains an inscription 'Articles once sold will not be taken back'. FINE! The only option then left with us is to throw away or approach the Consumer Courts where consumers' cases are filling the court rooms—giving a **Hope** to have a **Hope** against **Hope**. There are shops which sell only duplicate articles and they sell not only in their shops, but also they promote their duplicates through *'Door to Door'* sale by their sale boys and girls who always claim or pretend to study a course in business administration/ management for which the sale of duplicate items becomes a part of the curriculum. God, you alone can save the people!—the Country.

People want to possess many things and sometimes, beyond their financial capacity. People who live in a lower economic stratum of the society want to go to the next higher stratum and this may make some to have recourse to foul or unfair methods even by committing crimes. Studies have proved it to be true. Why? It is because the **Push Factor**, i.e., *Acquisitiveness* (accompanying emotion is a feeling of *ownership*) is in everyone. They have the **Push Factor** called *Self-assertion* (accompanying emotion is a feeling of *superiority*). These **Push Factors** have their corresponding **Pull Factors** too. Owing to India's financial development today, many children are born and brought up in some affluence. They can have anything purchased or possessed. Those who cannot acquire them, make attempts to possess them *via* their delinquent behaviour. Albert Cohen says that 'the children from the lower economic class accept the goals of the middle class. As they have not received the type of socialization and consequent **ego** formation which the middle class children had in their development, they have an *Ego* which may be crime prone'. The **Pull Factors** are the availability of everything in the market. As there are people to purchase things by any means—fair or foul— there is scope for the sale of duplicate or third rate articles. The

Chinese products may be of inferior quality and people sell them without any guilt feelings. The people are cheated and those who cheat others do not experience guilt feelings and to that extent, they are psychopaths.

There is a demand, but there is no sufficient supply. As a result, people market anything—fake and false—and thus the sale is not limited to articles alone. They sell false employments, prayers, gods, pious articles, etc. In society, one may see any number of fake companies, duplicate articles, adulterated materials, false promises, cheating enterprises, untrue advertisements and propaganda, unscrupulous cure by divine intervention and what not? The **Pull Factors** are plenty and the children brought up in such an atmosphere develop an *Ego* which is duplicate-prone, adulteration-prone, fake-prone, false-prone, etc., and they do many nefarious activities without any guilt feelings.

The strategies suggested to reduce crime and delinquent activities may be—

- Strict checking of all qualities of the articles sold and executing strict action against those who produce and promote fake or duplicate items in society.
- Perfect surveillance against the nefarious activities including those committed by false or fake companies, organizations, individuals and 'isms'.
- Control of the market and sale of goods by many departments with their coordinated actions.
- Inculcation of values in children by parents, teachers and other value-developing organizations.
- Promoting legal, moral and social literacy among the people to fight against a culture of cheating others.

PEST CONTROL AND POLICE FIRING

–5° celsius is the temperature outside today at Bentonville and there is ice everywhere. The entire area is seen as white Himalayas in our cinema. I do not think that any insects, reptiles or mammals can live here unless they are created with a capacity to withstand this extreme climate. A few days ago, we went to a zoo and we could take our car inside the zoo and drive. A variety of animals and birds were in the zoo and we drove our car seeing them. Some came to us and many visitors in front and behind us took photographs of the animals. We could not photograph them as we forgot to take our camera. I asked Martin and Neethie: "How do these animals, reptiles and birds survive the extreme climate? They did not answer my query as they did not know the answer. They told me that the zoo would be closed for outsiders during the extreme climate. Anyway, today, when I looked out, I could see not less than 500 sparrows-like birds flying in the sky. Of course, God's special creations with capacity to withstand any extreme cold climate!

I do not see mosquitoes here and I think that ordinarily, they cannot survive here in this extreme climate of coldness. Or, they must be specially created mosquitoes. I saw a small spider inside the apartment and then I asked: "How come spiders here?" Mary replied my question: "Specially created spiders" for Bentonville, Arkansas. Neethie added to Mary's comments saying that the pest department was very serious about pest control and they could be called if pests were seen. Good. They have immediate remedy for their problems. The people are also conscious about the pests and they take care of their protection.

In Kerala or India, pests are a real problem and what do we do against the pests? I have little or no information about the working of a pest department in India and any serious activity to control or destroy pests. When some epidemic like chicken guinea attacks the people, the mosquitoes are blamed for it. Then the Corporation Authorities come up with an occasional fogging to kill the mosquitoes. The Health Department has some projects against mosquitoes/malaria. From my compound at Mannammoola where I live, I find centipedes, millipedes, pests of many descriptions, reptiles, mad dogs, worms of all categories, snails of every type, wastes thrown to public roads, flies of many kinds, rats and what not? Should we not think about a permanent pest department which is ever active and vigilant? Or should we continue to declare regional *bandhs*, road blocks, *hartals*, *dharnas* and mass destruction of public property to see the eyes of authorities open. Or, are we to think that the pests can be controlled by suppressing public reactions and agitations by police muscles, lathi charges and as a last resort, by police firing?

Every individual has an **Ego** formed out of the **Push** and **Pull Factors**. The **Ego** is the activating force or energy and in simple terms, it is the product of the **Push and Pull** Factors. Like the individual's ***Ego***, there is a **Societal Ego** which every society, sub-society or sub-sub society has. **Societal** means 'pertaining to large social groups, or to their activities, customs etc.' A region, religion, State, nation has an ***Ego***. A race, caste, sub-caste has an ***Ego***. For example, a communal riot or a racial conflict may arise out of a hurt ***Ego***. There exists inter-State rivalry, inter-country rifts, inter-religion fights, inter-faith attacks and behind each one of them, there is the working of a **Societal Ego**.

Every society must have all the instincts which an individual has. Every society must have its own emotions to every instinct. The media, especially the visual media today activate a lethargic society, or government by provoking them to do a particular thing in a particular way. When the roads in a State are in a dilapidated condition, the media bring it out and attract the Government's attention to it. Thus, the inertia is taken away. When the media brings out the inertia or the opposition political party exposes the inaction, the Government becomes active.

How is the **Societal Ego** formed? The **Push Factors** in the society may be *Escape* (accompanying emotion is *fear* which may be seen at the time of an epidemic or towards the waste stored in public places), *Repulsion* (accompanying emotion is *disgust* which may be seen in unhealthy environments, pollution of water, etc., etc.). The **Push Factors** in the opposition political party may be *pugnacity* (combat with an accompanying emotion of *anger*). The **Push Factors** can be anything causing fear, disgust or anger in people. Owing to the interaction of the **Pull and Push Factors**, people organize *bandhs*, road blocks, *dharnas*, mass protests, etc., and they cause serious damage to the law and order situations without any guilt feelings. Children who are born and brought up in a culture of violence develop an ***Ego*** to do anything for social goodness without any guilt feelings. In this case, the pests in the country is a serious problem and the governments in power do not take any effective steps to control or prevent the attacks of the pests. They have some *adhoc* arrangements or adjustments to solve a social problem *hic et nunc*. That is not enough and the **Societal Ego** formed in a particular State or country may be responsible for mass scale attacks and they do it without any guilt feelings.

How to solve the pest issue? Here are some suggestions:

- Read the pulse of the people and solve the issue.
- Study the **Push** and **Pull Factors** of the general public and initiate steps to remedy the situation.
- Evaluate the **Societal Ego** from the history and educate the people about civic sense and citizen's responsibility. Any destruction of public property is a crime and very much a moral evil which has a guilty consciousness.
- People's **Ego** must have guilt feelings when they commit offences.

An inactive government may cause the development of a **Societal Ego** without guilt feelings.

ROMAN KINGS AND ABOVE THE LAW

Waste management is a developed science and there are universities which offer Master's Course in that branch of discipline. I am told that the students who study M.B.A. in waste management do not waste their time in seeking placements. Any way in Bentonville and for that matter in the entire USA, I think that the waste management is well programmed. In **The Link** at **Rainbow Curve** apartments here, there are, it appears to me, more than 100 apartments. There exist extremely fine arrangements for waste collection and disposal. In Singapore, the arrangement is still better and in Dubai and Sharjha, it is indeed fine. If all these countries can perform a responsibility in an enviable way, why do we fail miserably in that area? Hygienic environment is a human right and no authority can deny it to the citizens.

In Thiruvananthapuram where I stay, the waste management is far away from being satisfactory. Wastes are thrown to public roads, to public lands, to water, to road sides, to private property, to railway tracks, to road side drainage canals and where not? When I go from Mannammoola to Peroorkada (about one kilometre) I find waste being thrown to road sides—smelling and many a time with nauseating smell—from Peroorkada to Kaudiar (two kilometres), even dead dogs, intestines of chicken with feathers, market wastes, decayed vegetables, rags, human excreta, dead animals, rats ....may be seen. The entire city is contaminated with waste of all descriptions and kinds/categories. Public protests are seen and heard against waste disposal. People helplessly suffer the foul smell and many have skin diseases. The environment is polluted, the water is dirty, vegetation around is smelling and the T.V. visuals are horrible and public anger-causing. There are laws prohibiting the polluting attitude and activities of the people. I am told that the punishment is ₹ 10,000 or so. The law is not effectively enforced and the people are worried at the callous indifference of the authorities in the matter. Foreigners visiting the capital city ask: "How do the people live here?" The position is not different in Kochi, Chennai, Kolkata and all cities in the country. In rural areas, waste collection, control and disposal is unknown. No enforcement of the laws! What to do?

When the public agitation is there, the police enter the scene. Cases are registered against the strikers and the peace is disturbed. While cases are registered against even innocent people, or against the agitating and aggressive members of the public, the bureaucrats/officials who are to perform their duty are not proceeded against. No case is registered against them for their inaction, lethargy, omission to perform their responsibility. Are they above the law? Or the law can be enforced only against the enforceable? Yes, all these officials having power and authority are the **Roman Kings** and **Above The Law**!

What about the situation in other cities? The situation is no better in many cities and towns. No toilet facilities, no waste disposal plants, no arrangements and precisely because of that, people agitate at them. Nevertheless, they tolerate to some extent the lethargy and inaction of the authorities of local administration and governments in power. Here too, the public behaviour is to be interpreted as the effect of the **Societal *Ego*** formed.

The **Societal *Ego*** has two areas, namely (1) tolerating, and (2) agitating. How? The **Push Factors** are doubtlessly *Escape* (emotion is *fear*), *Repulsion* (*wonder* is the emotion), *Pugnacity* (combat) (emotion is *anger*). The public have *Appeal* too (emotion is *distress*). What about the **Pull Factors**? People suffer the waste and the foul smell. Many do not have any toilet facilities at home. Some have their nature's call answered on road sides or in public. They throw their waste to the public places, roads or to the other man's land. All these **Pull Factors** have mitigated the rigours and strength of the **Push Factors**. As a result, people develop an *Ego* which has tolerance, i.e., an act or capacity of enduring or endurance just like many people have a tolerance to the noise, sound pollution, road blocks, *hartals* and *bandhs*, etc. But, now, owing to the awareness of more hygienic life styles and construction of clean toilets and providing of more facilities for hygiene in many newly built houses in the country, the society started to develop a **societal *Ego*** with **Push Factors** of *escape, repulsion, pugnacity* and *appeal,* etc. **Pull Factors** are more in favour of hygienic environments and people invest a lot of money for water closets, latrines and bath rooms. There is the growing demand for public lavatories and bath rooms in bus stations, railway compartments, hotels, cinema halls and they conduct *dharnas*, agitations, processions and *hartals*, etc., demanding the construction of sufficient toilets, bathroom facilities, waste disposal plants, scientific waste management, etc. The earlier generation and their **Societal *Ego*** tolerating the waste and its foul smell is getting vanished and a new generation with a new *Ego* of not tolerating the unscientific waste management is coming up. As a result, they, sometimes, violate the rules and laws regulating waste management. They throw the waste to the offices of the authorities and protest against the attitude and approach of authorities. They do not experience any guilt feelings for what they do out of public interest, rather feel proud of their law violations. Time is not far away that the **Societal *Ego*** reacts against the administration.

The suggestions to reduce the law violation in this specific area may be—

- Massive investment of money and resources for waste disposal in cities and towns on a war-footing.
- Lavatories and bath rooms should be constructed for the public to make use of them freely free. There should be proper maintenance and cleaning with lotions and disinfectants.
- Children should be taught and educated about personal and social hygiene. The public must be exposed to awareness programmes so that a **Societal *Ego*** pregnant with a pro-cleanliness attitude is formed. People should have a guilt feeling if they violate the rules of public cleanliness. Children with such *Ego* formation are seen in other countries. They never allow people to violate the laws of hygiene and public cleanliness.

SMALL CAUSES AND SMALL CLAIMS COURTS

There is a body Fitness Centre for The **Links** at **Rainbow Curve** and the residents can make use of it. It is a well-equipped Centre here and I used to go there every day exactly at 3 O'clock and return by 4 O'clock tired. Mary is ready with a hot coffee which I enjoyed with pleasure. There is a programme by the CBS television channel and it is all about Small Causes or Small Claims cases. **Judge Joe Brown** and **Judge Judy** are there to decide the cases. Being a criminologist and an Advocate by profession, I used to attend keenly the proceedings of the Court and study the quality of the decisions. To quote from the *Facebook.com* about the Court: "...justice is served daily on the dynamic, tough-talking, no-holds-barred Judge...The Judge adjudicates real cases between real litigants from all across the nation. Litigants are bound by the Judge's insightful rulings and inspired by his mandates to take responsibility for their actions. He shows the litigants' unique ways in which they can deal with their mistakes and forces wrong doers to reflect on the consequences of their behaviour".

The Court room proceedings is a spectacular reality telecasted by, as said earlier, the CBS television. Judge Joe Brown and Judge Judy deserve special mention. The small claims cases are decided judiciously and legally. The small cause's cases are finalized. Usually, they relate to small contract violations, car damages, rent problems, dog issues, loan repayment, etc. It is interesting to see how the Judges decide the cases just by questioning the litigants and by evaluating the evidence produced by the plaintiff and the defendant. There is no lawyer to complicate the issues. The Judge is, as I understand, the Prosecutor, Defence counsel and the Decision Maker.

When I watch the reality proceedings in the Court, my mind is in Kerala and other States in India and the petition inquiry by police. The police claim that it is a method of instant justice delivery without any expenditure. But the oft-heard allegation against it is that the instant justice delivery system with little or no expenditure has become cheap owing to several reasons. First of all, the police have no legal power or authority to conduct petition inquiry and adjudicate on the matter. Secondly, daily a lot of time is spent on petition inquiry so much so that the more important duties of police are conveniently neglected or overlooked. Thirdly, the quality of the decisions becomes a matter of dispute often. Fourthly, the police officials become, as the allegation goes, susceptible to temptations and the politicians cash on their susceptibility. Fifthly, the police, it is said, misuse their power and abuse their authority even to the extent of coercing people by the use of third degree methods and thus the petition inquiry by police has become a curse for many more than a blessing or an instrument of instant justice delivery at no expenses. Of course, the police department claims that the use (abuse?) of their **"Good Offices"** in settling small causes or deciding on small claim cases pays rich dividend. I doubt very much as my studies do not give me evidence to endorse their unsubstantiated claims. The police decisions without legal sanctity and power become no decisions at all for those who want to ignore them. They are enforced on the 'enforceable' only.

My suggestion is: '**Why** can't we introduce the American Court System to adjudicate on small causes or to settle small claims cases?'

The issues discussed here relate to—

(1) Why do some people obey the police and why do some others refuse to obey?
(2) What can be done to settle the small causes or small claims?

The first and the simple answer to the first question is the effect of the *Ego* in the people on police decisions in petition enquiries. Let us analyse the issue deeply. What about the general impression of people and their opinion of the police in India. My studies prove that the police have—

(1) An unenviable image as administrators of justice. Many people have no trust on the police and their decisions are not always transparent.
(2) Introductions and recommendations work with the police and thus the justice can be manipulated.
(3) Petition enquiry may be a method by which instant justice can be administered by police. More often than not, they do not maintain any records. Once the justice is administered, the matter is closed.

(4) Political interference works. The police, being a muscle power, the so-called instant justice is sometimes administered under threat or torture.
(5) There is no accountability for the police. There is also lack of transparency. The decisions of the police are enforced or executed under the colour of their authority or pseudo-authority. Hence, they become the uncrowned kings.
(6) The police is the investigator, the prosecutor and the decision-maker. Hence, the approach is faulty.

My suggestions may be—

1. The police power to conduct petition enquiry must be stopped forthwith as they do not have any legal powers to do so.
2. There are courts like the Consumer Protection Forums and similar courts must be introduced to settle small causes raised in petitions. Their procedure and decisions must be transparent and there is the need to enact new laws for the purpose.
3. The American system decided even small claims of civil nature. The same can be introduced here with necessary changes.
4. Facility must be provided to the police to devote their time for higher and more serious matters. Their valuable time should not be wasted for such matters like petition enquiry.

TERROR CAUSING 'ISMS'

In Dallas, Texas, we have a home of our own and it is in a community having 15 Malayalee families. For Thanks Giving, we decided to go to Dallas, 6 hours' drive from Bentonville. We started at about 9.30 a.m. and had our breakfast on the way in Oklahoma State. Neethie and Martin—they drove the car and we reached Dallas in time. On the next day, a Malayalee friend came to our home. Mary offered him a cup of tea and we had some Malayalam chit-chat outside the family members. He came for collecting a contribution, i.e., $ 100 for the X'mas celebrations in that community. He phoned to Martin earlier and came at the appointed time.

I asked Martin: "Do you have contributions?" He said: "Yes, for functions like this in the community". "Fine"—I said and sighed. Martin asked me: "Why do you sigh?" and then I told him about the coercing and compulsory contributions/donations in our State. In my view, they are not contributions or donations; rather in criminological terminology, they are **'Terror Causing 'isms'** which is very much different from terrorism. Kerala State is almost saturated with **'isms'**—namely, Marxism, communism, communalism, Leninism, Naxalism, *Goondaism*, regionalism, socialism, rationalism and what not? And to them, we may add **"terror causing 'isms' "** too. Some people unknown to us come to our homes demanding compulsory contributions for the political party meetings, demonstrations, conventions, for literary and linguistic activities, for religious festivals, for cultural programmes, for labour union activities, for charitable works and thus goes the litany of needs. The usual *modus operandi* of these people is to come in groups with printed receipts. They cruelly demand money and if we give less than what they ask, then they look at us harshly—so harshly that we get frightened or threatened. Some utter filthy or foul words whereas some others express them with their body language, eye-contacts, facial expressions, etc., and thus we have an *unsettling* of the human mind. We start worrying whether or not they may damage our property, stone at our home during night hours, *handle* us on road, etc., and thus the terror caused by them is technically called **"Terror Causing 'isms' "** by me.

My questions are:

(1) How do the people in other parts of the world manage their political activities?

(2) How do the people in other parts of the world manage their literary and other cultural activities? Certainly, they are not *via* compulsory, coercing, or causing terror in people unknown to them. Why can't we follow the same strategy?

(3) What is the compelling necessity or interest for the people who are in no way connected with such activities to contribute money for their so-named party works, festival celebrations, charity activities, etc.

(4) Why do they come—showing no respect to others—without permission and coerce the people to contribute?

Once, I had seen a person dressed well showing his privates when the demanded donations were denied. People who come home to collect contributions by causing terror must be checked by law, if needed. We should not allow vandalism to thrive amidst us in any manner. Only those interested in special or specific activities may willingly or voluntarily contribute and leave aside those who are not interested or connected. Will it ever happen since it is the politicians and political parties who sponsor such activities?

Most people are cowards and they can be threatened or frightened. ***'Escape'*** is an instinct in animals and they have *'fear'* as an accompanying emotion. Man too has the same. As he is intelligent, he sees and foresees the danger. No doubt, *escape,* is a **Push factor** and the **Pull factors** are his own experience which he has heard or seen in society. The media reports everyday bring a lot of news relating to *goondaism,* destruction of property, damage to other belongings, etc., of those who refuse to give compulsory contributions to political parties, literary activities, protests, processions, etc. Thus, an ***Ego*** is formed in everyone to go along with the current and not to swim across the current. Those who have *'repulsion'* followed by *disgust* do not express it as it is dangerous to do so.

People have *'Self-assertion'* as a **Push Factor** (accompanied by a feeling of *superiority*) and some show it by becoming active in political, literary, cultural or religious activities. Some express *"acquisitiveness"* (following emotion is a feeling of *ownership*) by misusing their position and role in such activities. If they do not get their **Push Factors** satisfied, they become aggressive, arrogant, abusive or angry. All those emotions are the accompanying emotions of the **Push Factors**, especially, the *'pugnacity'*. This is the reason why they cause destruction and the **Pull Factors** sometimes justify such behaviours.

The **'Ego'** of the one who expresses **"terror causing 'isms' "** is different from the **'Ego'** of the person who is at the receiving end! He may have *'repulsion'* accompanied by *'disgust'*.

FILTH THAT CUTS THE BONE

Neethie showed me a **Blog** when we were in Dallas and it was all about a religious institution. Many Malayalees are members of that organization and the **Blog** contained filth-abusive words or foul expressions against some religious leaders and community makers. The language is so mean and cheap that it is difficult to hear such penetrating expressions even in the fish markets in Kerala/India. When I read the **Blog**, I felt so sorry about our fellow brethren in USA—that they have come all the way from that subcontinent to shout against one another, in filthy language!

Can aggression go to this extent of calling abusive words? Let the psychologists who studied verbal aggression in abnormal and criminal psychology answer the question. Certainly, there might have been something wrong in the developmental period of those who employed such verbal slaps to maintain their homeostasis at the moments of frustration. What is wrong in our culture?

Political aggression, communal riots and religious bigotry, labour disputes, students' unrest, agrarian clashes, inter-denominational fights, fights among political parties and among communal forces, terrorism, Naxalism, fundamentalism, regionalism—and everywhere we hear slogans of all categories, *jhatthas* and demonstrations, shouting of verbal abuses, etc., so much so that aggression—physical, verbal, sadistic, vicarious—has become a part and parcel of our social life and cultural upbringing. Children who are born and brought up in such a culture continue to behave in the same way even in a foreign land, if that is possible, forgetting that they are being watched by the whites, blacks, Mexicans and others from very many countries. What an impression they will have about the culture and finer aspects of life in the God's Own Country!

Decency and common sense do not permit me to reproduce the filthy expressions in the **Blog** here. If I do so, I will be doing an injustice to myself, my country, my people and my brethren living in USA. My humble advice to them is not to wash the dirty linen in public—not to publicize their negative feelings and ill-feelings in **Blogs** in full or part indecency. When one humiliates another, he humiliates himself and his behaviour affects all in that community adversely. Why should they preach religion if they can't have religious thoughts? The **Blog** is a mixture of religious thoughts, functions, prayers, prayer songs, etc., and filthy, abusive, indecent expressions and words which the most wretched people on earth or in any culture will be afraid to use. May God forgive them and let them project the noble and the sublime culture of Kerala-Malayala Nadu—our country and her heritage everywhere.

Filthy words are plenty in any language and such foul words are always sex-centred. *Sex*, doubtlessly, is an instinct with *lust* as an accompanying emotion. Filthy sex is expressed in words, writings, pictures, drawings, symbols and in many other ways. One sees such undesirable expressions in the **Blogs**. All including animals become aggressive and they may resort to several methods to get out of their aggressiveness. Aggression is expressed physically, verbally, vicariously, etc., and those who write the **Blogs** in filthy language do so verbally. Why?

In modern times and in current environments, filthy language, foul expressions, sexual films, C.Ds, conversations, cinema dialogues, T.V. serial shows may be plenty so much so that the sex-industry in India is indeed very rich. It has been estimated (about 1½ decades ago) that India has a sex-industry worth ₹ 43,000 crores. If so, the **Pull Factors** in the sex-industry may be in favour of accepting/enjoying such foul words and filthy expressions in the **Blog**. Look at the chat language in the internet—the SMS in the mobile phones—the advertisements on roads and elsewhere—police language or language of the law enforcement departments other than the police—market talks and *goonda* language—slogans in *jatthas* or processions and agitations and attacks on Government—bars and toddy-shops, one listens to the foul language and sex-centred filthy expressions. Children born and brought up in a culture approving sex-centred foul language develop an *ego* which does not feel guilt when they listen, talk, write or read filthy words and expressions. The **Blogs** are written in Indian languages and I have seen Malayalam **Blogs** and the purpose seems to be that they ought to be read by Indians who may not have guilt feelings when they read the **Blogs** or enjoy them.

Indians seem to have a tendency to point at others saying that they are not O.K. whereas, they fail to note that the reality in Indian culture is worse and far away from being satisfactory. They find fault with the loose sex-life of others in foreign countries, disrupted family life, broken family relations at home, interpersonnel rivalry, etc., in other countries while they shut their eyes on hard realities seen amidst them.

MISSING CHILDREN AND THEIR FATE

In WALL*MART store at Dallas, I found a Board which contains two dozen photos of children from five years to fifteen years of age exhibited under a caption ***Missing***. I made an enquiry about the what, why and how of the ***Missing*** and I thought that it was put by the police just like they publish the photographs of missing persons including children in railway stations, bus stands, newspapers and television networks in India. I was told that they were the photographs of the *Missing* children from the WALL*MART store there. The parents go there with children and they are found to be deeply immersed in looking for items to be purchased by them. They may forget their children for a moment and the children may go here and there. Sometimes, the kidnappers of children cast their net and see to it that the children are kidnapped. Occasionally, they are found to be ***Missing*** owing to other reasons as well.

At Thiruvananthapuram, when I visited a Mall, I was told by the employees there that, sometimes, children would be found *Missing* there too. The story was almost the same as we heard in WALL*MART store at Dallas. People may be alike in all countries and cultures. The human nature may be the same everywhere down the millennia. But, most unfortunately we read in newspapers and listen in T.V. telecasts that the children kidnapped by beggars disfigure them for the purpose of begging. There is a Malayalam movie '*Kakoothikavile Appoppanthadikal*' in which a similar story is depicted. When I saw it years ago, I thought that it was only a fiction. But the news appearing in these days confirm the saying (cliché in fact) that 'facts are stranger than fiction'.

What happened to that child in Alappuzha, Kerala ? His case was investigated by the C.B.I. for a long time. Nothing is certain and nothing is proved! Are the kidnappers of children an organized group? For what purpose do they abuse or misuse our children? The number of children who is found *Running Away* from their homes, schools, etc., too is on the increase! The number of young girls kidnapped too is incredibly high. Girls of tender age elope with their lovers or fake lovers or go with people who promise them employment, chance to act in films, T.V. serials, song albums, modelling, anchoring, etc. They too are found to be on the upward trend although the girls thus kidnapped, promised employment are seen sometimes in brothels, found dead and their dead bodies thrown as anonymous, abused for blue film production and other pervert sex works in sex industry, the boys are seen sometimes among the pickpockets, hooch-producers, and illicit traffickers of girls, carriers of drugs and among those involved in all other sorts of nefarious activities. Are our parents aware of these evils and do they take appropriate steps to check the problem? Do they need information and if so, what do the educational institutions, police, N.G.Os and the Governments do in this regard? Think about it and think about it loudly.

Children are a vulnerable lot. Children are misused or abused by the elders who find instinctual satisfaction when they do so. The news about sexual misuse of children by many including their parents are beyond human imagination. Relay rapes are reported on girls of tender years of age. Girls below 18 years are transported for sex-work and a study says that nearly 200 girls are transported every day in India. Girls from other countries too are transported to India. A few years ago, the girls were between 18-25 years of age and the situation has changed now so much so that girls above 10 years of age are in demand in the sex-industry. The sex-rackets are operating profitably and they employ very many means to recruit girls of tender years for tender flesh trade.

What are the **Pull Factors** and what are the **Push Factors**? Children are exploited in the labour markets. They are misused for begging. They are employed as domestic servants and exploited sexually. They are misused as guinea pigs for experiments and recently, the skulls of some children without brain were detected. They were suspected to have been misused for experiments.

Children are kidnapped from bus stations, railway platforms and cabins, school premises, homes, markets and the number of missing children is going up. In some States in India, **missing children's bureaus** are created and it shows the gravity of the issue under discussion. **Pull Factors** are many and what are the **Push Factors**? Some children run away from their homes without thinking much about the after-effects of such a running way, girls who run away never come back in the way they leave their homes. In my view, the running away is an "instinctive act' [*Escape*] which is followed by *"fear"*. Many children have any number of explanations for their running away and they may be far away from being real. *Repulsion* is an instinct with *'Disgust'* as an accompanying emotion. Many children who run away from homes have repulsion as an instinct. Earlier, I did make some studies and then, I was to think strongly that *'distress'* was the only emotion that accompanied, many a time, the running away children. They had many *appeals* as **Push Factors** and they were not fully honoured. Some wanted to 'self-assert' their **ego** (self-assertion doubtlessly is a **Push Factor (Instinct)** with a *feeling of superiority* as an accompanying emotion). In **Wall*Mart** or any other supermarket, the children may be kidnapped for the purpose *"acquisitiveness"* (instinct) with a *'feeling of ownership'* as an accompanying emotion. Such kidnapped children are caught by the police and sometimes it is learnt that they are stolen and sold by the kidnappers. They have language barriers and cultural differences. Those who kidnap the children do not normally have any guilt feelings. They apply the demand-supply theory in crimino-economics to explain their criminal activities.

OLD AGE LIFE OR A GARBAGE CULTURE

During 1986, I visited a friend of mine at New York and he had a love affair with a white lady. She had her old mother and an aunt. Seeing the aunt staying alone in an apartment at Bronze,

I asked: "Why is she alone?"

"No one to look after her "—my friend's fiancée said.

"We have a use and throw culture"—she continued. "The garbage will be collected by the collectors of garbage"—she laughed and said casually.

Thus a number of old people living alone or in old age homes everywhere in America could be seen. It is there many of the Malayalee nurses used to work during their initial days of American life at that time. Earlier, Bishop Mar Clement Thottungal, C.M.I. of Sagar diocese told me when I was doing my M.A. in Criminology and Forensic Science in Sagar University, Saugor (1973-1975), that his apostolate in USA was with the old who had no one to look after—forlorn and forsaken. He used to narrate to me his most touching experiences when he used to administer extreme unction to the dying souls. The dead bodies of the old had no place in the home of their children. Now, I do not know how the old is treated in USA and what I learn is that everything has gone from bad to worse from 1986 to 2011.

What about Kerala? And to some extent, India? During 1986, we did not think much about the problems of the old. They were looked after very well by their own children. As time elapsed, home nurses were employed to nurse old parents, amidst objections from the parents. Now, they are admitted to old age homes and one sees old age homes for all economic categories of people from all walks of life—from the poor to the rich. It has become almost a business for some although some do it as a humanitarian service. The old are neglected and many live a lonely life without any one to talk to them. I have visited some old age homes and seen some in televisions. I have read articles about the life of the old in the old-age homes and I have written articles about it. Old people are a real problem in our culture too and the "garbage culture" is spreading very fast in India. The "Use and Throw" attitude make many desperate and many children have no option and guilt feelings to throw their parents to old age homes and they visit 'Jyothishaalayas' to find out the best day to transport the old to a 'home'. "Thinkalazhcha Nalladivasam" [Monday, the Best Day], "Allkoottathil Thanie" [Alone in the Crowd] etc., were Malayalam films showing the ill fate of the old in Kerala culture. I, for one, think that the Government must come forward with good plans and programmes to offer care and protection to the old. This is so because, we are now fully westernized in that sphere of life as in America—everything goes from bad to worse as far as the old age is concerned.

No one wants the old in India too. The land-based economy in the State of Kerala has already vanished and in other States, it is in the process of getting vanished. *Naxalitism,* agrarian unrest, agitations on land, etc., may be a manifestation of man's desire to have a change in the economic policies of land. As the land-based economy is going away, one sees a sort of job-based economy in India so much so that many job-seekers leave their parents and parental homes for getting employed. Resultingly, the number of the old goes up incredibly high. What to do with them? *"Do away with the used material"*—seems to be a strategy and policy resorted by some youngsters. They think of even '**mercy killing**'. The rate of suicidal death among the old is going up higher and higher in these days. The problem is as severe there in India as it is in U.S.A. Of course, the situation is different in rural America as it is in India. It is in urban areas in India as well as in U.S.A., the old are neglected, avoided and abandoned more.

What are the **Push Factors**? Of course, *escape* and *repulsion* play an important role here. Why does *Escape* play a role here? Unless one's **ego** has a moral content, man wants to get away (*escape*) from the old, who are always a nuisance to the young. This is the reason why it is insisted that the **Pull Factors** ought to be those respecting and honouring the old. In the *Old Testament*, the respect to the parents (old) is found to be the fourth commandment. The teachers, parents, value-creating institutions make or must make all attempts to provide an environment which ought to contain respect and honour to the old. In U.S.A, the *Moral Ego* of the people is such that they do not have any guilt–feelings if at all they neglect the old and the infirm. The same or similar *Moral Ego* creeps into the Indian culture. People have *'Repulsion'* [an instinct] towards the old with *'Disgust'* as an accompanying emotion. They do not want to nurse the old so much so that the old becomes a waste to be buried or burnt away.

In India, old age homes are constructed as they are in U.S.A. It has a business motive and a market psychology works here. *'Eliminate the old'*, if that is possible, seems to be the approach or attitude of some among the young. The murder of the old, especially, if they stay alone or away from their children, is going up. The children seem to be not bothered of their old parents. *"Dispose them of at the earliest"*—seems to be an attitude and approach of the young. The children are not very much concerned of the inheritance of wealth from their parents. In olden times, the children were concerned of the inheritance of property from their parents. Those children whose ***Ego*** is moral have guilt feelings if their old parents are neglected or thrown away. So long as the instinct of *'escape/repulsion'* works very strongly in an environment pregnant with **Pull Factors** like avoidance, disrespect, contempt, etc., to the old, development of an ***Ego*** containing a moral sense uprightly formed in the right direction is not that easy—rather is indeed very difficult or extremely difficult.

THE AGED AND THEIR SAFETY

Today is a sunny day—a Sunday and Neethie took us to church—the nearest Catholic Church, St. Stephen's for services. A beautiful abode of God in every sense. I found many old women (no men), beautifully dressed and lovely in look. A rough estimate of their age conservatively calculated would be above 70, above 75, above 80 or '80-90' and they came to church alone—no one to accompany them—even to drive their cars. I noticed that many of them donating 50 or 100 dollars to the church as their offerings for that Sunday.

I asked Neethie: "Why so many old women?—no one to look after them?—no one to help them?—coming with a lot of money to offer!—walking with sticks–driving in difficulties—coming to church?"

She said in reply that they could be the old folk who lived alone—without any one to look after. Their children might be away or would not get time to spare. This is a curse here. Amidst the riches and wealth, no one has any time or interest to care the old! *Sufferings, Sufferings, Sufferings* !

Yes, immediately I had a flash to our State and country. Just before I left to America, I wrote an article about the murdering of the old who stayed alone in the State. At Ernakulum, four or five old women who lived alone were murdered during a week and many senior police investigators told me that an investigation of such murders was difficult. The reasons were—

(1) There is no one to say anything about the *modus operandi* of the murder or the property lost, if any.
(2) No one is interested in the progress of the investigation.
(3) If at all children are there for the murdered victim, they are least interested.
(4) Most of them want to dispose of the dead body and to leave the country or State by the next available flight or train, as the case may be.
(5) The investigation becomes just a police 'baby'. No one else will be coming forward to help, cooperate, support or give evidence.

I asked Neethie: "Are these old people safe and secure at their homes? Or apartments?"

She said: "Every house might have an alarm fitted and the

police will come within 3 minutes if the alarm is heard. Moreover, many homes or apartments here do not have gold ornaments or cash in dollars. They might have a laptop, computer and a T.V., washing machine and a few credit or debit cards... The thief or murderers do not want them. The Indian especially the Malayalee families here have gold ornaments and there were reports of burglaries there."

Yes, there is a point in what she said. Our homes in Kerala or India may be richer in gold and cash in rupees. Certainly, they attract thieves and murderers for gain. Hence, take them to safe places or bank lockers and that is the only way to reduce the plundering and murder of the old living alone in the State/Country.

Old Age and Garbage Culture—that was the topic of our previous article. Here, the safety of the old becomes the topic of discussion. In India, are the old safe? The *blade* companies, i.e., investment schemes promising exorbitant interest rate cheat the old and pensioners by offering temptations without any intention to fulfill the promises—loot the old. The hospitals running only on mercenary considerations and business motives put the old to the intensive care units/ventilators, sometimes, solely for the purpose of looting them. The old are neglected and are thrown to a room without anyone to look after them. If the news appearing in the media is correct, the life of the old is in serious danger. They are administered medicines and are made a prey to experiments by multi-national drug manufacturers. Religious institutions, more often than not, loot them by offering spiritual euphoria and promises. Of course, they are the **Pull Factors.**

BRIBERY AND CORRUPTION

There is so much uncertainty and fluctuation in the climate in Arkansas that no one can make any prediction of what will be the climate tomorrow. The weather forecast is as good or as bad as the weather forecast in our country. When I went to the Body Fitness Centre in our apartment complex, there was very good sunlight and the temperature was –10° Celsius. After about 40 minutes, when I returned from the Centre, there was snowing. I had then a feeling: 'The climate change here is almost like the corruption, corrupt practices, corruption money-splitting, corruption money-fixing, bribery, etc., at the lower or middle level of Government administration in India'. Of course, in an age of corruption and malpractices, it is only through corruption and malpractices that the wisdom can rule. People are prepared to be subjected to corruption as they find that there is no other option left with them. My studies about corruption cases in Kerala and in India give me ample proof that—

(1) People are well prepared to offer corruption money in a 'decent' manner. However, they do not favour 'indecent' demands and exorbitant amounts which they cannot afford to.
(2) Like a blackmailer, the corrupt officer repeatedly demands corruption money at each and every step to be taken further in the same file—without any morality or moral principle.
(3) Accept corruption money and do nothing for the actualization of the promises made prior to acceptance of the corruption money, in other words, corruption within corruption is noticed.

Kick-backs or nexus dealings are accepted as 'good and glorified' trade practices or transactions. In the present scenario in Kerala/India, people helplessly approach the Vigilance Departments only in rarest of rare cases—just before their drowning in the deep sea—when they are cheated—or in situations enumerated above. The cases registered per year by the Vigilance Department and given in the *Crime in India* publications of the Government of India show that they are of a negligible number. Is there corruption even in the registration of cases? The staff in the Vigilance Department may be handful although they may be overburdened with small-small cases. Anyway at Bentonville city in Arkansas, I wish to sing with the English poet:

> "If winter comes, can spring be far behind". No, it can't. Likewise, if there is bribery in an office, can corruption be far behind?

No. It cannot be, because the *Bribe* of the British India was intended only for the lowest level of functionaries in Government services. The expression *Bribe* is a disgrace for the high, higher and highest level officials. It has no status and for them, 'corruption' is the word used. If there is bribe in an office, certainly there is corruption at higher levels. If that is certain, the ordinary people have still uncertainty in another aspect. Like the climate in Arkansas, can we predict the nature? No one in Kerala/India, except some astrologers (exaggeration admitted) there, will be able to say something about the fluctuations and uncertainties of higher corruption centres in Government offices. When one offers money, there will be bright sun light; immediately afterwards, there will be snowing, ice-fall and what not?

What about the political corruption? Is there any politician punished for corruption in that vast country called India? If at all a few are punished, they are only handful. When the houses of the politicians are raided, crores of hidden money may be unearthed. The undue delay in investigation of cases bury the corruption cases for good. The corrupt politician becomes the ruler tomorrow. Under his administration all corruption cases against him are either withdrawn from the courts or converted to glorified ones.

What about the bureaucratic corruption? Like many politicians, some bureaucrats who are born in gutter and brought up in slum become multimillionaires over a short period of time. I have any number of such examples to show the hidden or unholy nexus among the political leaders, bureaucrats, business men and organized criminals. The nexuses make all of them rich and richer.

What about the corruption in the religious field?—in charity works?— in multi-national companies and enterprises?—in sex work and illegal trafficking?— in the sale of liquor and contraband items?— in income-tax and other areas of tax-evasion? Where does everything go wrong or become motionless? The laws become sterile and the corrupt rule the country.

Self-assertion (accompanying emotion is feeling of *superiority*), *acquisitiveness* (accompanying emotion is feeling of *ownership*) are seen in everyone including the politicians, bureaucrats, 'religious' men, *Mafia*, crime-racketeers and so on. If they have very conducive **Pull Factors**, certainly, they will get themselves actualized so much so that the *Ego* without any moral sense or guilt feelings will develop. In India, one finds an abundance of such **Pull Factors** so much so that people having no guilt feelings get themselves glorified. It is the corruption market that is seen in the whole country and people who are not corrupt cannot happily survive. What to do and how to go about become the concern of the people and the nation now.

FROM DIVORCE TO DESTRUCTION

'A house is built by hands, but a home is built by hearts', said the Parish Priest in a Latin Catholic Church in Dallas at the X'mas mass. He was giving a sermon on family life and cited the Holy Family of Joseph-Mary–Jesus as the best model to follow. Yes, the homily was fine as I used to think that 'a house is constructed by bricks, but a home is built by emotions'—emotions of love, concern, care, sharing, sacrifice, understanding, listening etc....and the words of the Parish Priest at Dallas are plenty to show that a home— a sweet home—is the Holy of Holies when a switch, a single switch regulates everything and that unique switch is the emotions of the Family of Nazareth.

A lot of stories are heard about American families and I do not know how far they are true; nevertheless, many of them cannot be totally false. What I hear about the American family life is not nice to write here as I do not want the Indian and particularly the Malayalee children to read it. I am concerned with our families in Kerala, India. Is the marriage still sacramental? Or only contractual? It seems to me that some people are inclined to think that the marriage is contractual and one can break the contract at any time at his/her desire. Yes, marriage for a life time—that may be an old concept—seems to be unacceptable to some as the divorce rate goes incredibly high in the most literate State, Kerala, in the country. Many Malayalam films/T.V. serials project this theme and the older generation still prays that what they see in films and serials should never become a reality ever. But, look at the causes of divorce in Kerala. They are not, many a time, what are stipulated under the civil law or under the canons of any religion. They create very powerful causes to get divorces at any rate. In a study conducted by me in an area of 160 sq. kms., I found that out of 60 unnatural deaths (murder and suicides), 21 were of those who were married and they had or were suspected to have illicit or adulterous relationship with a person outside the wedlock. Can you believe that the family courts in Kerala are flooded with divorce applications and several lawyers mint money by becoming divorce lawyers. Malayalam films show such lawyers too in their cinemas.

In Indian pulpits too, we hear about the unacceptability of western values and their decline of family structure and life. I admit it, nevertheless with a question back: 'Are we in a way better than the westerners in our family concepts?' I think that we too are moving to a situation that our couples as well start thinking now or in the near future about *'Your Money, My Money'; 'Your Children, My Children'; 'Your Business, My Business', 'Your Look Out, My Look Out', etc. O.K., "Shut up and let us part with"*. In Kerala, desertions were found in the past in plenty and then it was called the "poor man's divorce" and "divorce in a secret way", etc. Now the poor man too goes to courts to get everything legalized and the divorces in a clandestine way become more open and acceptable. The value creators, society makers, religious men, moralists and so on must fight against this epidemic **(Pull Factors)** which will take our families and family life to destruction.

What about the families in India? Women complain of patriarchy so much so that women are treated like slaves. Of course, ours was a country where *sati* was practiced and it was stopped by enacting laws against it. Even today, *sati* in some form is seen in some parts of the country—or that is what the journalists report. Whatever that be, one sees suicides of newly married brides. Dowry harassment is reported and dowry death takes places. Family suicides do occur in many parts of the country. Kerala is notorious for it. Mother kills her children and later commits suicide! Father kills his children and afterwards commits suicide! In other words, family murder-suicides are reported in an alarmingly high way. Though in India, divorces do not take place as they are seen in U.S.A., family suicides, family-murder suicides, suicides do take place. Desertions were seen more in the past than they are today. The number of disorganized families, problem families, broken families, separated families is on the increase. Family courts are flooded with suits and besides, there are criminal cases pending before the courts of Magistrates in larger numbers. From 2000, the cases registered in family courts have gone up two or three fold so much so that more and more family courts are now established everywhere in the country. In some States, family counselling cells have been formed in police departments just to settle family issues. Further, many N.G.Os are coming forward for family therapy and the number of counsellors and family therapists are on the rise. Many religious institutions and value creating centres are active in family therapy and in settling family issues.

What a misfortune indeed! Father, step-father, uncles and neighbours exploit sexually girls of tender years of age and some of them are punished for raping their own daughters. Cases are reported that parents jointly pressure their girl children to become sex-workers and they offer them to be raped. The old are neglected in their own families and amidst all these family problems and aching issues, we accuse the westerners telling that their families are at disarray and lost. It is like the one who has elephantiasis on two legs accusing the one having the beginning of elephantiasis saying that he is neglecting the care of his health. What a pity indeed! Burning of the newly wed brides has been a problem in India so much so that the law was amended to make all unnatural deaths of brides taking place within seven years of marriage to be treated as a murder and investigated. Thus, some suicides were proved to be murders committed in a calculated way within the four walls of the house. The Supreme Court of India verdicted that a case could be registered when a harassed woman by husband or his near relative (Section 498A) made a complaint and afterwards, it has been noticed that several mothers-in-law have been put in jails as they were falsely accused of cruelty against the women. A study proves that some of them are really innocent and the question is what happens to Indian families? We had a joint family system and still we have it. We are shifting to more and more nuclear families and the problem persists– perhaps worse than what is seen in the west.

What are the **Push Factors**? Many instincts—like the escape, repulsion, pugnacity (combat), sex, parental, appeal, submission, self-assertion, food-seeking, acquisitiveness, constructiveness, laughter, etc., are powerfully in operation so much so that the various accompanying emotions in the positive or negative way—in an indifferent manner—may be expressed or exhibited. *Fear, disgust, anger, lust, humility, feeling of superiority* in various degrees will be seen. If the family lacks the capacity to share, to adjust with the situations, to accommodate with the spouse and children (if any) to understand one another, certainly the situation may go out of the gear causing serious rupture or accident. A child born and brought up in a family which respects values and honours traditions/customs, adheres to the laws and rules of life, norms in society and culture will be successful in family life. The schools, teachers, media, neighbourhood contacts, religious institutions, literature, etc., will be helpful to mould an *Ego* which is rightly formed in the upright direction. We may devote our time and care in these areas in the years to come.

MARRYING FOR DIVORCE

"Hi"—we, Mary, Neethie, Maria and I heard an young girl of 27-28 addressing so and smiling. A young handsome man of the same age was with her—very good looking couple made for each other!

Neethie told us that they were her associates in WALL*MART and they married about two or three months back. They were in real love for about ten or more years with a lot of datings, etc. They lived happily.

Yes, Neethie told me that her American associates simply did not or could not understand the concept of *'Arranged Marriages'* of our culture. They often asked her: "How could a man and woman live together and love each other sharing their lives till they died without knowing each other prior to marriage?" Quite reasonable question indeed!

Yes, it is a question asked by many Americans to whom I used to say that Mary and I married on November 20, 1977, i.e., about long 33 years ago and our life has been a real message to Americans. My parents had more than 50 years of married life—until their death—with eight children and many grandchildren. My wife's parents had nearly 75 years of married life. All of us married without *'Dating'* and knowing each other prior to marriage. We had a trust that all would be O.K. For, our parents made a lot of inquiries about the character, reputation, income, family status, credibility and thus a hundred questions were asked and answered prior to our marriage and their taking a decision together about our marriage. They usually did not go wrong and thus the marriages in India are not between two individuals but between two families.

Most unfortunately, Americans do not and cannot understand the secret of Indian marriages and their success of living together until death. Many still think: 'To say that one can love one person all his life is just like saying that one candle will continue burning as long as they live'. My counter question is: 'Why don't they see the live examples just in front of their eyes before they start doubting?'

Sociologists in India assert that the success of marriage and family relations does not have any positive correlation with dating and mutual knowledge prior to marriages. If they are positively correlated, then why do many American marriages fail and end up in divorces? Divorces do take place within no time in American culture and stability in married life is a topic of live discussions among the American sociologists.

In India, people, in general, are still proud of their stable family-life and marriage until death. Nevertheless, the attitude to such marriages is getting changed and some are inclined to think about divorces. They do divorce in these days and as seen from the family court records, some do not have hesitations to approach the courts for getting divorces.

May be owing to the influence of the western culture, some young men and women, now a days, think of knowing each other prior to their marriage and then? Inter-caste, inter-State, inter-denominational, inter-religious, international, inter-continental marriages are taking place in the Marriage Registrars' offices and no doubt, it is owing to their 'knowing each other' prior to their marriages. God alone knows whether or not such marriages will last long! Are we going to shatter the institution of marriage in the years to come? Sociologists will and they must answer the question or let us think aloud and arrive at a conclusion.

Sociologists have attempted to answer the question. Nevertheless, what do the criminologists see and say about the marriages in India now? Today the traditional functions of the family are shattered and equality of women and men is more recognized now. Gender justice is acknowledged and women liberation movement is seen in an intense way in many parts of the country. Feminist advocacy and women empowerment have paved the way for the collapse of patriarchy which is still honoured and respected in many families. Laws are enacted in favour of women and there is reservation for seats in local government administration. There is a move for reservation of women's representation in the State Legislatures and the Parliament of India.

More and more universities are established and educational institutions are started exclusively for women. There is increase in the enrolment of women in higher educational centres and more and more women come out of such institutions professionally qualified and that too in an enviable way. The result is that more and more women become economically independent. The joint family system is crumbling down and nuclear families have come in large numbers. Resultingly, the old generation living with the newly come-up nuclear families may not be there so much so that there is lack of control. Moreover, the concept of family becoming a shock absorber is not seen as it was in the past. Members of the family give more importance to their economic stability and financial independence. Some do not want to have children and they go to the extent of abortion to prevent unexpected child birth in the family. The concept of "Living Together" gets into the family slowly and the number of "unwed mothers is going up". The inter-caste, inter-State, inter-religious, etc., marriages do take place and of course one sees cultural differences in many families. The children born and brought up in such cultures live a life of confusion and thus the old concept of "Home—an abode of sweet emotions" gets changed. The homes are converted into houses and the criminologists may find the idea that 'marrying for divorce' may not be rejected *in limini* by the new generation couples. Why so?

In order to answer the above question, we need to analyse the **Push and Pull Factors**. The **Push Factors**—being the instincts—do not change. They are the same in the past and even today. What is seen today is the change in **Pull Factors**. Owing to an interaction between the **Push and Pull Factors**, the *Ego* gets changed. What is a family? The concept has undergone a lot of changes. This is owing to many factors like the value deterioration, media influence, gender equality and many other similar factors. Is marriage a religious institution? Is it only a contract? Is it sacramental? Is it sociological? Is it cultural? All these questions have a variety of answers and many people are confused. Some people argue that divorce is acceptable and desirable when other options are not possible. What about the children born in the wedlock after a divorce? Some answer the question saying that the children in divorced families need not necessarily be anti-social or criminal in outlook. What happens in the west? Amidst the divorces, the children are brought up. What about India? In spite of the so-called stable family, anti-socials and criminals are seen. According to some, divorces or separation in family life need not necessarily create criminals in society. Even in a pious and stable family, one sees a lot of criminals. The *Ego* of the individual is important and if the *Ego* is formed in an upright way in the right direction, the number of crimes can be reduced, if not eliminated. Today's India, may be tomorrow's U.S.A. and today's U.S.A. may be tomorrow's India. Therefore, the criminologists are not prepared to make assertions about the marriages and divorces in future India although they may subscribe to the view that the divorce rate is likely to be increased in the years to come.

MEDICAL CHECKUP AND VEHICLE CHECKUP

We were having a drive through the freeway from Dallas to Bentonville at a speed of 70 miles per hour. That is the permitted maximum speed in freeways. Neethie was very strict in keeping the speed limit and I was more serious to see that she did not violate the law on speed limit. We could see some policemen hiding themselves to catch the violators of the speed limit. They had speed detecting gadgets with them and once they caught a driver, they came with evidence to convince him that he was driving at an over speed. There were 'wiser' drivers who kept an electronic gadget with them to identify the presence of the hidden policeman sufficiently in advance. They were really smarter not only in escaping a ticket from the police but also in violating the laws. Forget about such mental cases.

The traffic policeman is a decent law enforcement officer who books a driver only if he has violated a law and only if he has dependable evidence to prove the violations. They do not stop all vehicles going through the freeway and harass the road users as we see in our country. In India, for instance, checking of motor vehicles by stopping all vehicles going through the road, retaining the road users for hours together, asking them a number of unnecessary questions, finding out some violations of law and then booking them—fining them for violations etc., could be seen more in the past than at present. There is no justification for such vehicle checkings and there is no rationale necessitating such checks. If the police have evidence of violating a road law/vehicle law by a driver, then book him rather than booking all drivers driving their vehicles through a particular road. Whenever, I give lectures to police officials, I used to insist that there should be decency even in detecting road violations.

"Check only one violation at a time or book a violator of law if there exists visible evidence. Vehicle checking is not a medical checkup in which the doctor examines the patient from all sides to find out some disease or malfunctioning for effective treatment or for extracting money. In vehicle checking, the examination is done to correct the erring driver and if needed, to punish him and not at all to treat him medically. Be decent and dignified—this used to be my instructions to the police officials.

The Mobile Courts are not medical checkup centres although many check the vehicles from left and right, from up and down, from behind and beyond to find out, somehow, some defects solely for fining the road users. This is not the right approach and in every sense, it is an atrocity on road or abuse of power or misuse of authority. By checking vehicles, one can find out some defects which may be violations of law. It is not for that the Mobile Courts are intended. It is intended for nobler purposes and more over to ensure the safety and security of the people on roads. Certainty of punishment is always better and more effective than severity of punishment and the Mobile Court is for that purpose and that purpose alone.

The roads in Africa are excellent. There is timely maintenance—said a friend of mine from Africa. The roads in U.A.E. are fine and there is enforcement of road laws/rules there—told another friend. The roads are horrible and accident-prone—said a foreigner who visited India recently. Yes, the drivers are accident friendly in India so much so that the road accidents are alarmingly high in the subcontinent. I am told that Kerala has more road accidents than the same in other developed countries. There is no maintenance of roads and corruption, corruption, corruption everywhere on roads. The lip-stick tarring done on roads, drunken driving, road rule—violations, lack of road culture, too many vehicles, unscrupulous law enforcement officials, violence on roads, road blocks, dearth of road signs and markings, no proper planning—and thus the roads have become accident prone/friendly. The processions, agitations on roads, street corner meetings, way-side sellers, foot-path markets, pedestrians and bystanders, beggars and *goondas*, unprincipled drivers, thrill-seekers make the roads not usable for vehicular traffic. One may see manually operated cycles to container vehicles on roads in India. Two wheelers are plenty; three wheelers make a living by their driving, private buses carrying passengers violate many laws to make profits, lorries, tipcarts, trucks, vehicles of the handicapped, tankers carrying petroleum products are seen on the roads at a speed fixed by them and not by law. The speed laws or road rules are not respected by many drivers who express road rage when they see others violating the rules. Many know the laws, but none observes them or obeys them. For, according to them, the one who observes the road laws or obeys the traffic regulation will not be able to drive a vehicle on roads. "Driving vehicles by adjustments" is the strategy now followed. Deaths on roads are very high and those who become handicapped owing to vehicular accidents are beyond imagination. Who is to be blamed? Some unscrupulous criminals murder people by misusing vehicles and creating road accidents. They make use of motor vehicles to kill even witnesses in criminal cases knowing fully well that they can escape punishments as they will be dealt under a Penal Code enacted in 1860 (when automobiles were not available) and under an Evidence Act enacted in 1872.

Curiosity, Self-assertion, Laughter, etc., become the **Push Factors** in many. Everyone is important for himself/herself and they are impatient too while they drive on roads. Some of them feel that they have the ownership of the road (i.e., the emotion accompanying *Acquisitiveness*)– a **Push Factor** and precisely, therefore, are reluctant to follow the road rules and regulations. Some drink or are under the influence of drugs or liquors and they do so without any fear of punishments.

The **Pull Factors** are many and various. They can be the lack or failure of law enforcement, inadequate road system without any proper planning or signals, incorrect planning and road markings, dilapidated road surfaces with gutters everywhere, lack of proper driver-training and licensing, too many vehicles on roads, unbelievable density of vehicle population, corruption on roads, dearth of law enforcement officials, road rage, projection of false ego and thus the **Pull Factors** may be anything from *A* to Z. Road accidents may become the No. 1 killer in the country. Resultingly, people look at vehicle accidents lightly and say *"after* *all a road accident"*. They do not have any guilt feelings if at all someone is killed in a road accident or seriously injured in vehicular accidents. People are inclined to look at accidents as *"accidents only"* and this *Ego* attitude is dangerous indeed.

In order to reduce the number of road accidents, we must modernize the roads and road-system. There should be proper signals everywhere and the detection gadgets like cameras, speed-detection devices, etc., must be fixed on roads. Enforcement officials should be beyond corruption and the licensing ought to be free from malpractices. Drivers must be properly trained and they must be instructed properly about the road laws and rules emphasizing to respect the road etiquette and road culture. "Be dignified" while driving and thus reduce the number of vehicle/ road accidents. Some of them are not accidents, rather are road murders.

ROBBING CUSTOMERS TO MAKE OFFERS

Visit any Malls here, one will be just shocked to see the offers, 20 per cent OFF, 50 per cent OFF, 70 per cent OFF, BUY 2 and GET I FREE-Life Long Warranty and Oh, God ! These Malls are meant only for offers!! I asked Neethie: "What is the profit for these people if they give 70 per cent OFF ?"

She said in reply: "Appacha, it is business and offers too are business for them".

"Do they cheat us?"—I asked again." There is a feeling among the people that these business men put a very high price and then make offers. Even when they give all these **Offers**, still they benefit. It is a sort of cheating served in a golden plate in a glorified manner. Don't you agree?"

In Kerala and for that matter, any city in India, during festive seasons, the market is flooded with all sorts of **Offers and Offs**, exchange offers and every offer is attractive—very attractive. When one takes his old item for exchange, he gets an amount which may not be enough for transporting it to the shop. Once I purchased a saree for my wife for an offer price and believe me, it got fire when it had a contact with a sofa-cum-bed covered with rexin. Qualitatively, all third rate products are sold out during the festive seasons under **Offers**. Clearance sale with a lot of offers and once we purchase them, we feel that we are cheated.

Offers are given by hotels, hospitals, health clubs, textile shops, electronic shops, grocery shops, other shops, tourist resorts, etc., and there are door-to- door sale girls and boys who make Offers and Offs. Daily newspapers carry notices containing information about Offers and Offs. But, I find a difference between the Offs and Offers here in USA and the same there in Kerala (India). In USA, if the customer is not satisfied, he can return the products and many Malls take them back without questioning. In Kerala, once an item is purchased, it is never taken back whatever may be the defects of the purchased item. 'Once cheated, then cheated forever'—and often no sympathy or consideration towards the purchaser, particularly when the product is purchased during a *Sale* or under *Offers*.

We do not have proper laws to regulate the *Offers* and Offs. There should be effective and proper laws regulating *Offers* and Offs, because many jewellery shops, Malls, clubs, etc., make Offers and Offs in one count and take away our money on another count. "Robbing Peter to pay Paul", i.e., robbing customers to give *Offers and Offs* to them is a calculated and glorified cheating that gets an accelerated momentum in these days.

"Yes", Neethie said: "This is business and business is money for the business man. *Offers and Offs* too are a business" without any regulations whatsoever!

Look at the advertisements on T.V. or other print media. We see a lot of *Offers and Offs*. When one visits a Mall, there is the mike announcement making Offers. Offers and Offs come home *via* notices, telephone calls, SMS, sale boys/girls, e-mails, etc. The businessmen who know how to sell their produces know how to make offers and offs. They know that the people in general become a prey to their Offers and Offs. Some businessmen mock at other businessmen through advertisements expressing how the customers are cheated by Offers and Offs. These unscrupulous businessmen then make Offers and Offs to sell their products. What ethics do these businessmen have becomes out of question in these days as they think that everything is justified in business. There exist no effective laws to regulate the business or if at all there exist some laws, they are not enforced properly or meaningfully. Corruption is seen everywhere and there exists an unholy nexus among the leaders, businessmen and bureaucrats. The Offers, Offs, promises, guarantees by insurance companies, investment schemes, money-chains, multi-sale markets, chitties and kuries, flat-mafia, tourist resorts, racketeers, film and T.V. serial syndicates, hotels, sex industry, etc., are incredible; still many become prey to such calculated tricks and cheatings. Hospitals, medical shops, doctors, pharmacies, medical laboratories, legal firms, chartered accountants, religious men, retreat centres, political leaders too make many Offers and Offs to attract people. Faith therapy, healing ministry, black magic, *mantravada, Elas-sale, gem-business*—all have their eyes on Offers and Offs. What to do and how to go about?

Acquisitiveness (followed by a feeling of *ownership*) can be a **Push Factor**. It can be any other instincts (drives) which man has. The business world is contaminated with Offers/Offs and feels not guilty if at all others are cheated. The *Ego* is formed in such a way that many accept the frauds as desirable. **Faith** is exploited and the common men are cheated. Man is intelligent, but some are more intelligent. More intelligent people give their interpretations and they make everything morally justifiable. The less intelligent people become victims of these Offers and Offs without thinking for a moment that everything in business has profit as the only motive.

India is a good market for anything as we have a high population. Precisely, therefore, we will see a lot of Offers and Offs by the businessmen. The governments are aware of the organized cheating, but are, more often than not, silent about them. For, the Offers and Offs bring fortunes for the political leaders, law enforcement officials, law makers, law interpreters and adjudicators. Everything is business and money in India and the *Offers and Offs* too come under business and money.

ECONOMIC RECESSION AND EMPLOYMENT INDUSTRY

The economic recession in USA affected adversely their employment market and potential. Many became unemployed and it affected very badly several countries including India. Unemployment is a social problem and it has powerful impact in causing crimes—sometimes in an indirect way. Criminology of 1930-1960 in the west devoted a lot of time in studying the relationship between unemployment and crime. But in India, particularly in Kerala, researches after India's independence took another direction and studied how could the unemployment be converted to vote bank and abused for political advantage.

"Unemployment in Kerala" according to me is an industry—an industry to manufacture manpower for political advantages. The more are the unemployed people, the more frustrated they become. The politicians misuse or abuse the energy of the frustrated unemployed to strengthen their political party. They really want energetic people to shout slogans, to conduct *dharnas*, to participate in demonstrations, strikes, *bandhs* and *hartals*. The employed people do not get time to waste and to actively involve in many political activities which are often negative and destructive in character and nature. Unemployment is a live problem against which the politicians trigger the unemployed. The Naxalism and similar problems like the agrarian unrest, communal clashes, political strikes, labour disputes, etc., need manpower to fight and precisely for that, the politicians want the manpower of the unemployed which in India is readily available in plenty. Although they promise employment during their election campaigns and plead for more employment potentials, many of them do not mean much by that and they are not at all serious. For them, 'unemployment' too is an industry and they really want more and more unemployed youngsters throughout the State. Many States outside Kerala did develop industrially and the Keralites are at a standstill, sometimes going back with strikes, stoppage of work, destruction of property etc. Some people who want to live without working get political patronage. The notorious *'Nookukkuuli'* [i.e., getting wages for just seeing the head-load work by others] demanded by some class (so-named) of 'unemployed' people supported by political parties, is an example in point.

Hence, though 'unemployment' is a serious problem throughout the world today, it is an industry manufacturing people to strengthen political party membership in Kerala. There is all likelihood for further strengthening of the 'unemployment industry' in the years to come for political mileage. In such an industry, the economic recession is a blessing in disguise—a God given gift in every sense for the politicians.

If one goes to any prisons in India, he may see many convicts who were unemployed at the time they committed the offences for which they were incarcerated. When one looks at the *Mafia* crimes in various areas in India, he may see that, the *goondas* misused *by the Mafia* kings are unemployed. Ask those who are in a *jattha* (political procession particularly), most of them will be unemployed. Many who are deeply involved in the manufacture of hootch, its sale and transport are unemployed. Women engaged in sex-work, mobile prostitution, various forms of frauds, cheatings, etc., are found to be unemployed. Employment, seasonal employment, non-profitable employment, marginal employment, under-employment, unemployment—all of them are connected to various kinds of crimes. This observation does not attest the view that unemployment is a cause of crime—employment is not a cause of crime. The unemployed may commit crimes of their choice whereas the employed will commit crimes of their choice. It has been observed that all who accept corruption-money are employed whereas all who offer the corruption money may or may not be employed ones. The question is the *Ego* of those employed or unemployed. If the *Ego* is formed in an upright way in the right direction, they may not involve in the commission of crimes.

Instincts are powerful in all, no matter if they are employed or unemployed. *'Food-seeking'* is an instinct with *appetite* as an accompanying emotion. *Roti, kapada, makan*— this is heard in India and *roti* implies the instinct of food seeking. The unemployed want *roti* to eat and the instinct (the **Push Factor**) works strongly. The **Pull Factors** may be criminal as well as non-criminal. If one engages in criminal activities, he may be able to make money for *roti*. For this, his *Ego* must allow him and that is the reason why some people prefer to die in poverty rather than committing crimes.

Politicians in India want unemployed adherents in their political party. They want to abuse them. In order to have maximum number of unemployed followers, they are reluctant to improve the employment market. Anybody who is unemployed and who is seeking *roti* is likely to be more susceptible to temptations. The unethical politicians inject the instincts (**Push Factors**) like *Repulsion* against the ruling government, *Pugnacity* (*Anger* as the accompanying emotion) etc. and make them fight against the ruling party. They cash on unemployment.

A society having unemployment, poverty, overcrowding, no development, etc., is likely to cause crimes as they work as **Pull**

Factors in people having strong **Push Factors** with inadequate formation of *Ego* in them. How does *Naxalism* flourish in some parts of India? How did the *Naxalism* which prominently flourished in Kerala in the past had a natural death now? The reason may be seen in the **Pull Factors** as well. Many from Kerala left the State seeking employment elsewhere whereas many in other States are migrating to Kerala for employment. No doubt, if the employment potentials are improved, many crimes can be reduced. *'Roti–Kapada–Makkan'*—certainly all must have them if crimes must be reduced. Recently, it has been noticed that some of the migrant workers to Kerala State involve themselves in the commission of crimes and they are found committing burglary, theft, chain-snatching, sex-crimes, murders, etc. They drink a lot and behind every crime they commit, the working of the **Push Factors** and their interaction with the **Pull Factors** can be seen. What about the guilt feelings? This depends upon their Ego Formation in an upright way in the right direction.

THIRUVANANTHAPURAM (TVPM) MEANS CHEATING MULTIPLIED BY 4 ?

Getting out of the international airports in Singapore, UAE, USA or Canada, we may see many taxi-cars. Get into any one of them and they take you to the destination and normally, they charge you the fare shown in the meter. One who travels in the taxi is not worried whether or not he is taken to his destination *via* the direct route or through a curved route. He is not at all bothered about the quality of the meter too. It is taken for granted that the meter is O.K.

Getting out of the airports in Bangalore, Chennai, Mumbai or Delhi, we may see any number of taxi-cars, perhaps more than what we see in other international airports in the world. There are pre-paid taxi services and counters everywhere. Everybody is tensed until he reaches safely his destination. Why? Reasons are many and various. If the taxi is prepaid, then the meter will be alright. If not one doubts—

(1) Whether or not the meter is qualitatively correct?
(2) Whether or not he is taken through the direct route to the destination?

(3) Whether or not he is taken through a roundabout way to his destination?
(4) Whether or not he will have a fight with the driver at the point of destination?
(5) Whether or not he will be attacked on the way? And thus his questions are many or his suspicions are numerous. The answers are 'anxieties' and doubts.

I am from Thiruvananthapuram and I notice that there, the anxieties and tensions of the passengers are seen at the railway station too. I had them several times and I have been cheated by auto -rickshaw drivers, had to fight with them often, had to argue with them for the taxi fare and at times call my friends and people around to settle the issue...the police to take legal action, etc. The police too give warnings and instructions to the passengers to be beware of cheatings. The same situation exists in other railway stations, bus stands and airports in other parts of the country.

For a *tamasha*, people in Thiruvananthapuram used to crack a joke. Thiruvananthapuram was earlier known as Trivandrum, the short form of which was TVM. When expanded, the TVM becomes in Malayalam language—**Thattippu** (a form of cheating), **Vettippu** (another form of cheating) and **Moonchikkal** (a third form of cheating) [Out of them, the third word is a slang in some part of the State]. Thus, Trivandrum (TVM) means **Three Cheatings** put together. When cheatings were multiplied and expanded to many other areas, as the *tamasha* goes, the old Trivandrum was renamed as Thiruvananthapuram (TVPM) and in reality, that was to keep up the history and tradition of the place. Anyway, the short form of the newly renamed Thiruvananthapuram thus became TVPM, i.e., **Thattipu** × **Vettippu** × **Pattippu** × **Moonchikkal**. Out of them *Pattippu* means a fourth type of cheating. Thus Thiruvananthapuram (TVPM) has become *cheating* multiplied by 4. Though the above narration or interpretation is a comedy or a humour, it is to be taken seriously. A State contaminated by various types and forms of cheatings and frauds must find out ways and means to put them down as they are infamies. Administration and people must join together to fight against this malady—a curse in every sense.

Cheating (i.e., cheating multiplied by 4) is seen from Alpha to Omega in human transactions. Cheatings in markets may be seen in underweighing, adulteration, sale of unusable items or duplicate articles. The markets are flooded with articles of inferior quality. Go to a hotel. There, one may get food prepared in unhealthy conditions, food mixed with materials which are poisonous, old and used food, dirty food, food whose utility period has expired and thus the hotel business has become a business for cheating for some. Even in liquor, one may see adulteration, insects and centipedes/millipedes, etc. Visit a railway platform/bus station. Yes, one can see a variety of cheatings right from the moment of purchase of the ticket till he reaches his destination. The passengers are looted–intoxicated for the purpose of robbing them– sexually abused and sometimes, murder takes place. Terrorists bomb the trains and buses. Go to a religious centre where the pilgrims are tempted to involve themselves in illicit activities. The pilgrim centre itself becomes a centre of cheating. Go to a hospital. The patients are looted in very many ways—even subjecting them to experiments. Allegations are heard about Kidney *Mafia* and organ transplantations in some "well reputed hospitals". What about the lawyers? Some people say that the lawyer's profession is a lier's profession– if that is true one can add that his profession contains, sometimes, a heavy dose of cheating as well.

What about the insurance companies?– mediclaim policies?– investment frauds?– multi level marketing ?– money chains?– flat construction and sale?—cinema acting and cheatings? gold sale and jewellery?–textile sale?– offers and offs in sale?– chitties and kuries?—NOC rackets and false employment bureaus?– pipe money and con-tricks?– tax evasions and white-collar crimes?– organized racketeering and sale of contraband articles? I think that now TVPM should be multiplied by 1000 or 10000 instead of 4 in order to picture the quantity of cheatings in India.

Why do the people become prey to cheatings? Any animal or bird can be trapped and thus children catch hold of birds, squirrels, rats, fishes, etc. They put the bait and the birds, fishes and animals become victims or they are cheated. Instincts operate in them and this weakness is exploited. The same instincts work in human beings as well. Of course, they can be trapped. The **Push Factors** may be any instinct and the **Pull Factors** may be anything that attracts the **Push Factors**. If the *Ego* is not rightly formed, people become prey to the **Pull Factors**. Satisfaction of the instincts is a need for animals and men. In the case of man, laws are made to control people in satisfying their instincts. Some religions bring the concept of devil to explain the working of the instincts in men. Thus, one sees the demonological theories explaining crimes on the basis of devil's instigation and man's innate depravity to withstand the temptation or the instigation of devils. The innate depravity is otherwise called the weakness of the *Ego*. If the *Ego* is formed in an upright way in the right direction, certainly the devil's instigation (i.e., the instinctual pushes) can be controlled and thus the crimes can be reduced.

PUBLIC PARTICIPATION IN JUDICIAL DECISIONS

Today I feel highly satisfied. I went to the Body Fitness Centre and did watch the proceedings of the Small Claims Court which is telecasted by the CBS television. An interesting case indeed! Two girl friends used their mobile phone with an understanding that they would share the telephone bills. Somehow or other, they became inimical so much so that one did not share the bill as agreed. Consequently, the bill came to be nearly $ 1000 including the disconnection charge and reconnection charge, etc. I am not interested to go to the details of the case and the arguments *pro or contra*.

The most interesting part of the proceedings has been that the television anchor asked the viewers to the programme: **Take A Stand** and the viewers could decide the case by themselves. After some time, the anchor said: *"Will the Judge rule in favour of the plaintiff or in favour of the defendant?"* That was written on the T.V. screen as well. It was not over there. The anchor requested further: *"SMS Your Verdict"*. A telephone number was given.

Those announcements were given before the judge took a decision? I do not know whether the Judge saw the people's verdict before he pronounced the verdict or after. In either case, it was good. If the Judge saw the people's verdict before, he could consider it too before his decision. If he saw it after, then it would be a control for his later decisions. The system was assessed by me to be better than the former Jury Trial in Indian criminal justice system.

We are advocating transparency in judicial matters. As it is today, anyone can watch the entire proceedings in the Courts directly and the trial is open except in certain cases when the law permits *in camera* trials. People read the press reports and listen to court proceedings from the television news channels. In fact, they do not have any opportunity to witness the proceedings in the live media. The law also does not permit such type of transparency in judicial matters. All said and done, there take place media trials of many cases and the general public make their views, evaluations, opinions, decisions and judgements. After a verdict is pronounced by the Court today, there take place media discussions about the quality of the judgement. Truly, whenever, the judges are accused of being unjust in some cases in some way, the people form bad or wrong or true impressions of the judiciary.

Viewing the entire live television proceedings in the CBS network, I am inclined to think that it is a good proposal if we accept and adopt the same policy of transparency in judicial matters too (we have transparency in legislative proceedings today). YES—

Take a stand.... Will the Judge rule in favour of the plaintiff or in favour of the defendant?...SMS your verdict.

This is called the **Public Participation** in judicial decisions-more transparency and more trustworthiness.

There was a time when discussions were going on whether or not the proceedings in the Parliament of India and the State Legislatures was to be telecasted live. After a lot of arguments in favour or against, a sober and wise decision was taken to telecast the proceedings 'live'. Let the people – tax prayers – see what is going on there; what do their representatives do in the Parliament/ State Legislatures? how do the people's representatives perform their duties and responsibilities for the voters and the constituencies? Of course, transparency in democracy must be a declared policy of administration. Most unfortunately, people see what they ought not see in the *Holy of Holies* of a democracy. Slogan shouting, boycotting, sit-in-strikes, attacks on other fellow representatives, speaking in filthy languages, throwing of the microphones, martial arts and attacks on watch and ward, shoutings and hauling and the people get an impression that the law making institutions becoming law breaking institutions. Policemen under the designation of *"Watch and Ward"* are posted to maintain law and order in the Houses in certain States. Ridiculous indeed!

Now discussions are going on whether or not the proceedings

in a court of law should be telecasted 'live'. There are arguments—*pro and contra*— and I am of the firm view that they ought to be telecasted. Let the people in a democracy see what is going on in their institution of justice administration. There is no need for any clandestine dealings during the administration of justice. The judges are accused of bribery and corruption; the lawyers are blamed for their unholy nexuses with vested interests and some of the judgments are criticized for their deficiency in quality. Anything done in a clandestine manner will have its own aberrations and defects. The media must be allowed to videograph everything that takes place inside and outside of a court of law and justice. If everything is clear and neat, why should one be afraid of its exposure? Justice must be done and it must appear to the people who are the patrons—tax payers—that everything is just and fair.

Any human organization is manned and managed by people with flesh and blood. The judges are no exception to that general rule. They should not enjoy any special privileges which the people's representatives in the law making Houses do not enjoy—the officials in the law execution branches do not enjoy. Law making, law enforcement, law interpretation and adjudication are the different phases of the justice administration. As such every sub-system ought to be transparent. The judiciary alone should not enjoy privileges which other subsystems do not have in such matters.

The judges, lawyers and prosecutors have instincts. The **Push Factors** in the judicial officers are exposed to the **Pull Factors** in society prior to and during their entry to judicial service and afterwards. The formation of their *Ego* may be in an upright way in the right direction or otherwise. Those officials having an inadequate *Ego* formation will administer justice in an unenviable manner—even in an unjust way. Allegations are plenty and the judicial officers are accused of showing partisan attitude and political affiliations jeopardizing administration of justice. Innocent people, resultingly, may be remanded and later convicted. In order to control such undesirable acts, it is always advisable to telecast the court proceedings in the media. Let the people participate in the decision-making of the judiciary— *"will the Judge decide the issue in favour of the defendant or against him?"*. This is more needed at a time when judicial criminology and crimes become a live topic of discussion and academic studies. The *Gown* of a judge is not a guarantee that justice will be done. Today, the visual media telecast the decisions of the courts in a loud voice. My studies show that the telecasts do help to ensure just justice to people. If so, why not telecast the live court-room scenes?

NOT JUSTICE, BUT 'JUST ICE' OR 'ICING JUSTICE'

The former Chief Justice of India and his kith and kin were accused of amassing a lot of wealth from unknown sources. It got fire-wild fire-owing to media discussions and some lawyers' approach to the issue under discussion was found to be very violent. Allegations were raised even against half a dozen judges/chief justices of the Supreme Court of India for corruption and malpractices. Everyone spoke about the sanctity of judiciary and loss of public trust in the existing judicial system. The issue became slightly dim and then came up another issue. If media reports were true, two judges of the High Court of Kerala accepted corruption money to pronounce judgments in favour of an ex-Minister who was accused of a sex scandal commonly known as the ice-cream parlour case. The issue became a topic of hot discussion in the media and people from all walks of life spoke mostly against judicial functionaries, public prosecutors, Government pleaders, police officials and the rotten system as a whole and the judges in particular. Yes, once one of the former Chief Justices of India said in a public address that 20 per cent of the judicial officers were corrupt. Ever since, the number of judges–higher level and subordinate level—accused of various kinds of nefarious activities, corrupt practices, partisan attitudes, political affiliations was incredibly high. The nexus among the affluent, the influential, the powerful and the **Judges** was found to be unbelievably strong—so much so that injustice, wounded justice, less justice, no justice, waste justice and miscarriage of justice could take place instead of fair, holistic, equal and total justice.

Is it not painful to hear such sad episodes about our judicial functionaries? The allegation so far has been that many judicial officers were little educated and lacked expert knowledge in law and legal practice/administration. They were not well trained people in police, forensic and investigation sciences. Their knowledge in behavioural sciences was almost nil or was far way from being satisfactory. Their *Ego* was very unrealistic and most of them thought to be the Roman Kings and above **Grammar**. Their judgements were qualitatively of inferior nature and thus the litany of people's dissatisfaction might be very long. Nevertheless, they could tolerate all such defects and demerits if they were free from corruption and malpractices. Each judge is a **Legion** and his defect is spread like an epidemic. The poor people lose their trust in an impartial judiciary and everything becomes ritualistic to administer 'justice' as it is popularly called. Some people say that it is not **Justice but, 'Just Ice'** or **'Icing the Justice'**. How unfortunate it is to see and hear such allegations !

Yes, it is unfortunate to see and hear allegations against the judges from the Chief Justice of India (in his speech at Kollam), of State Ministers, Members of Parliament, Members of the State Legislature, Media-men, religious leaders and so on. It is more unfortunate to see and hear such allegations against the judiciary from the ordinary man on the street, the illiterate, the downtrodden and the handicapped in society. To whom should they approach if the judiciary is rotten?—if the idols are crumbling down?—if the *divinities* do things which the *mortals* are afraid to do.

Caesar's wife shall be above suspicion and so do the judges in justice administration. If the judges become corrupt, then justice becomes an item for sale. People will purchase it whatever may be the price for it. When one of the former Chief Justices of India makes a statement that 20 per cent of the lower level judicial officers were corrupt, his allegation could not be ignored just like that. Yes, *Acquisitiveness* can be a **Push Factor**, nevertheless, will it be so powerful to sell justice? The **Pull Factors** may be anything from poverty to affluence. Affluence of money makes some to commit crimes and it is contrary to 1940 American thinking that poverty was a cause of crime. The present day research studies prove that affluence becomes a cause of crimes by the affluent whose crimes will not be generally known by the common public. If a poor man commits a crime, his crime generally is of a poor nature or category. When the judges commit a crime—particularly the crime of corruption—it will be done in a clandestine way that the man on the street does not come to know anything about it.

Sometimes, the *Ego* of the judges who are forced to write an unjust judgement and the mental conflicts which they undergo are shown in films and theatres. Fine. For, that is meant for stage-shows while the reality is quite different. Allegations are heard from the stage of recruitment of the judges. Allegations are there in the appointment of prosecutors and government pleaders. Many things centre around money, influence and introductions. Resultingly, the **Pull Factors** can be from those who are their god-fathers. Their *Ego* values will be of those who appoint them. Corruption plays an upper role here so much so that they administer **'waste justice'** to the people who come to them for **fair and white justice**.

JUDICIAL CRIMINOLOGY AND CRIMES

Bureaucratic crimes have been in existence ever since bureaucracy came into being but were identified as a special category of crimes only recently. When Edwin H. Sutherland, an American criminologist defined white collar crimes as a special category of crimes committed by people of high socio-economic status during the course of their profession or occupation, I do not think that he aimed at bureaucratic crimes. Of course, Sutherland's description of white collar crimes has an economic motive at the base; but, I do not notice such economic motives alone for bureaucratic crimes. Bureaucratic crimes, according to me, are the crimes committed by bureaucrats during the course of their job as such bureaucrats. Of course, they need not be traditional crimes as defined by criminologists. White collar criminals do not usually commit traditional crimes or if at all they commit such crimes, they are then treated as such, i.e., as people who commit traditional crimes.

When I wrote the book *Police Criminology and Crimes*, I concentrated very much to enumerate the crimes committed by police during the course of their job as such police officials, i.e., under the colour of their uniform and under the cover of their authority and they numbered hundreds. Criminalization of police is one thing and police crimes are quite another thing. I also wrote another book titled *Indian Police and Nexus Crimes*. Then I never thought that I might have to think about judicial criminology and crimes. They are new areas of research and study. Once, I remember to have read that the colour of the skin was a powerful force influencing judicial decisions among the whites in the west. Many lawyers have told me, time and again, that religion, caste, sub-castes, etc., too have been powerful forces influencing decisions in judiciary. Certainly, it is a serious matter of research and study, if they work as powerful forces behind judicial decisions.

Judiciary to me means the **Bench** and the **Bar**. I have written books on ***Less Justice, Miscarriage of Justice, Wounded Justice, Injustice***, etc. There is an oft quoted saying: 'One who is close to the church is far away from God' and I am inclined to think that the saying is, *mutatis mutandis*, applicable to judiciary as well. Some lawyers may do anything to win their case, because they think that it is their business, livelihood, time and money. Some judges may not write everything disposed in their courts. They write only those things which they think 'necessary' and they apply the principle (?) that 'the law is what the judge says'. One may find that it is not always just and fair to think that what the judge writes must be just and fair in every case disposed of by him. Convicted cases are acquitted and acquitted cases are convicted and all is done on the same facts in issue, but interpreted and viewed or appreciated differently by different judges.

Recently, allegations against higher, highest and subordinate judiciary—against senior and junior lawyers—are heard in plenty in India and one notices that there is some truth in many allegations. Perhaps, the crimes committed by the **Bar** and the **Bench** during the course of their job are more than the crimes on which they argue the cases and write judgments. A time has now come to develop a branch called **Judicial Crimes** and **Criminology** and more **Blogs** on this area will have to be written.

Why do the judges and others in judiciary commit crimes? The reasons are many and various. They are —

1. They can afford to commit crimes during the process and progress of criminal justice administration without fearing anyone.
2. They enjoy immunity from any liability over the decisions they take. There is only an appeal against their decisions and usually no action is taken against them.
3. They are in a comfort zone even when they commit crimes.

The Contempt of Court Act comes to their rescue when they are in trouble.

4. People are afraid to criticize the judges and their decisions. For, people's criticisms against the judiciary have bad consequences on the people's trust on the system.
5. Presently, the judges are safe as there exists no special institution to conduct inquiries and award punishment to the erring judges.

I am remembering of a real incident that took place in an affluent country in the west. A girl from the Royal Family was in an open jeep and she had a short skirt. Owing to heavy breeze, her short skirt went up showing her inner garments. A magazine photographer took a photograph and published it with a note: "The under clothing of the Royalty behaves exactly like the commoner on the street". Yes, one portion of her under clothing went up while the other portion did not. Just like that, I may say that the instincts in judicial functionaries behave exactly like the same in ordinary people. The judicial officers commit crimes because their *Ego* is not uprightly formed in the right way to the right direction. Some religious men who undergo several years of spiritual training and **Ego** formation go wrong. The reason is found to be the inadequate formation of the **Ego** in spite of strenuous spirituality and moral upbringing. The judges are recruited and posted to function as judges without any meaningful moral training or **Ego** formation in an upright way in the right direction. Of course, a proper **Ego** formation at later years may be difficult to be achieved and, therefore, the recruitment must be made more objective by conducting personality and aptitude tests, etc. Remember always that legality needs not necessarily be morality. A judicial decision without morality will be criticized. Justice with a moral sense is what is required now to reduce judicial crimes.

As the instincts push the judges to behave in a particular way, the **Pull Factors** too can drag them to undesirable destination if they do not possess an upright **Ego** rightly formed in the right direction. The law is what the judge says—this is a wrong concept. The law is what the conscience (uprightly formed in the right direction) of the judge tells him. A criminal judge may discard the dictates of his own conscience to administer injustice, wounded justice, less justice or to miscarry justice.

Judicial criminology and crimes deal with the crimes committed by the **Bar** as well. The lawyers with their **Ego—Push and Pull Factors**—may assist a judge to administer injustice, wounded justice, etc. In spite of the crimes committed by the **Bench and the Bar**, people treat them as *'honourable men'* and the system moves on administering *"justice"* in many ways—objectively, subjectively or otherwise.

FOX AS A JURY AT A GOOSE'S TRIAL

'When an elephant is dead, even a frog will kick at it'—this is a simple saying and is fully visible in India. Many judicial officers are under fire now and there are any number of them under suspicion as their integrity is in doubt. Everybody knows that there is little accountability for judicial actions in India and no transparency for many things done under the cover of judicial authority or under the colour of judicial power. No social or judicial auditing worth appreciating and very many judges and judicial functionaries are very much in the comfort zones.

Just recently, the former Chief Justice of India's Supreme Court was subjected to a media trial for alleged amassment of wealth from unknown sources by his daughters/sons-in-law and so on. A case has been filed for investigation of his unaccounted wealth. The Income Tax department is at work making their own inquiries and investigation. All frogs are kicking the dead or better the dying elephant. To add insult to injury, two former judges of the High Court of Kerala were blamed for corruption and malpractices in pronouncing verdicts related to a notorious sex scandal case involving an ex-minister of a State. That case was finally disposed off about 15 years ago by the Supreme Court of India. Of late, a former Minister of the State and a sitting M.P. of the ruling Federal Government at Delhi made a public address in which he made a statement that he was a witness to the acceptance of corruption money by a Judge of the Supreme Court of India. All these buried cases are digged up and a media trial is going on in T.V. channels and newspapers. All frogs have gathered together.

Politicians and not statesmen are in the front row to comment on the judiciary, judicial functionaries and functions. Crocodiles in large numbers cry and sometimes the foxes cry because the chicken is wet. They seem to be disturbed because the public lose their trust in the judiciary. The so-named politicians, i.e., the people who think that the State belongs to them unlike the Statesmen who always think that they belong to the State—who are notoriously known for various nefarious activities, criminality and crimes of all descriptions including nexus crimes and *Mafia* activities come and collect together to kick the judges in hot water. They conduct a 'trial' of the judges in public and make attempts to convert everything to their political party's advantage. Among them one notices people of dubious character and integrity as well. In my view, if the judiciary is to be bettered or the judicial functionaries are to be corrected, then that noble task should not be entrusted to politicians of questionable purity. 'Fox should not be the *Jury at a Goose's Trial*' and what I notice in the media 'trial' is a calculated attempt to encash the situation for political mileage and not for the welfare of the people or for the benefit of the society. All of them shed barrels and barrels of tears.

No doubt, if the judges are really at fault, they must be exposed and punished; but it should not be the politician's task to do so. Satan accusing the sinner ! It is the right time for the Government in power to make an independent machinery to investigate all allegations against the judiciary and to bring the crime-doers to justice. I have been advocating for it time and again through my published books and articles. No doubt, there should be proper accountability, transparency and auditing for judicial functions and functionaries and for that purpose new legislations must be brought out, if needed.

Politicians are very important in a democracy and no democratic government will or can function without politicians. They are a *sine qua non* for any democratic government to function. Their opinions count and will convert many people to vote for them. The eyes of the politicians are always on the vote bank and they go to any extent to collect votes for their party. They encash the police for their advantage and the recent trend seems to be that they want to cash on the judiciary too for their advantage. They criticize the judges and judicial decisions in political languages which in many ways will affect adversely the public trust on the judiciary and the system of administration of justice. Any constructive criticism is always welcomed, all destructive criticisms calculated to diminish the public trust on the judicial system must be discouraged.

I feel irritated and sometimes lose my control (**Push Factor** being *Repulsion* with an accompanying emotion called *'Disgust'*) when I see criminal politicians appearing on the T.V. screens to conduct a media trial of the judiciary, judicial officers and judicial decisions. I hate those 'literary' men who speak "this and that" against the judiciary. I abhor those 'journalists' who try to commercialize the news for mercenary considerations. They misuse their media and abuse their tongue-power without conducting any researches in the field. Any criticism against the judiciary ought to have rich and sound research basis. Beating at the bush should not be the approach of well meaning citizens in a democracy.

People may express emotions like *'Fear, Disgust, Anger, Distress etc.* against the judiciary and judicial officers. Every emotion will have proper basis too. Nevertheless, they should advance their constructive criticisms to improve the system and not to damage or destroy the system. Democracy does not have an alternate system to substitute the judiciary and precisely, therefore, the system must be retained with corrections and changes. Politicians burning the effigy of the judges, conducting *dharnas* and *jatthas* to the courts, etc., are of bad taste. Expelling serving judges in stage shows, public trial of judicial officials, using abusive language and filthy expressions against judicial officers in general deserve highest condemnation and disapproval. At the same time, the injustice done by the judiciary should be exposed and proper inquiries conducted. Remember always that any adverse criticism calculated to damage the judiciary can and will stick mud on the system. Therefore, the judicial officers must take extra care and caution so that their decisions are not qualitatively inferior inviting all sorts of kicks even by the frogs and rats in society. No judge is a superhuman being as he is mortal, nevertheless, his judgments have an immortality and superhuman nature.

BLACK AND WHITE

Black Money and **White Money**—they are very much known to us. Black market, white collar crimes are very much familiar to us. What about black work, i.e., doing work and getting money by evading income tax? Black sheep and black lists are amidst us. In

Bentonville, Arkansas, we have today very heavy snowing about 18″ snow on roads and the atmosphere outside the home is –17 °C. Really cold outside the apartment at the **Links on Rainbow Curve**. Nevertheless, standing near the glass window, one can experience the hot rays of the hot sun. Really hot and I do not know how can it be !—'**Hot** and **Cold**'! After spending some days inside the apartment, we decided now to have our lunch outside. Thus, we went to a Chinese restaurant where we saw an item of food "**Sweet** and **Sour**". Many people taste it with pleasure. Leaving the restaurant, I do observe a number of **White** and **Black** people.

Now I start thinking for a moment—

Why do the **Black** and **White, Hot** and **Cold, Sweet** and **Sour** follow me like a shadow?

Of late, I saw a news item in the T.V. that certain companies were in the black list of the Indian Government.

Yes, I can recollect the past. During 1970s, Kerala had a lot of Gulf returnees and many of them started individual **Blade** business and **Gold** pledging institutions [*Blade* here means getting deposits from the people offering extraordinarily huge interest rate, i.e., a sort of investment schemes to cheat the public]. They had a lot of **Black** money and they wanted to whiten it, i.e., money laundering was their aim. Some had 'pipe money' too [pipe money means money illegally brought to India without the knowledge of the Reserve Bank of India]. Most of them gave loans to the needy people for exorbitant interest rates and many of them had a natural death as the loanees refused or failed to repay or return the principal and interest. They formed even associations and the loners could not realize the loaned amount through the courts of law which was highly expensive. *Goondas* and *goondaism* started to grow then and the purpose was to realize the loaned amount and interest without the intervention of the courts of law.

When individual loaners died a natural death, institutions sprung up like anything. They started to accept investments for which they offered incredibly high interest rates. Many investors deposited their money and miserably became tragic victims of investment frauds. After amassing the deposits and black money thus put in such investment schemes, most of them vanished into thin air and oblivion. Thus the depositors were cheated.

The **Black Money** which the investment racketeers accumulated found expression in another investment scheme which was then notoriously called the '**Teak-Goat-Mangium**' frauds or some other similar schemes. When the '**Teak-Goat-Mangium**' investment schemes met with a tragic premature death, the cheats took to another direction and thus suddenly came up a new investment scheme known as **Tourist Resorts**, followed by **Flats, Tourist Boats** and what not? The '**Total For You**' racketeering is the latest in that line and in all such **Blades**, investment rackets and *mafia* activities, massage centres, flesh trade business, boat houses, five star resorts, star brothels, sex industry, reality shows, album productions, cinema actings, modelling, sale of health nourishners, jewellery and liquor business, *Hawala* and real estate, terrorism, religious fests and miracle *dramas*, etc., etc., one sees **Black Money, Money Laundering** and **White Money**... and thus the **Black** and **White** !!!

In Criminology, I am of the firm view that no police department functions without violating the laws. According to me, law violations by the police become more or less a necessary condition to execute the law. In other words, law enforcement *via* law violations—this is what is called **Black** and **White** in police administration. A question arises "to what extent can the police violate the laws to enforce the laws?"

According to me, no judiciary can work without administering injustice, wounded justice and less justice. Injustice administration today becomes a part and parcel of justice administration! Is it not true?

In my view no government will work efficiently without violating the laws it has made. No business can be done by observing all the laws. No man can become abnormally rich over a night without violating the laws. No gods can survive without devils around them. No good exists without a 'bad'. No night without a day. No pit without a hill. This is nature's law and no one can ignore it. Hence, think about a man. No criminal is a criminal always and no law abider is a law abider always. Crimes are natural, necessary and inevitable in any society—in any culture— everywhere—all times.

Every **Push Factor** (instinct) has positive as well as negative contents. No instinct is good or bad in itself. A new born child behaves instinctively just like animals behave. His/her instincts (**Push Factors**) are shaped or modelled according to the **Pull Factors** which may be sociological, cultural, legal, educational, etc.

Hence, theologians argue that God created man in his own image to do good controlling his instincts and this process is called socialization/*Ego* formation. Hence, if the *Ego* is formed in an upright way in the right direction, he has a conscience with moral values. If he violates the laws and commits crimes, he feels guilty and tries to correct himself to become law abiding. **Black and White** will be there, but must be controlled or checked so that crimes are reduced.

Too much of "**White**" in any society is abnormal and too much of "**Black**" in any society is abnormal. ***Vertus Stat Medio***, i.e., the virtue is in the middle and, therefore, a society with '**Black** and **White**' is a normal society. People live and survive in such a society by promoting goodness and by controlling/reducing badness.

FLOURISHING SEX INDUSTRY !

Sex crimes reported in USA are plenty and incredibly higher than the same reported in India. Owing to several factors—especially, social, cultural, religious and traditional—the sex crimes are rarely or sparingly reported in India and thus do not catch the attention of police to set the law into motion. When you go anywhere in USA, the boys and girls mix and mingle more liberally and without much sex barriers constructed between them. Premarital interactions between boys and girls and knowing each other closely are a must before settling the marriage between them. In spite of the mixing and mingling of two complementary sexes, sex crimes are on the increase, sometimes in a frightening way.

What about us in India? In India, there exists a lot of restrictions and controls in the mixing and mingling of boys and girls. Social, cultural, familial, religious and parental controls make the boys see girls only from a distance and *vice versa*. Yet, sex crimes are on the increase. Though the statistics relating to sex crimes may not be apparently that frightening, criminologists are of the firm view that the unreported sex crimes are beyond human calculations. Whatever that be, as said earlier, a report about sex industry in India, published a few years ago, says that the industry is having a turnover of more than 43,000 crores of Indian rupees annually! Formerly, girls between the ages of 18-25 were in demand whereas now the age has been lowered down to 10-18 (?) years! About 200 girls are transported from one part of the country to another everyday (?) and recruitment of new ones to the industry is in full swing. Those who run the industry have huge income and thus the industry is flourishing incredibly well. Sex albums, sex photos, blue films, C.Ds, DVD productions, sex works, mobile sexual recreations, door to door sex, casinos, etc., are a part of this sex industry.

In spite of all these, the news about sex crimes appearing in the media may be quite alarming and disturbing. Sex crimes are committed at home, work places, schools and colleges, industrial estates, hotels, resorts and massage centres, railway cabins, tourists' spots, star hotels, brothels and thus practically there is no place where the crime is not taking place ! Connected to them are the kidnappings, abductions, elopements, false recruitments, forced entries, cheatings, fake promises to give chances to act in films and T.V. serials, production of song albums, modelling, and reality shows, etc. Almost all types of people from every walk of life from the rich to the poor, from the powerful to the powerless, from the influential to the helpless are accused of involving in many forms of sex crimes. What to do?

We cannot keep the male and female in two water tight compartments. In earlier years, the girls enjoyed less freedom and they were under the strict and continuous control of their parents. The situation has now changed a lot and the instinct of *sex* (following emotion is *lust*) finds expression in very many ways. The family planning pills and devices have accelerated the instinctual satisfaction of sex. The clandestine or open facilities to go for abortions may be another factor for the industry to go up.

Whether or not one accepts the Freudian explanation of sex energy is not the issue there. An inordinate sex-urge can lead to sex offences. Victimologists may argue that the victim precipitation and victim participation may result in sex-offences. The *curiosity* (an instinct accompanied by an emotion called *wonder*)—a **Push Factor** is nursed and nurtured by internet sex, cyber sex, mobile phone sex, video and CD sex, etc. Today gang rapes as well as relay rapes (one rape followed by another at distant places) are reported. The industry is flourished by sex albums, sex-stimulating literature, sex-stimulants, sexual talks, etc. Sex-work in seven star hotels, call girls, door to door sex, rent-a-girl system, cheese-cake girl culture, cabaret dances, etc. are plenty and the law is sterile in many respects. The law enforcement officials are reluctant to enforce the laws strictly as they become handicapped under the influence of the powerful in society. A culture of sexual activities in dignity has come into being.

What about the **Pull Factors**? The **Pull Factors** in society are plenty. One who wants to enjoy sex, he gets a lot of opportunities so much so that the concept of sin/immorality connected to illicit sex has almost vanished away. Instead of sin, some call it to be sexual recreation in which the sinner-sin relationship does not come to play. Earlier, people used to say: "Everything is justified in sex and war" and they said so only in licit sex activities. But today, many subscribe to the view that anything is justified in sex and they mean "illicit sex" as well.

Sex is an industry today just like the sugar industry, jute industry, coir industry, etc., and the industry is run for profits. Hence, liquor with sex becomes more profitable. The helpless law enforcement officer sees everything but keeps silence which is very much needed for his existence and survival in the law enforcement department. Swim along with the current—not against the current—is the strategy followed by many with respect to sex crimes.

How to control the sex crimes? Controlling the sex crimes means controlling the sex industry—controlling the powerful and the influential. This is difficult if not impossible. The only option is the **Ego Formation** in an upright way in the right direction. Prevention is impossible, reduction is difficult, but **Right Ego Formation** is quite possible

CENT PER CENT CORRUPTION AND NEXUS CRIMES

There is a joke about an Indian Minister making a visit to the United States. He was invited by the Minister (Secretary as he is known here) in USA for a dinner and thus the Indian Minister paid a visit to his house in Washington D.C. It was really a mansion and the US Minister told him the story of how he could manage to construct such a huge house in the centre of the city.

He said: *"Look, you see a bridge there. That was constructed on my orders and I got 10 per cent of the total budget for the construction of the bridge. That is allowed in law here"*.

The Minister from India said: *"Oh, I understand"*.

After three years, the US Minister visited Delhi and he was taken by his Indian colleague to his residence for a dinner. The US Minister was wonder-struck literally to see a very huge mansion, triple the size of his house in Washington D.C. Seeing the US Minister's eyes and expression on his face, the Indian Minister said: *"Look, you see a bridge there?"*

The US Minister replied; *"No, I don't"*.

The Indian Minister: *"Yes, there is a bridge there. It was constructed as per my orders. CENT per cent! That is allowed here"*.

The US Minister replied: *"Oh, I understand"*.

What is happening in India? Ministers are accused and arrested for corruption. High bureaucrats are prosecuted for corruption and malpractices. Very high political leaders are caught for nefarious activities and as Mark Antony in Shakespeare said: "They are honourable men!"

These 'political kings' have followers who shout slogans in favour of them and for them. The helpless law enforcement officials watch the *drama*. High level judicial officers and police functionaries are under suspicion and prosecution. Long ago, I wrote a book titled: *Indian Police and Nexus Crimes* in which the questionable activities of police-politicians-businessmen and bandits for amassing exorbitant wealth were exposed. Now the nexus crimes are seen in all walks of life, politics and administration, which include judiciary as well. The cent per cent corruption is everywhere and the black money is deposited in foreign banks. Perhaps more black money can be seen circulating within the country of huge size.

When corruption is detected, like the Satan quoting from *Bible* and accusing the sinner, one political party leaders accuse the other political party leaders in the media openly with an understanding that *"you scratch my back; I will scratch your back"*. The people are fooled by this scratching dramma and, yes, all is well that ends well!

In Indian democracy, one political party or a coalition formed by many political parties rule the State/country for minimum 5 years at the end of which there will be a general election. During the five years of rule, there may be changes in the chief Ministership/ministership, etc., as the policy is the *"survival of the fittest"*. At the Central Government level there may be changes in the portfolios of Ministers. Whatever that be, one government registers cases after cases against the former government and allows a sort of never ending investigations to start at various levels. Such investigations have only media importance and news significance for votes. The government in power withdraws cases after cases registered against everyone by their predecessor government when the new Government comes in power and authority. No politician is ever punished or a politician is rarely punished and the drama continues fooling the electorate everywhere.

Any minister or any government may be for a short period of maximum five years and, therefore, 'accumulate as much wealth as possible' seems to be each one's declared policy. The cent per cent episode narrated above may be an exaggeration and a humarist said recently that there are only few things which God, Almighty does not know. One of such things is: *"How much money and wealth, politicians accumulate during their career"*. *Acquisitiveness and laughter* are very powerful instincts working in them. In order to accumulate wealth, they become susceptible to other instinctual forces **(Push Factors)**

What are the **Pull Factors** for accumulating wealth in a corrupt manner? The **Pull Factors** are plenty and a politician with an inadequate *Ego Formation* becomes corrupt to the core without guilt feelings.

In Malayalam language, there is a saying—**Chakkalathil Poru**—which means 'Fight in the Expeller's House". Husband and wife in an Expeller's house join together and fight each other to exploit those who come there for extracting oil from the grains or seeds. Almost in the same way, two political parties fight each other and they register criminal cases just to exploit the voters. The crimes committed by the political parties are too many now so much so that there emerges a new branch in criminology called **Political Criminology**. In every State in India and in the country as a whole, the political parties and their leaders are too many so much so that coalition Government alone is the only option at present. This system helps them to accumulate wealth in an easy way– **cent per cent**– while everyone looks at their crimes silently.

NEXUS CRIMES AND HONOURABLE MEN

See any news channel in the T.V. about India and one may hear about nexus crimes, corruption and politicians' vandalism. Nexus crimes, i.e., unholy nexus among leaders, bureaucrats, businessmen and bandits to amass wealth and money in various forms, are reported in abundance. In one case it is more than 1,50,000 crores of Indian rupees and in another case it is about 2,00,000 crores of Indian rupees. Politicians are involved and the Ministers of the ruling Government are accused of having nexus partnership in such criminal activities. Of late (2011), it is learnt that a Joint Parliamentary Committee inquiry is going to be instituted. Most surprisingly and frustratingly enough, political parties are supporting the nexus transactions and justify the nexus partners. Whether, the political party benefited or the politicians benefited [or both] is a question of dispute. Investigations will be conducted and many meaningless investigations will go on endlessly and infinitely. The Governments may come and they may go. The investigating officials will come and they also will go. The interest and enthusiasm seen presently will gradually be lessened and there will come a time when the investigation of nexus crimes becomes *"no body's baby"*. Is there any case so far registered and investigated by any investigating agency culminated in the conviction of a political leader? If there is any, the politician may be of an insignificant type with no followers. Just recently, a politician was punished in Kerala by the Supreme Court of India after about two decades of legal battle. Now, a lot of political parties come forward to support him and his political followers organize strikes, road blocks and *dharnas* against the verdict of the Court. Some religious leaders too speak in favour of the politician who was punished for his alleged nexus dealings. The media is full of such nexus crimes, justifications, rationalizations, glorifications and what not? He is made the **'Hero'** of the time. While the Parliament has problems in transacting business because of the 'stilling' of its activities by vested interests inside, no one, it seems, is bothered very much about it as everybody is after a never ending—meaningless—purposeless investigation of nexus crimes.

Nexus crimes may be seen in other parts of the world. But, everywhere the same patterns are noticed so much so that nexus crimes make all partners **"Honourable Men"** in society. This is perhaps the curse of the democracy today.

A satirist once said "In a Kingdom, the King alone is a Cheat and in a Democracy, every Leader is a Cheat". Though his joke may be an exaggerated version of the politicians' crimes in a democracy, one may notice that there is a lot of truth behind the exaggeration. The civil servants in the democracy participate in the commission of crimes and rob the country and the people alike–and they have no evil consequences. The corruption is more at the higher and highest echelons of administration, but it goes unnoticed as it takes place in an invisible way or in a clandestine manner. People are not directly affected adversely by nexus crimes whereas they are affected badly by the corruption or bribery at the lower or lowest level of civil administration. The nexus crimes and corruption at the top levels are investigated or inquired by Joint Parliamentary Committee or Administrative Boards whereas the corruption at the lower levels is investigated by ordinary policemen. Nexus crimes have news value and nexus criminals are honourable men. Nexus criminals are not viewed as criminals, rather are respected as leaders, i.e., gods on Earth or Kings on Earth. They become rulers which give them opportunities to loot the country.

The crimes–especially the nexus crimes–committed by the top levels of democratic administration are not defined in law. If at all the crimes are proved after investigation, they are dealt with under the criminal laws of the country which were enacted centuries ago–and that too, not at all to deal with the *'Kings of Democratic Governments'*. When the Indian Penal Code was enacted in 1860, India was under the British colonial rule and democracy was not established there. All these newer crimes came into being after India became independent and democratic. Political criminology in a democratic set up is different from the same in a colonial rule. Under the colonial rule or in the kingdoms there will not be any "Honourable Men" as one may see them in a democracy.

Nexus crimes in a democracy are committed by a group of people and, therefore, there will be corporal liability or responsibility. Again, corporate crimes are not well defined in the Penal Code. Disputes and discussions are going on about corporate *mens rea* in such crimes. Politicians are leaders in a democracy. Although they enjoy *de facto* powers and authority in a democratic set-up, they do not have any *de jure* power or authority in nexus transactions. Hence, making politicians as nexus partners in the commission of nexus crimes cannot or does not make any sense or meaning. Therefore, they are safe and live in comfort zones. These 'honourable men' have accumulated wealth with them and, more often than not, their political party comes forward with necessary financial assistance and needed people's support. They accept donations and contributions from vested interests and political followers with the ultimate result that the conduct of the case before any authority does not pose any problems for many. The so-named authority ceases to have any authority over them when they form a government. We are in a vicious circle and we cannot get out of it. What to do and how to go about in such a situation remain to be an enigma today for political criminologists. Yet, the instincts and the *Ego Formation* of the nexus partners assume importance as the etiology of nexus crimes. Yes, the birds of the same feathers gather together!

CONSENSUS CRIMES AND JUSTICE

'Consensus' means in Dictionary the general agreement or concord and it appears to me that consensus works very deeply during the administration of justice. When I listen to the news in the media, I hear a lot about the *consensus,* i.e., the politician-police concord during the registration and investigation of criminal cases. The agreement is that the entire case will be investigated from its registration in a perfunctory manner or in a haphazard way so that the case will be discharged or dismissed or acquitted ultimately. The whole mountain will be in labour and what comes out will be a dead human flesh. It has been noted that even the Ministers of the ruling governments, National level or State level politicians, district level political leaders interfere with the registration and investigation of criminal cases. They may even produce fake suspects for the police to arrest as the prime accused in the cases registered.

Though we have the independence of judiciary and the prosecutors are free to conduct criminal cases in an independent way for administering justice to crime doers, the truth is that, as the allegation goes, they are approached or pressured to enter into *consensus* with politicians who offer them a lot of promises. The politician-prosecutor tie-up is extended to the police for arriving at a general *Consensus* or *Agreement* to torpedo the administration of justice and delivery.

Consensus with judges too becomes a live topic of media discussions and press conferences. Most unfortunately, the allegation against some of the judges is that in some of the cases, they are offered with corruption money, human comforts, luxuries, positions and new assignments, etc., to destroy or defeat the sublime purpose of administering justice. Thus to cut a long story short, a desperate situation, it is strongly suspected, has now emerged that the fence has started eating the crops, i.e., what has been intended to protect or guard the crops eats up the crops! In other words, there is no one to guard the guardians! Resultantly, people lose their trust in police machinery of the States. They demand always—sometimes going to the Courts of Law—C.B.I.'s inquiry/investigation in almost all cases to the extent that in a recent case before a High Court of Judicature, the C.B.I. has informed that they had no officials to spare for taking up the criminal investigation of fresh cases. The State Governments in large measure resort to the investigation by the C.B.I. and it indicates that they too have started losing the trust in their own police machinery. The State Governments in some cases appoint special public prosecutors to conduct the criminal cases or they remove one and appoint another Public Prosecutor to conduct the cases. They mean again the same thing. It shows the distrust of the Governments in their own lawyers. Many politicians including some Ministers make public utterances, media interviews and speeches signifying their distrust in judges and the quality of their judgements. All these point to a hard and unpalatable fact that all of them suspect a sort of consensus among the various sub-systems and the politicians. The motivating factors can be anything from monetary gains to positions of importance in life. It is a fact to be reckoned with that many who act upon the **consensus** are respected, honoured and placed at high pedestals, posts or positions after the purpose for which the **consensus** is arrived at. The growing demand of the people today is that the **consensus** among the sub-systems or between the sub-systems and politicians must be treated as crimes called **consensus Crimes** punishable under the penal laws of the country.

Democracy has three pillars—Legislature, Executive and Judiciary. Each one performs the functions independently and it should be so to ensure fair and just justice. Independence of the judiciary is a noble concept and it should be there. What is the meaning of politician—police nexus or concord? It means that the police is *politicized*. *Politicization* of the police is a curse in any democracy. The purpose of *politicization* of police is not for administration of fair justice but for promoting and propagating the political ideology and to increase the vote bank. Political interference in police work annihilates justice administration. It has been heard that the police registers a criminal case only if they have the political good will; they investigate only if they have the political approval; they file the final report only if they have the political concurrence. The suspects are produced by the political parties; the evidence is collected and given by the political parties; the witnesses are made available to the police by the political parties and thus a politicized police behaves like political adherents of a political party in power.

What about the prosecutors?—the judicial officers? Allegations are heard against some defence lawyers coming in consensus with the prosecutors so that together they torpedo the criminal cases. A situation comes into being that the politicians make attempts to politicize the prosecutors for promoting their interest. If they become successful in their attempts, then arises a politician-police-prosecutor nexus. Sometimes, the politicians are able to get the full support of the defence counsels as well and thus the consensus will be extended to include the defence lawyers too. The witnesses are approached and their goodwill and support are ensured and one sees the politician-police-prosecutor-witness nexus/ consensus. If the judicial officers too are brought to the consensus network, then everything becomes successful as far as administration of justice is concerned! People are becoming more and more suspicious of this sort of *'Group Song'* or *'Group Dance'* performance in the area of justice administration. News comes in the media about the waste of money in the pretext of administering justice. It means that the system is rotten and there is the immediate need for correction by a major surgery by virtue of which the independence must be reestablished and the consensus must be dismantled. Will it be ever possible?

Consensus crimes are not defined in the penal laws and, therefore, the *'group song/dance'* administration of justice does not become a crime today. Media is said to be the fourth estate and an independent media is the fourth pillar of democracy. Some political parties have their own media making attempts to rationalize, legalize, legitimize everything they do. Attempts are made (sometimes unsuccessfully) to include the media too in the consensus network and if it happens, then there is no meaning in having a democracy in any country. In such situations, the Constitution becomes meaningless and justice administration ceases to have any value or worth. Hence, treat consensus crimes as crimes and punish the consensus criminals as criminals committing very serious or heinous crimes in society.

THE BIRTH OF 'CONVICTION' CRIMINALS

'Conviction'—one of the meanings given in the Random House Webster's Dictionary is ***a fixed or firm belief.*** Therefore, a **'Conviction'** crime means a crime committed as a result of a conviction— like the Naxalites, fundamentalists, fanatics, terrorists, insurgents and so on. There are laws and international understandings about how to deal with such criminals who are put under the above categories. Of course, they are law violators out *of firm convictions*, i.e., salvation only through terrorism, insurgency or Naxalitism, etc. Insurgency, for example, means "insurrection against an existing Government, usually one's own, by a group not recognized as having the status of a belligerent". News coming from Assam, Jammu and Kashmir, Bihar and Nagaland, etc., show that insurgents are at work. We have in India terrorists and many terrorists' attacks are reported time and again. In USA and other countries too, terrorists are seen, but my concern at present is not about such 'convictions or criminals' who commit offences out of their belief in a philosophy.

The news coming from India shows that we are badly affected by **'Conviction'** criminals of a different type, most of them are 'honourable' men. The *Mafia* Criminals, Crime Syndicates, *Hawala* Criminals, Nexus Criminals are at work and they are convinced that their success in life depends upon the ruining of the nation's economy. The bureaucratic crimes intended to amass wealth are crimes calculated to destroy the country. The *Hawalas* are for it. Political leaders who misuse their career to sell the country's wealth for their personal or party advantages are 'conviction' criminals who are in a way more dangerous than the Naxalites, terrorists, fundamentalists and so on. The Naxalites, terrorists, fundamentalists and so on consciously resort to violent acts to destabilize and destroy the country whereas the *Hawalas, Mafias,*

Nexus partners, the unscrupulous Bureaucrats, Political or Religious Conviction Criminals make use of economic terrorism, political fundamentalism, religious fanaticism, etc., to destabilize the nation or destroy the country.

When we listen to the T.V. news or read the newspapers, we are shocked to know that such 'conviction' criminals' are involving in nefarious transactions resulting in the loss of several crores of rupees to the Government. If anyone supports the terrorists, insurgents, fundamentalists who try to destabilize the Government, then action will be taken against them. On the other hand, these new 'Conviction' criminals are honoured sometimes as leaders and they are mistakenly supported by the political leadership at the national level, Chief Ministers, Ministers and so on. The law becomes sterile and law enforcement becomes barren. They become heroes and are knowingly or unknowingly adored by many. Where are we going to?

Economic terrorism, it appears, is a new concept in crimino-economics. The economic terrorists terrorize the people who helplessly suffer the consequences. The national wealth is pocketed and thereby economic instability is created. How much money is there in the foreign banks deposited by Indians? The amount is beyond human imagination when many Indians live under starvation, semi-starvation or are seen under the poverty line. The word terrorism is not presently associated with economics or finance. Economic destabilization of a country is indeed dangerous and is worse than terrorism. Hence, the new concept known as economic terrorism.

Naxalites, terrorists and fundamentalists claim that they commit several acts to save the country—of course, by destabilizing and destroying the country whereas the bureaucratic criminals, economic offenders, political crime-doers do many things in the pretext of stabilizing the nation. In the process of doing so they pocket national wealth. This is what is now called the *"bureaucratic terrorism, political terrorism"*, etc., but they are in comfort zones enjoying very many privileges which the *Naxalites*, fundamentalists, insurgents and so on do not enjoy.

As pointed out earlier, once a Director General of Police from an Indian State said that the Hawala money coming to his State annually was more than ₹ 50,000 crores. Some who heard his statement responded that the D.G.P. was underestimating the amount. What about the container money reaching the sea/air ports in India? News comes in the media saying that the Indian money printed outside the country by another (hostile?) country is dumped into Indian territory. How? Their intention is nothing but, probably, destabilization of Indian economy. How do they do so? Do they have the political support? Do they have the bureaucratic support? What about the money received by the religious organizations and NGOs in India? Does anyone know the channels through which the foreign money comes to India? The authorized ways are different from the unauthorized ways. If weapons are brought to India, it is viewed with seriousness. In my view, the money dumped into India is more dangerous than the weapons. If bureaucrats, politicians, businessmen, religious leaders and so on are found to be responsible by aiding or otherwise, they are conviction-criminals more dangerous than the terrorists and insurgents. They are "conviction criminals" because they are sure that they are going to destabilize the country by economic terrorism. Beware of such criminals, for they are convinced of the nation's ruin and their environment by their involvement in the commission of crimes.

THIRD DEGREE METHODS AND POLICE

I used to watch American T.V. at Bentonville and I see the police stories. I can see the policemen employing force, torturing people even to the extent of shooting at the suspect. One day I met a policeman and asked him: *"Do you torture people?"*

He replied: *"Yes, in public and never in secret in police custody."*

According to him, using force or beating people in public or torturing people in public's visibility is justified whereas torturing anyone, including the criminals or suspects, in police custody in a clandestine way is an offence under law. O.K., very good advice indeed!

Immediately afterwards, I took **You Tube** and watched the video pictures therein relating to police interrogation. Believe me or not, I could witness torturing the suspect during interrogation in police custody. I do not know from which country the video has been taken and shown in the **You Tube**. Any way it was not in India. Moreover, I could see a live telecast of a jail in which the prisoners were most cruelly tortured. There also I have no idea about the country from where such a scene has been videographed.

Concurrently with the torture news, I could listen to the torture death of a person in police custody in India and the difficulties which the C.B.I. faced to take action against two senior police officials of the Indian Police Service (They were alleged to have involved in that torture death). Torturing in police custody is a crime in India from 1860 when the Indian Penal Code came into being. It was due to the recommendation of the Torture Commission instituted by the British in 1855 to inquire into the alleged torture in police custody in the erstwhile Madras State.

I used to teach police officials about **James's Law of Police Interrogation**, i.e., the Police Defence Mechanisms (PDMs) cause Suspect's Defence Mechanisms (SDMs) which in turn cause the PDMs and the process goes on until one of them is made inactive or inoperative. In other words, police interrogation becomes successful if and only if the defence mechanisms found working in the suspects are made inactive or inoperative [See *Wikipedia*, the free encyclopedia and refer police interrogation]. It is a law which gives a theoretical basis for police interrogation and it helps the police interrogators to apply the law in their scientific and psychological interrogation.

For applying the above law in practical police work, police interrogators need to undergo special training. The police officials should be academically qualified and qualitatively suitable to become professional interrogators. There should be special recruitment to the post of police interrogators and the law should be amended to that effect. Instead, the approach today seems to be to train police officials as Jack of **All** Trades and Master of **None**. Resultantly, they starve on Sundays as the saying goes. Unless and until professional interrogators are recruited and appointed—the law on interrogation is amended—the curse of torturing the suspect in secret in police custody will continue to haunt the investigation works in India. The crime will be a perpetual persecutor for the police and the killer for the people in police custody. What to do and how to go about?

In employing third degree methods on a person under custody, one sees the naked exhibition of human instincts, i.e., *Repulsion, Self-assertion, Laughter,* etc. The one who has an upper hand in a given situation–has the power and authority to control the situation–can certainly afford to become aggressive. This is what is seen in torture under police custody. Police interrogators who lack adequate *Ego Formation* in an upright way in the right direction employ torture without any guilt feelings. I know some police officers who express grief and experience guilt feelings after torturing suspects in police custody. They are the personnel who had an upright development of their *Ego* or *conscience*.

Police officers who advocate the employment of torture in police custody sometimes advance an argument that they do not have any *mens rea* while they torture the suspect. Right and they are right in thinking so. I hope that they will admit the fact that they are violating the law when they do so. The law enforcer shall not become a law violator. Their sole intention is to bring out the truth. Fine, yet a question back. The end does not always justify the means. It means that the 'means adopted too must be justified'. Here, if the tortured is an innocent person, then what justification does a police officer have in such a situation? Exhibition of the animal instinct in an animal way is not a human act. No amount of torture during interrogation will be a substitute for scientific and psychological interrogation for which the police interrogators should have the necessary aptitude, knowledge, skill, technology and knowhow. The uniform, psedo-authority, exercise of excessive authority under the colour of the uniform or under the cover of the power cannot be an alternative for acquiring scientific knowledge in the subject. The custodial deaths and deaths under custody are going up in India and allegations are plenty against police torture. It may be remembered that the suspects have a lot of rights under custody and no police officer can violate them. If they do so, they are committing violations of the human rights law. When police officers violate the human rights laws, they cease to be police officials, rather become criminals in uniform. *Criminalization* of police is a topic of discussion in these days and psychologists say that the police torture of a suspect in custody, etc., may be the impact of *criminalization* of police. Criminologists subscribe to the above view and add further that *criminalization* is a process by which a neonate to the police service is made to commit crimes without guilt feelings. Certainly, *criminalization* is not the formation of *Ego* in an upright way in the right direction.

GOING TO HEAVEN AND LOVING SUCCESS

I went to Bentonville Public Library and found a beautiful reading room where the wisdom of several generations down the millennia could be seen. I just took a book and read:

> "Everyone loves to go to heaven, but no one is prepared to die".
>
> *"Everyone loves success, but many do not like successful people".*

I read them again and again; reflected on them again and again–having seated on a chair in the library. For, two days ago, I listened to a T.V. talk in which a person in a religious garb (I do not know whether or not that person is really religious) was speaking about how to go to heaven or attain *Moksha*. It was a wonderful talk worth listening and one might be inclined to die at the earliest and for which he would have no option, but to commit suicide. Anyway, I was not prepared to die by such a short cut method for going to *Moksha*, yet I thought that he could successfully impress the listeners by his speech.

I came back home and again listened to a T.V. discussion in which I could listen to two political leaders belonging to the ruling front and the opposition parties in India talking about making the Nation a heaven or *Moksha* on earth. I found them accusing each other and the political party to which each one of them belonged. Both of them claimed success, but none of them really liked successful people either in their own party or in the opposition party. It was a sort of verbal abuses and hence I switched off the T.V.

There is a growing feeling and a real reality that some political parties in India are richer than the State Governments in power. The Governments coming to power have no money and they are in perpetual debts and hence no *Moksha* for them. At the same time, the political parties are abundant in richness and they have black and white money. Or they know how to convert black money to white. Some politicians are richer than many business magnets and we have any number of such news items to prove the observation. All love to make the Nation a *Moksha*, but many do not do anything positively to achieve the objective. They become richer and fatter.

There is a growing feeling and a real reality that many so-named religious leaders and speakers are richer than some of the political leaders and many rich or affluent people in society. The offerings, donations, contributions, etc., received in the name of God are beyond the imagination of any man. They take all of us to *Moksha* or heaven after death. It has been found that the richest *Mafias* identified so far were in the name of religion.

Both 'politicians' and the so-called 'religious men' are jealous people and they do not really like or love successful people, if they do not become the ultimate winners. The number of crimes committed by both of them to make the Nation a heaven on earth or, if that is not possible, to take the people direct to heaven after their death is innumerable and beyond human conception. Their success is the success in committing crimes in perpetual hopes-hopes against hopes or hopes that will remain always hopes!

Anybody in any executive uniform is a privileged person and tries or can try to exert power, authority, pseudo-authority, assumed authority, etc. He may or can make promises which he knows will not or cannot be executed. Politicians, policemen, traffic wardens, school going children, lawyers, religious men, *sadhus* and *sannayasees*, priests, *poojaries* and god-men, human-gods, *avatars* and other spiritual men—all have their uniforms. Depending upon the status of the uniformed person, the instincts in him/her work. If he/she does not have an adequate *Ego* uprightly formed in the right direction, he/she involves in all sorts of crimes or becomes susceptible to them.

Beliefs, false beliefs, superstitious beliefs, delusional beliefs, etc., are different in different ways. God-men, *Avatars*, human gods, priests and spiritual men/women have their *modus operandi* to create beliefs, false beliefs, superstitious beliefs and delusional beliefs in people. By their calculated move and psychological approaches, they become successful in cheating others and they do so by activating the instincts in them. Animals can be activated by instincts and thus I have seen in my younger days how male pigs are activated sexually in piggeries by presenting female pigs. Likewise, the "religious men" activate the believers by presenting oral or written testimonials. *Escape, Repulsion, Curiosity, Pugnacity,* etc., are the instincts thus made operative. Researchers in psychology say that addiction can be many—such as drug addiction, song addiction, prayer addiction, T.V. addiction, corruption addiction, etc. Spiritual men's cheating tricks work well with their ardent believers or prayer addicts. News reports are seen about various types of cheatings committed by 'spiritual men' and they include sexual cheatings and rapes as well. There exists no law to control spiritual cheatings of various types, rather these spiritual cheats are adored and adorned as god-men or spiritual leaders. The crimes committed in the name of religion, for religion, on behalf of religion are numerous and they continue to multiply in very many ways without any fear. The spiritualists, god-men, human gods and fake religious leaders and so on live in comfort zones without anyone to control or question them.

What about the politicians? They too cheat the people in many ways by their promises knowing fully well that their promises will not be fulfilled. In a country in the west, one voter filed a suit for damages against a politician who violated his promises during the election and the case was decided in his favour. Both 'spiritual men' and 'fake politicians' are suffering from an inadequate formation of *Egos* as they do not have a conscience formed in an upright way in the right direction. They do many things with a hook which will bring to them only advantages, privileges and pecuniary achievements.

JUDICIAL CRIMES— A CURSE IN INDIA

'Judicial Crimes' are not defined in any Penal Codes, for there existed no such crimes till date or if at all there existed such crimes in reality, they were not taken serious note of. If at all they were taken note of, no action was initiated against the culprits. Hence, those who successfully committed judicial crimes under the colour of their uniform or under the cover of their authority and position have been living in comfort zones. No one had the courage to peep into (why to think of investigating them) the safety areas of judiciary. As said earlier, they were the Roman Kings and above Grammar! They were on the elephants and the urchins on earth were helpless.

In India, 'Judicial Crimes' are widely discussed in these days. 'Judicial notice' has a special and specific meaning in law practice. 'Judicial Crimes' are not to be defined or viewed in that sense or way. There may be a number of traditional crimes which lawyers, judges and those employed in judicial service commit. They too are not categorized under 'Judicial Crimes'. For example, manipulation of records by lawyers, production of concocted evidence or tutored witnesses, acceptance of corruption money and false evidence afterwards, etc., are classified under traditional crimes and precisely, therefore, they do not have any place in 'Judicial Crimes'. I may prefer to give a specific description (not definition) to 'Judicial Crimes' here.

'Judicial Crimes' are the crimes which one may get by combining **nexus crimes, consensus crimes and white collar crimes** put together. 'Nexus crimes' have the political leaders, bureaucrats, middlemen, *goondas* plus business men put together and they work as nexus partners. The unholy relations that exist among them bring money and other advantages for the nexus partners. In 'Consensus Crimes' one notices that there is an agreement among the crime-doers and the beneficiaries. In 'White Collar 'crimes, the crimes are committed during the course of one's profession or occupation.

Thus, the 'Judicial Crimes' have—

(1) *Nexus Crime Partners*: i.e., the political Leaders + Judicial Officers+ Business men + Middlemen (*Dallal*) and Gang squad (*Goondas*).
(2) *Consensus Crime Partners*: i.e., the Judicial Officer, on one side and all others mentioned against (1) above on the other side.
(3) *White Collar Crimes*: The crime is committed during the course of the profession of the judicial officers.

The ultimate result is that all in the Syndicate are benefited monetarily and otherwise. People do not know anything much about it as they are the most honourable men on earth—the '**Idols**' in the people's mind. Hence, a 'Judicial Crime' is a crime of a special nature and it has nothing to do much with the judicial notice, judiciary, and judicial officers and so on except that the crime is committed by judicial officers with ulterior criminal motives.

In short, any judicial officer who takes a decision with an ulterior motive other than administration of pure, just and fair justice commits a judicial crime. This discussion is limited only to judicial officers which means that the Bar or Lawyers are not included. Examples :

1. A judicial officer having affiliation with a political party takes decisions always in favour of that political party;
2. A judicial officer having parochial interest takes decisions accordingly;
3. A judicial officer—a strong devotee of a particular religion takes decisions favouring his religious belief.
4. In the west, some time ago, the colour of the skin was a deciding factor for some judges. While hundreds of black people were ordered to be hanged by white judges, a similar decision for a similar offence was taken only against a handful of white offenders by them. Why? The colour affinity was a deciding factor. Likewise, in India, allegations are sometimes, heard that the caste, sub-caste, denominations, sects, religion, communalism, etc., become deciding factors (?). Is it true?
5. Sex becomes a factor in decision-making. While many feminists and women liberators argue for women judges to decide on crimes against women, they admit in all fairness that sex is or should be a decision-making factor in justice administration. This attitude is not desirable.
6. Judicial officers suffering from *Ego* feelings, complexes, personality disorders, attitudinal problems administer justice in the way they want. Of course, justice is a nebulous term which may be interpreted 'this way or that way' as a judge decides.

Thus, the Judicial-Crimes can be very many and various. Decisions are taken, but fair and pure justice is not administered. Are our judges qualitatively fine to take impartial and just decisions?. Are they educationally up-to-date to arrive at right decisions? Is the recruitment system perfect or at least free from defects? Do they update their knowledge by inservice courses? Can the judges take a decision without fear and favour? Are they influenced by the media trials and propaganda? If any one or all of them are not O.K., then the ultimate result will be Judicial-Crimes for which there exists no remedy—not even a relief. Innocent people are punished and imprisoned sometimes and the judicial officers live in comfort zones. How unfortunate it is to see that decisions are not taken even after several decades in some cases! Adjournment–adjournment–adjournment always and no one knows for whose benefits the adjournments are lavishly allowed. Is it because of partisan approach or parochial attitude that the judges become liberal in certain cases? Are they afraid to take a decision? Do they feel "less" in front of learned lawyers? Do they have anger or antipathy towards or against some lawyers? Do they want to favour some lawyers? Why don't they write down everything asked during the examination-in-chief or cross examination? Some of the judicial officers write what they want—nothing more, nothing less. How can they take a decision unless they write down everything? How do they appreciate the evidence?

Remember that "man takes decisions on another man and his acts". Yes, the one who is in the palanquin is a man and the people who carry the palanquin too are men with human flesh and feelings. Judicial officers taking decisions with ulterior motives—with nexus partners—with consensus—during the course of their profession like white collar criminals—do commit Judicial Crimes, no matter they are defined in law or in statutes.

CRIMES OF LAW ABUSE OR LAW ABUSE CRIMES?

"Whoever, knowing or having reason to believe that an offence has been committed intentionally omits to give any information respecting that offence which he is legally bound to give shall be punished with imprisonment of either description which may extent to six months or with fine or with both"—this is Section 202 of the Indian Penal Code-1860. This section of law received wide publicity recently (2011) and the background is as under:

A sitting Member of Parliament in the ruling Government at the Centre and a former Minister of a State Government in India made a public address in which he openly stated that he was a witness to a corruption case in which a Judge of the Supreme Court of India received several lakhs of Indian rupees for awarding a verdict in favour of some Abkari Bar owners. The incident took place about 18 years ago. The statement was made at a time when many high ranking judicial functionaries were under fire—were accused of corruption and malpractices. Anyway, his open platform statement got fire and became a wild fire. Many political higher-ups too were alleged to have involved in the above illegal transaction.

Many political leaders, some advocates, a few vested interests raised their voice and demanded the registration of a criminal case against the sitting Member of the Parliament and the section of law was the one quoted above for not informing the commission of a crime 'in time' to police. Moreover, they wanted the registration of the case only against that particular M.P. and nobody else who was alleged to have been present or received the corruption money, offered the corruption money, etc. I am not at all interested to enter into the merit of the case, nevertheless I have the following doubts or questions to clarify or ask and certainly, they need answers.

(1) In cases of torture, manipulation of records, concoction of evidence, tutoring of witnesses to give false testimony before a court of law, several police officials know the commission of such crimes and no one files an information to register criminal cases for investigation. In fact, they are bound to inform the commission of such crimes. There are several judgements from the criminal courts stating that such manipulations have taken place, yet everybody including the courts of law is silent. Why?

(2) In corruption cases, many in Government offices know about the offering of money, corruption money splitting, corruption money fixing, etc. Without such knowledge, no corruption in an organized way can or will take place. Every one working in such offices are legally bound to give information of such offences; but they do not give. Why?

(3) In political corruption, several politicians know the extent and intensity of the crimes committed. In domestic violence, many know about wife-beating, torture of women, dowry harassment, etc., in road accidents, many are aware of the culprits and thus the final question is—"if cases are going to be registered for omitting to report crimes known to a person, then how many crimes will have to be registered everyday throughout the country?"

What is the relevance of registering a case when the offence itself is not established? First of all, one must establish the commission of the offence and then only one gets the cause of action to proceed against those who kept silence about it. Even in such situations, a case should be registered against all alleged to have involved in the transaction and not against the one who made the statement.

Anyway, remember that the section of law given in the Indian Penal Code 1860 was not at all intended for the abuse of the law for making political mileage. This sort of **law abuse or abuse of law** for parochial or partisan interests is called 'Crimes of Law Abuses' or 'Law Abuse Crimes'. New and newer crimes are added to the old Penal Code of India-1860 which itself is a museum piece.

Allegations are there against the police saying that they register false cases against the citizens. After trial, the cases may be acquitted or in some few cases the cases may be convicted. In both instances, miscarriage of justice has taken place. What action is taken against the police for registration of false cases and waste of time for investigation, prosecution and trial? What type of crime do the police commit in such cases?

Concoction of evidence is an oft-resorted strategy in many criminal cases. The cases may be acquitted or convicted. In both situations, miscarriage of justice takes place. What type of offence has been committed by police and how many cases have been registered for concoction of evidence?

No one commits a crime in vacuum as many know many things about the crimes and criminals. But, no one reports them to the police often or if at all reported, they do not cooperate with the police. How many cases have been registered against the citizens for omitting to report crimes known to them?

In public order crimes, many in the crowd know who committed the offence, but none reports it to the police. If one takes into account the crimes committed down the decades– from 1947 when India became independent—how many cases had to be registered against people who omitted to report crimes in spite of their knowing of them. Impossibilities ought to be considered as impossibilities.

Coming to the present case, what benefit is there for anyone if a case is registered against an M.P. who omitted to report a crime known to him about two decades ago? If at all a case is registered, how is the police going to prove the offence before a court of law? It may be a waste of time, energy, money and manpower for the sub-systems administering justice. The *tamasha* is that a case against a viewer (maximum he can be a witness) is taken while the actual culprits accused of having committed the offence are overlooked. What type of justice is that or better what type of crime is being committed by the sub-systems intended to administer fair, just and proper justice? Can we call it crimes of **Law Abuse**?– or **Law Abuse Crimes**? If it is not a crime of **Law Abuse or Law Abuse Crime**, then what should we call such types of crimes?

PUBLIC LIES AND PERJURY

Perjury in law is "the wilful giving of false testimony under oath or affirmation before a competent tribunal, upon a point material to a legal inquiry". In simple language, telling a lie or falsehood before a Court of Law is called 'perjury' which is a punishable offence in India. Many do give false testimony and they escape punishment. Everybody knows about perjury, but all take a lenient, liberal, tolerating or indifferent attitude to the perjurer. In street corner meetings, many politicians speak lies and falsehood. The people are fooled, cheated, misinformed and the offence of telling a lie or falsehood in public addresses is not a punishable offence. In religion, telling a lie or falsehood is a sin and in many religious platforms, the so-named religious speakers (or better, the speakers in religious garb) say a lot of lies, falsehood, stories and concocted stories containing only lies and lies only to convince the followers of their religious faiths. Such lies are treated as '*Virtues*' and not lies. Precisely, therefore, telling lies or falsehood in 'Religious Talks' are not made punishable offences. Many who appear in press conferences speak lies and only lies and they are not made punishable offences. In media interviews, lies and lies are spoken, but no offence is committed. Hence, the lies and falsehood have received public acceptance and the sanctity of virtues and not sins or offences in any way under any interpretations whatsoever.

In these days, there are channel discussions, channel interviews, channel live telecasts in the visual media. The interviewed tell lies after lies and accuse many for telling lies and falsehood. These liars are supported by vested interests who continuously tell lies and lies and they repeat the lies without any shame and interruptions. People are either confused or convinced of the lies and falsehood and these channel talkers leave the platforms with their *'Heads High'* for telling lies, lies and lies to the channel viewers. It is also made no offence in India hitherto.

Now comes the Question; **"If telling a lie, many lies and lies or falsehood before a court of law during a trial or otherwise is punished under the law of perjury, why not the lying in the media or in public addresses or religious platform speeches or lying to the public in whatever form be made an offence?"** As it is not made an offence, many are not afraid of telling any number of lies and falsehood before the public in public addresses, media interviews, media conferences, and religious platforms or in statements issued to the media/press. This sort of offence should be called the **Offence of Public Lying** as we call the lying in courts ***'Perjury'***.

Hence, if perjury is defined as what is given above, then the lying to the public must be defined as: *'lying to the public by whatever means, consciously or in a calculated way to protect the self interest or vested interest.'* In every sense, it is a more heinous crime than perjury and, therefore, the punishment should also be more severe than what is given for perjury in the penal laws.

Some people mock at statisticians who speak the truth by accusing them as telling lies. For, according to them statistics is a lie. Forget about their ignorance of statistics and forgive them. At the same time, many misuse the public platforms to promote and propagate lies and lies alone. No action is taken against them. During an election campaign, how many lies are told to the public about the achievements and failures of the ruling government and opposition? No one verifies any lie and no action is taken against any one. Why? Is it not a crime to utter lies to mislead the public?

Take the election manifesto and see the promises. None of them may be fulfilled and no action is taken against the political parties for making false promises and promoting and propagating lies to the electorate with an objective of obtaining votes. If they say that one lakh employment will be created during the span of 5 years if they come in power, they are bound to keep up the promise. Otherwise, it will be considered as a public lie calculated to cheat the public.

See the visual media and the advertisements. They make false claims and promote lies about their products without any honesty or research evidence. Believing the lies, people become victims/preys to their advertisement tricks. Lies are told about soaps, detergents, tooth pastes, health nourishers, medicines, ayurveda products, beautifiers, cosmetics, furniture, jewellery, automobiles etc. Every advertiser is fully aware of the lies and they are intended to cheat the public. Hair growing oils, body slimming gadgets, liver protecting medicines, shampoos, mosquito repellents are sold after repeated lies being told in television channels. Even educational institutions and tutorial colleges have such motives. What action does the law take against these liars on public platforms?

What about the religious tricks on platforms? Just go through the pages of a newspaper and see the advertisements. One may see hundreds of liars with God's gifts to show miracles, to offer protection, to ensure prosperity, to annihilate enemies, to obtain jobs, to find out life partners, to get children and my God, unimaginable indeed! How do these liars exploit gods and their spiritual powers? What action is taken against these liars? In the print media, the news comes with lies and interpretations. The I.S.R.O. episode of espionage activities contained many lies and no one took any action against the liars. In the west, once a Government had to appoint a commission of inquiry to convince the general public that the lies promoted and propagated against a Dam were lies and not truths. What about the Mullaperiyar Dam? People listen to many versions and how many of them are true or how many of them are lies? Will there be any action taken against the liars, if any, when truth comes out.

If public lies are not treated as lies, there is no meaning in treating perjury alone as a crime. The perjurer always says that he is employing his defence mechanisms to maintain his homeostasis when he is under mental conflicts or frustrations. Criminologists are researching into the possibilities of making *"Public Lies"* as offences under law.

THE LATEST PENOLOGY

When I was a Member of the Sentence Review Committee of the State of Kerala, chaired by Justice V. Hariharan Nair, Retired Judge,

High Court of Judicature, Kerala, a case came up for our consideration. An old lady of 72 (years of age) who was convicted for life imprisonment for burning to death of her daughter-in-law by pouring kerosene on her head wanted pre-mature release from the prison. Her husband, 81 years old, was alive. He was sick and badly needed the presence of his aged wife for nursing him. She too was sick and had spent more than 10 long years in the jail and was legally eligible (?) for getting pre-mature release from the prison.

On examination of the above case, we could learn that she was most suitable for pre-mature release. Nevertheless and most unfortunately, we could not recommend her for pre-mature release because the law did not permit it. For, anyone convicted for life imprisonment for an offence against women was not to be granted pre-mature release. Regretfully, we refused to recommend her genuine case to the Government and while the Chairman was writing the so-called unanimous refusal words of recommendation, I made a comment in a feeble voice: **"Yes, her burial can be at the expense of the State and it is the net result of this refusal"**. The Chairman and other members smiled or frowned at my honest but painful comment— I do not remember.

Imprisonment as a punishment has a history of its own. It has a history of just over 300 years as it was in 1704 that the same was accepted as a punishment for offenders. When the Indian Penal Code-1860 was enacted, imprisonment became the only punishment that could be given either alone or along with other types of penalties for all kinds of offences. The imprisonment was punitive to begin with and gradually it became *punitive-correctional, corrective, corrective-reformative, corrective-reformative-rehabilitative and now for socialization and reintegration of crime doers back to society.* Of late, the purpose of imprisonment has become 'to develop human personality in an upright way in the right direction'. Quite recently, an aged and sick politician and a former Minister of a State Government in India was punished for one year's imprisonment for an offence which he was alleged to have committed about 20-25 years ago. Again a high ranking police official who was 76 or so was punished for life imprisonment for an offence he was alleged to have committed about 40 years ago. Then the questions arise:

(1) Do the aged and infirm crime doers need to develop their personality in an upright way in the right direction at the fag end of their **life? Or** better, can it be developed?

(2) What type of **'Justice'** is administered to a crime doer for a crime committed about 25-30-35-40 years back? Can it be called **'Justice'** by any definition or description? When a law is enforced, the justice should not be denied'—is a basic and fundamental principle of jurisprudence.

(3) The history of punishment has travelled a long way from retribution, i.e., an eye for an eye, a tooth for a tooth approach to the development of the personality of the crime doers. If so, imprisonment is only a means to an end, the end being the development of human personality in an upright way in the right direction. When the objective cannot be achieved or is not required, then there is no meaning in awarding a purposeless imprisonment to the very old and the infirm. What do you say?

(4) Are they sent to prison for their burial at the fag end of their life or for developing their personality just before going to their grave? Is it not better to award death penalty and finish them permanently than forcing them to suffer the punishment and thus to die a miserable death?

The international community may deliberate on the topic and give a full stop to this cruel and inhuman punishment to the aged and infirm at a time when the people come forward with all sorts of special care and protection to the aged. Is this the latest **Penology**?

No doubt, it is time now to review the policy relating to the ends of criminal justice administration or objectives of punishments. During 1973-76 when I was doing my M.A and LL.B. courses in the University of Saugor (as the University then was known), I had to study the ends of criminal justice administration. Now, it is 2011 and the same text-book is used to teach the ends of criminal justice administration in many colleges and universities. All over the world, penology has given way to correction and now further to *development of personality in an upright way in the right direction*. Yes, a lot of water has flown under the bridge and still, the courts are under the impression of punishing the criminal, incarcerating the punished, etc. They are not concerned with the development of the personality of the inmates at the Centre of Personality Development (That is how the prisons are now called by some criminologists). They are not very much concerned about parole, probation, ticket to leave system, group therapy, case study, psychiatric social work, counselling, etc. for the personality development of the inmates. Still, they use the Penal Codes and award punishments to the guilty with or without any purpose. Now, juveniles are not sent to prisons—human rights of the inmates are more recognized and respected—special training courses are organized to make the staff in prisons to adopt new strategies for the development of the inmates' personality. The U.N. Standard Minimum Rules For The Treatment of Prisoners adopted in 1957 have become obsolete now and the U.N. is serious about revising the Rules for betterment. Still, the judges are in the blissful ignorance of the latest development in the science of rehabilitation, resocialization and reintegration of the incarcerated to the society. They have the time worn deterrent, retributive, preventive and reformative approaches which are now taught in universities only from the points of view of history and examinations.

If the young offenders, women and so on are shown leniency by law, why cannot the old, the older old and the oldest old be shown mercy and consideration by the justice system? The number of older people committing crimes may be few and the less powerful, influential or affluent are normally incarcerated. Hence, the next discussion centres around special punishment policies for the aged and the infirm.

SPECIAL PUNISHMENT POLICIES FOR THE AGED AND THE INFIRM

A shoe-maker in Boston, USA is eulogized for the probation services. Through his committed and devoted dedication and zeal, several hundreds of offenders were released on probation of good conduct. Researches and studies in the special area of treating offenders show that probation has been the best method so far designed and devised for treating offenders. Its success rate is very high. For those who stay in a prison, the approach is to release them prematurely before the completion of their sentence, if found fine, and it is called 'Parole'. There are a number of NGOs and others involved in after care services.

The imprisonment has proved to be not a success in the development of the personality of the inmates in an upright way in the right direction. As Winston Churchill said: **"The mood and temper of the public with regard to the treatment of crime and criminals has always been an unfailing test of any civilization in any country"**. In the west, now social services, attending special training courses for the juveniles, etc., are awarded as punishments. Just recently, an ex-minister of a State Government in India was punished for incarceration for one year. The question here is: "Why not the former Minister of a State, a 76 years old sick person, be given probation of good conduct for one year instead of one year's imprisonment?" The fact that he has been punished means that he has been punished for the offence he committed and sending him to incarceration shows that the law became more retributive and cruel taking a sort of vengeance. Either the law is bad or the judge who punished him had a punitive approach—a training in the old school of penology.

Now, forget about the ex-minister who was punished for an offence he is alleged to have committed about two decades ago. Another case is about a retired Inspector General of Police, 76 years old sick man, who was punished for life for an offence, alleged to have been committed by him about 40 years ago. I am not at all concerned with the ex-minister or the retired police official. Mine is about the aged and the infirm as far as their imprisonment is concerned just before their death (?). We have special laws, concern and consideration for the juveniles, for women, for the mentally sick and so on and everything is done for the best interest of the convicted. We have thus the juvenile justice, gender justice, victim justice and there exist victimological compensation, restitution, etc. We have human rights laws and special courts for human rights cases to be tried. The question is: 'Why don't we have special laws, procedures and punishment policies for the aged and the infirm?'

It is an accepted fact that a crime is a human act and very much a social fact. Punishment for punishment's sake is no punishment at all. Purposeless punishments–especially incarceration, are counter productive. The purpose of imprisonment is not retribution or vengeance taking. The old and the infirm do not require any special treatments in the prison and they cannot be given hard work. Why should the general public be taxed to find money for maintaining the old and for treating them medically at the Government expense? It becomes a waste of money from Government Exchequer and should be discouraged. Even today (2011), an inmate in a prison needs more than one lakh Indian rupees for his accommodation and other needs in some States and if that is the general case, it will be more for the old and the infirm. Considering the nature of the problem and the issue under discussion, should we not think seriously about the punishment policies to the old, very aged and infirm convicts in prisons?

Under my supervision, a researcher conducted an empirical study on the aged in prisons. The study proved that they were affected by old age diseases of very many kinds and of very many descriptions. At a time the old are neglected or ignored by their children, kith and kin, it may be a nice idea to house them in a prison where they are ensured of medical care and proper nursing attention. Nevertheless, staying in a prison as an incarcerated convict has a lot of psychological disadvantages. Many of the old convicts interviewed for the purpose of the research study were suffering from guilt feelings and there was no reason to think that they would repeat the crimes if they were released prematurely. In spite of all the guarantees and comforts they received in the prison, all of them vociferously wanted to get a pre-mature release under any conditions stipulated by the authorities. They wanted to be among their own near and dear ones to spend the fag end of their life. Their pains, sufferings and problems were least known to the people outside and precisely, therefore, their old age incarceration had no deterrent effect on the potential crime-doers. According to some, they were sinned against more than sinning. For, the disposal of criminal cases took such a long time that the suspects/accused/punished/incarcerated suffered the punishment socially, psychologically, financially, etc., for several years since they committed the offence. My own studies in criminology give me ample evidence to show that there is a lot of truth in what those old people regretfully say. A man is mentally affected most when he is involved in a criminal case (No. 3), preceded by problems at home/family (No. 1), followed by health hazards (No. 2), followed by financial difficulties (No. 4), etc., and therefore punishment starts from the moment a person is caught by the police. The old, the older old, oldest old people cannot withstand the problems and difficulties connected with incarceration as they are found to be, as a rule, weak physically and psychologically. Hence, a more lenient attitude—say, probation of good conduct or parole—must be accepted. Laws may be amended to this extent incorporating the special punishment policies for the aged and the infirm.

CRIMINAL JUSTICE POLICY (INCARCERATION) FOR THE AGED AND THE INFIRM

The God, Almighty is always painted as *an old man-with grey beard and hairs. 'Respect the old and the aged'* is as old as humanity. 'Old is Gold', 'Old men for Wisdom', 'Old men's counsel is the Best', 'New brooms sweep better, but the OLD know the corners'—and thus there exist a lot of wise sayings glorifying the old-honouring the aged and respecting the old and the aged. Internationally too, there is a growing awareness about respecting the old not by showing sympathy to them, but by recognizing them. They get travel concessions, income tax benefits, special care in public transport systems, in hospitals, in health care, in medical laboratories, old age homes, etc.

Yes, 'the old age is when all telephone numbers in one's directory belong to doctors'. O.K., all said and done, no one sees anything specially done for the old either in administration of justice or in its delivery. They and the robust young are treated alike throughout the process and progress of the investigation, trial, prosecution and incarceration. It is a time now that Governments in many countries have formed special policies for the old, the infirm and the aged by classifying them as 'the old, the older old, and the oldest old' and so on. In such a situation, it is time now that we may give shape to a criminal justice policy and its delivery for the old, the infirm and the aged. I am now giving some points for deliberation at every stage of the criminal justice policy and its delivery hereunder.

Look at the points given here and consider them to make a policy for incarceration.

(1) Decide the age to specify who is 'the old, the older old, the oldest old' under law and who are to be treated as 'the infirm' and 'the aged' under law?
(2) If incarceration is intended for the development of human personality formed in an upright way in the right direction, then decide the needs and objectives of such an approach to them.
(3) If incarceration is with hard labour, what type of labour, what type of food, what type of medical care, what type of education and what type of leisure time activities are to be given to the old, the infirm and the aged?
(4) If incarceration is for correction, reformation, rehabilitation, resocialization and reintegration to the society back, then how must they be executed?
(5) If incarceration is not required, then what other methods must be enforced for administration of criminal justice and its delivery for the old and the infirm?
(6) Is incarceration necessary at all for the old, the infirm and the aged? Some of the old exploit it for getting expert treatment at Government expense or public exchequer.

I met a middle aged man and honestly he told me: *"Look, I am old and if I do not have anybody or anyone to look after me during my old age, I will simply commit a crime, confess it in the court and get a conviction to go to jail and, thereafter, I will gladly go to prison to get me treated at the Government expense. Jails, in my view, are better than many old age homes for the poor and the destitute in our country"*.

Incarceration has never been a panacea against criminality anywhere at any time. By trial and error methods, imprisonment was introduced as a punishment during the early years of the 18th century. To begin with again by trial and error methods—it was severely punitive—then punitive—then peno-correctional— correctional-cum-reformative–reformative-cum-rehabilitative.... and thus no one knows the reasons why prisons are in existence today. Prisons have proved to be a failure either in eliminating crimes or curtailing their extent. Crimes are on the increase throughout the world, nevertheless, prisons exist as an institution as a subsystem in justice administration. The sub-system is retained as the society has not devised or designed another institution for the offenders convicted by a court of law to stay. The prisons are of many kinds and they include the maximum security, medium security and minimum security prisons, etc. There are members in the custodial staff, in the correctional staff and there exist provisions for premature release (parole) and after-care services. Incarceration to a prison is no more considered as a punishment rather is treated as a means for the development of the inmates' personality in an upright way in the right direction. Under these current thinkings and philosophy, incarceration of the old, the older old and the oldest old must be assessed or evaluated. In a research study conducted to collect the public opinion about the incarceration of the old and the infirm, many suggested that imprisonment was meaningless as far as the old/aged people were concerned. According to some, there was no meaning in spending money from the public exchequer for the treatment of the old and the infirm in prisons. While the Health Departments in India do not have enough fund and finance to offer treatment facilities for the law abiding citizens in the general public, there is no moral justification in treating the convicted from public exchequer. In every sense, their stay in a prison is a burden and a financial liability for the government so much so that the expenses must be met by them or by the beneficiaries of their wealth and assets. Therefore, all sick convicts who are aged must be allowed to go to their near and dear ones under conditions stipulated by the authorities provided there are people coming forward to look after them. The courts must be given the authority to decide on the granting of **probation of good conduct** to the old and infirm. Anyway, it is desirable to appoint a Commission to make recommendations as to how the old and the infirm must be dealt with or should we still continue incarceration as the only option for the old, sick and the infirm.

APPOINTMENT OF THE CENTRAL VIGILANCE COMMISSION : ISSUES FOR RETHINKING

The Central Vigilance Commission appointed by the Government of India is just unseated on the basis of a judgement from the Supreme Court of India. The Court found (2011) that the newly appointed Central Vigilance Commission (hereinafter CVC) was an accused in a vigilance case and thus he had a 'Black Spot' in his personality. According to the Court,' Caesar's wife should be beyond suspicion' and so must be the CVC. There was a vigilance case against the CVC and it took several years for its disposal. At the time the CVC was appointed, the vigilance case against him was not disposed of. The appointment was made by the President of India on the basis of the recommendations made by a panel consisting of the Prime Minister, Union Home Minister and the Leader of the Opposition. In spite of the opposition from the Leader of the Opposition, it is said that the appointment was made. Now, there is a countrywide discussion on the issue, i.e., about the merit of the case and the quality of the judgement. Some political leaders go to the extent of demanding the resignation of the Prime Minister and the Union Home Minister. Here, therefore, there are some criminological issues for rethinking and they should be appreciated with the principles in criminal justice administration and its delivery.

The issues are—

(1) In the Holy *Bible,* there is the case of a woman of ill-repute and notoriously known as a prostitute brought before Jesus Christ. The people wanted to stone at her as per their retributive principles of justice to death. Hearing their arguments, Jesus Christ told them that the one who did not have a sin or have not committed a sin ought to stone at her first. Hearing it, everyone left the spot without uttering a word. Borrowing the same principle of Jesus Christ and applying it to the present case of appointment of the CVC in India, let us make a proposition for the **self-recruitment or self-appointment** by politicians who appeared on T.V. screens demanding resignation, i.e., let the one who has no crime or has not committed a crime must make a self-recruitment or self-appointment to the post of the CVC, then who will be able to make a self-appointment? The politicians were notoriously known as veterants in corruption. Forget about that issue for the moment. Let us go to the next issue.

(2) What is the delay that is found in the disposal of the above vigilance case against the CVC? Is that delay justifiable under *the scale of human conscience* to be called a normal delay? It is a principle that is accepted everywhere that

when the law is enforced, justice should not be denied. Human Conscience is the law here and if the delay is due to no fault of the newly appointed CVC, or owing to a defective system of justice administration and its delivery, who must be blamed for the miscarriage of justice? A never ending or ever continuing process of law is not the way or method of establishing that Caesar's wife is beyond suspicion. One can certainly be mad, but there should be a method in madness. Of course, there can be the delay in the disposal of a case, but there must be a 'method' in the delay. An inordinate delay is an inordinate delay in every case including the present one and judging the present case in the background of the inordinate delay, how far can one justify the unseating of the CVC as just, fair and reasonable?

(3) If one takes the history of appointments to the positions of the Chief Ministers, to the Home Ministers, to the Leaders of Opposition, to the Chief Justices of the higher Courts of Law in India and if we apply the principle of self-recruitment and self-appointment by following the law laid by Jesus Christ in the above parable which has more than 2000 years of existence, how many of the present ones will be eligible to hold the positions they have now? Many are not *'beyond suspicion'* and some are really people of suspicious integrity. Hence, this is the best time for each one of them to have an examination of his conscience before he stones at the CVC of India. Make a decision right now.

(4) The post of the CVC of India, no doubt, is a statutory position and the method of appointment is through a panel stated above. Can we not think of a better method to recruit the CVC and if so what is it and how should it be? If that is done, the issues will never become political. Presently, many appointments to various Commissions under the State or Central Governments are made from the lists of people who are not qualitatively **'Beyond Suspicion'** category, rather are party men politically. It is time now to think about more objective type of recruitment process to find out the apt and the best ones to those high positions in various Commissions in the country.

Anyone can approach a court of law for getting justice and that is valued to be the privilege of the citizen in a democracy. The causes of action or the reasons for approaching a court of law should be justified legally as well as morally. People who approach the courts with diabolical intentions do not do so with a clear conscience and precisely, therefore, their intention or motive is not getting justice rather getting their anger, vengeance, hostility, displeasure approved by the courts. Criminologists may be inclined to think that this sort of litigation is not meant for administration of justice, rather is an attempt to abuse the law and law courts to someone's advantage and another's disadvantage.

On technical grounds, one may win a case. There too, the question is; "Is fair and just justice administered by such litigations?" The obvious answer is an emphatic 'no'. The law in principle may be good, but the law in practice?. In my view, the law in principle and the law in practice must be good, just, moral and legal. In the case of the CVC above, one doubts whether or not the law in principle was interpreted in the way it ought to have been. In practice, delay has taken place, but is it in anyway owing to the acts of the CVC? If not, the law in principle—Caesar's wife should be beyond suspicion—has no relevance in the present case of inordinate delay. Doubtlessly, new recruitment procedures should be enacted. When a few Americans heard the fate of the CVC, they said: "Why so much delay in administration of justice in India?" Inordinate delay in administration of justice is injustice/ miscarriage of justice. Let it not happen in future!

THREE CRIMES: POLITICIZATION, CRIMINALIZATION AND COMMUNALIZATION

This is a time of '...lizations' which has got a high correlation to crimes and criminality. '...lization' is not a word in English Dictionaries although social scientists, namely political scientists, criminologists, psychologists and so on, make use of it by suffixing '...lization' to a word to give a particularly specific or specifically particular meaning. In simple terms, it is nothing but a *"process by which a particularly specific or specifically particular phenomenon or behavioural pattern comes into being and develops"*.

Politicalization in Dictionary means 'causing to be political; colouring with political' [Random House Dictionary]. ***Politicalization*** is what is meant by ***politicization*** and it is a process.

Criminalization means 'making punishable as a crime; making a criminal of'. If criminalization is a process by which a person is made a criminal, then the expression is true as the criminologists too mean the same thing.

Communalization means 'making communal'.

Now listen to what is heard in India often! After a crime has been reported to police or reported by the media, immediately comments are made as under—

"The criminal does not belong to our party"—say the politicians of major political parties. If they want to colour the criminal with politics, then it is ***politicalization***. They do it and thus it becomes a process by which politicization takes place and thus the political parties make many party-men. Making party-men *via* politicalization is to be treated as a crime as politicization is not a desirable act. This is **Crime No. I** in India today.

"So and so has been arrested because he belonged to our party"—say the politicians and "so and so was arrested because he belonged to our religion"—say thus by the so-named or so-called' religious leaders. They cannot see the crime and the criminal beyond their political party or 'religious affiliations'. This sort of an approach is an incentive—a real incentive—for many to commit crimes as they know that they have god-fathers to own or support them. Of course, they get party-men or members for their religion as the case may be. Resultantly criminalization takes place. This sort of an approach is to be made a crime as it is not advisable to develop such a feeling in criminals. Hence, this is **Crime No. 2** in India.

"This is an attack against... such and such religion/ community" and it can be a major religion, scheduled caste, a scheduled tribe or a suppressed community or even a religious group. This is called 'communalization' i.e., making everything communal so that they make more and more religion-centred or community centred party-men, fanatically religious men. This again gives greater strength and added confidence in criminals to commit crimes as they think that they will be supported by the communal forces in society. This is called communalization and is bad and hence **Crime No. 3** in India.

Look at the candidates found out for elections in the country and the type of the people's representatives to the Legislatures/ Parliament. Some of them have real communal background while others have really true criminal backgrounds. Both of them flourish in their career and develop quite comfortably *via* politicization, criminalization and communalization—three major crimes in India today.

Political criminals and criminal politics– both are under debate and discussion. Likewise communal politics and political communalism—both are under debate and discussion now. In any case, both are not the same. Political crimes/criminals and political communalism—both are not defined or described in any Indian laws. Nevertheless, people know what they are. Criminal politics and criminal communalism—both are real dangers to society and people know them well. Criminal politics may be politicians committing crimes with political motives. Likewise, criminal communalism means certain people commit crimes with communal motives. Crimes are crimes no matter they are politically motivated or communally activated. Precisely, therefore, they must be dealt with exactly like any other crimes committed under the existing penal or procedural laws with penal sanction of incarceration, etc. Any leniency shown on the basis of politics or communalism will bring havoc to administration of justice in a fair and just way.

Politicization of criminals or communalization of crimes and criminals– both pose great threats to Indian democracy. If crimes and criminals are politicized or communalized, administration of justice will become a vain hope—never actualized. Criminalization of politics or criminalization of communal feelings are crimes and should never be allowed. If no laws exist, new laws must be enacted to put down politicization of criminals, communalization of crimes or criminalization of communal feelings/politics.

GRASS-EATER CRIMES *vs.* MEAT-EATER CRIMES

What are the 'Suite Crimes? 'The immediate answer is "I do not know". Why? Many have no idea of such crimes taking place in palatial suites in the 5 star or 7 star hotels or Tourist Resorts where there exists very tight security. The ordinary policemen or the patrolmen do not have any access to such suites. Crimes and business worth crores of Indian rupees are being transacted there and the Penal Code, Magistrates' Courts, prosecutors do not and cannot usually go there. High level bureaucrats, Ministers of the Government, senior politicians, middle men/commission agents, top level police functionaries, very senior lawyers including some Judges of the higher judiciary and so on transact 'business' at very high levels. The Penal Codes do not define such crimes as they were enacted much before these crimes came into being.

On the opposite side of ***'Suite Crimes'***, we have the ***'Slum Crimes'***, i.e., small level hooch production, hooch distribution, hooch transportation, small scale gambling like cards play (under a tree in villages), fly-play (which means that the poor people bring beedies and they keep them in a distributive way at some place and they watch. If a fly comes and sits on a beedi, they see to it that all the beedies kept there by the participants are taken by the one on whose beedi the fly sits down. This is gambling technically as it is a chance play since nobody can say where the fly will sit beforehand), etc., theft of home reared chicken/coconuts, small scale shop-lifting, affray, etc., which are very clearly defined in the Penal Code. The bottom level policemen, the lowest level criminal courts, the newly enrolled lawyers and fresh prosecutors have the power to set the law into motion and see to it that the crime-doers are punished often with imprisonment which may extend to a few days/weeks/months or years. Thus the crimes of 'nuisance value' only are dealt with by iron hands whereas the crimes which sell the **Country** or ruin the **Nation** are just ignored like that and then promoted and encouraged. Of late, the 2G spectrum case in which a Minister at the Central Government is under CBI probe is just an example in point. Yes, ***Anchovy*** is caught, killed and eaten whereas the ***Sharks*** are lavishly fed.

In fact, the **Anchovy Crimes** are called ***Grass-Eater Crimes*** whereas the ***Shark Crimes*** are called ***Meat-Eater Crimes***. Why?

Worms which eat the grass or leaves, when seen even by little children of tender years, are caught and mercilessly killed. The special noise produced by mosquitoes irritates all of us and likewise the nuisance created by the *'grass eater criminals'* really annoy many of us whereas the *'meat eater criminals'* are not even known to the general public. The carnivorous animals (flesh eating), leaving a few types, live in thick forests and, therefore, their crimes are not even known to the common men in plane land.

"The nexus crimes, organized crimes, consensus crimes, some of the bureaucratic crimes, corruption at the high order, etc., are put under the meat-eater group of crimes." Ordinarily, no one has the courage to approach the 'carnivorous' animals and precisely, therefore, they commit crimes remaining in comfort zones. If at all some media men come forward, they will be subjected to many sufferings which ultimately push or pull them down. If they survive the crises, then some legal action will be initiated which usually will have a premature death and inconspicuous burial. The meat-eater crimes taking place in various spheres are many and no one is, it seems to me, punished. They will continue as leaders, administrators, public men, judges of 'integrity', high level business men and what or who not? They rule the country! The meat eaters are adorned or adored. They are the **gods** on **Earth**. They have their own **kingdoms** to rule and the penal laws are helpless, voiceless and ineffective. They are above grammar and hence—

Shark criminals Zindabad;
Anchovy criminals Murdabad!

Suite criminals Zindabad;
Slum criminals Murdabad!

Meat Eater criminals Zindabad;
Grass Eater criminals Murdabad!

From time immemorial criminal justice system in whatever form it existed made attempts to put down the smaller fries. The history of mankind is a history of human rights violations and a fight for human rights establishment. The 'Haves' always exploited the 'Have nots' and that is what is seen even now. Of course, there is a reverse move recently in some areas in the country.

Everyone is equal before the law and everyone gets equal protection under the law—very nice to hear these Constitutional guarantees in many democratic countries. But, the fact is that some are more equal and some get more protection. As repeatedly said elsewhere, the law in principle is not the law in practice. No law takes its own course. Every law is taken and the vested interests see to it that the law is taken in the way they want. Many speak highly about the Rule of Law while all want the Rule of Law coupled with the Rule of Justice. But, they do not get them in the way they must. Man administers justice on man and no man should be above the law. What may be seen is that some men are the Laws. They make the laws, execute the laws and adjudicate the laws and all others have to abide by the law. These thoughts are unpalatable, yet they are the unpleasant truths. Unpleasant truths may displease some; yet they must be exposed.

Money power, Muscle power and Mind power–yes, they are there. In administration of justice, mind power ought to have an upper hand. In reality, does it happen? Let the answer be given by the ***Shark criminals, Suite criminals and Meat-eater criminals.*** Do they get the punishments they deserve? In prisons, one takes note of more poor people—people who cannot afford to employ lucrative lawyers, who cannot purchase witnesses, who cannot manipulate records, who cannot concoct evidence, who cannot reach a consensus with the police and prosecutors. and thus the system of justice administration continues to move on.

'STATUS' CRIMES AND CRIMINALS

Is there a category of crimes called '**Status**' crimes? Newer and newer crimes are coming to the bright light although their definitions/descriptions are not seen in any books of law or legal literature. White collar crimes, Edwin H. Sutherland defined them, as said elsewhere, are crimes committed by people of high socio-economic status during the course of their profession or occupation, the purpose of which is nothing but financial achievement. But in 'status' crimes', it may be remembered that the crimes need not necessarily be committed by people of high socio-economic, literary or political status. It can be committed by anyone enjoying or suffering from any position in life provided he has a '**Status**' by being or becoming a criminal/crime-doer. The meaning of 'Status' as given in the Random House Webster's Dictionary is the position of an individual in relation to another or others, esp. *in regard to social or professional standing*. The Dictionary gives (further) another meaning too, i.e., *conferring or* *believed to confer elevated status.* It is in this sense, the expression **Status Crimes and Criminals** is used here.

There is a Malayalam movie titled *'Udayanaanu Thaaram'* which can be translated as 'Udayan is the Star'. *STAR* here means 'shining as a star or become prominent'.

Several unscrupulous politicians, 'religious' men-business-people, *goondas* and bandits of all descriptions, corrupt bureaucrats, *Mafia* kings, flesh traders, human traffickers, judges of questionable integrity, lawyers of dubious character, ministers of notorious criminal past, organized racketeers, syndicate criminals, 'professionals' of fake nature and so on come in the news in banner head lines. They become important and the crimes they commit get a 'Status'— not of a crime or a criminal but of a heroic act or elevated activity. Resultantly, they are not treated as first rate criminals, but as heroes—*Stars.* They appear in the media and on public platforms. They are praised or eulogized by many and thus they become *Super Stars.* The crimes they commit are canonized and they receive a special *Status* so much so that the corrupt, unscrupulous, dishonest, unjust *Heroes* become the role models or **Saints** in public. The *Status Crimes* they commit become glorified virtues and they become stronger and more acceptable leaders. One time *goondas* have become Ministers of the State, the corrupt professionals have become key bureaucrats, the unjust judges have become Commissions and thus the *Status Criminals* are conferred with more and more elevated *Status* in society. In contrast to these *Status Criminals* come the small scale cheats, pickpockets, burglars and those involved in small scale frauds. They are often seen behind the *Bars* and the *Status Criminals* are in high, higher and highest positions. They decide matters for others in the society.

What a tragedy in life and an irony in reality that those who deserve to be or better, should be condemned to jails/behind the *Bars* are venerated and adored by the mass—the common man!

> If wealth is lost, many things are lost;
> If health is lost, everything is lost
> And if character is lost,
> *Something is lost for some time.*

That is the modified version of an old saying that—

> 'If wealth is lost, nothing is lost;
> If health is lost, something is lost;
> And if character is lost, everything is lost'.

The modification became an inevitable necessity as one saw that the substitute for money was *Money* alone and nothing else. One who does not have money, as a rule, does not have status as well. Many great men who had the *Mind Power* when they lived on earth were not accepted by the people during their life time as they were not rich. *Money Power* is money power and a criminal who has money power can purchase many things including *status* in society. The crimes he commits will become *status-crimes* and sometimes, he will be able to convert his crimes to be virtues or laws. In a democracy, political parties rich in wealth survive and become richer and richer. They become so through activities which are criminal too. But, many a time, the crimes they commit become *status crimes* and the criminals become the most *'honourable men'* who will manipulate the law to their favour. The existing Penal Codes are not intended to catch hold of the *'Status Criminals'* as they are intended to book only the ordinary mortals. To obtain justice *via* the criminal justice system is really expensive and the *'Status Criminals'* who are affluent in wealth and money manage to get justice in a speedier way. How many politicians were punished so far? How many high level bureaucrats were incarcerated till date? How many business-men were put behind the bars? There may not be many as all of them are affluent *status criminals*. If status crimes and criminals are on the increase, it can be safely assumed that the criminal justice system is weak and need immediate strengthening.

Any democratic government is an expensive government. Once, the Election Commission of India said that 'the corruption has its roots in the electoral process' as the money dumped by individuals, institutions and political parties for the victory of their candidates is beyond human imagination. How do they get back the money invested? They get back their money invested by involving in the commission of various types of *"Status Crimes"* about which the ordinary man on the street is kept in blissful ignorance. Hence, some criminologists say that fair and just justice is difficult to be obtained in a liberal democracy—is difficult to be guaranteed to the electorate—is difficult to be ensured by all the three pillars of a democracy—is difficult to be administered in a fair and just way.

GOONDAISM AS A PUBLIC SERVICE

Goondaism is a real problem widely discussed in India today. *Goonda* in English Dictionary means a 'Rogue' or 'Hoodlum'. In Hindi, it is written as '*Gunda*'. Goon in Dictionary means (informal) a hired hoodlum or a thug; (slang) a stupid, foolish or awkward person. Gooney Bird means (slang) a goon who is also called *goony*. *Goon-Squad* means a group of hired thugs used to perform ruthless or violent acts. The act of goons is what we say goondaism and the *goondas* may be simulated ones, hired ones, appointed ones or self-employed as they are seen in our society. Such *goondas* are found in almost all cities in the country especially in Mumbai, Calcutta and Chennai.

During 1940s or around 1940, a number of studies was conducted in the west, particularly in USA to know the activities of *goondas, goonda culture, goondaism, goonda attacks, goonda personality, goonda rivalry, goonda fights, etc*. There were gangs in plenty there and when we read the literature on gangs in USA, we are inclined to think that we are witnessing in India what was there in the west during 1925-1940 as gangism–reborn here in the name of *goondaism* now. Of course, Indian *goondaism* has a difference now. We had the 'Goonda Act' during the time of the British rule here, but the *goondaism* as seen today is different from what it was during the pre-independence period.

Again, gang as given in the Dictionary has a meaning: "a group of youngsters or adolescents who associate closely, often exclusively, for social reasons, especially such a group engaged in delinquent behaviour". The *goondas* in India may be classified as follows on the basis of my studies and observations.

(1) ***Simulated Goondas***: They act as if they were *goondas*. They do so because they want to make an income or earning by being or becoming so. Actually, they do not enter into delinquent behaviour or they may even run away from a scene of delinquency. Unemployment, under-employment, making of easy money, living a luxurious

life without labour, etc., may be the **Pull factors** for the same.

(2) ***Employed Goondas***: They are employed by money-lenders, vehicle loan sharks, *Abkaries* and so on, the purpose of which is not at all for employing them for any criminal acts, but to collect the loaned amount or to capture the vehicles in case the loan is not repaid in time or to conduct their business smoothly, e.g., sale or transport of illicit liquor, contraband articles without any problems. They may become violent only if and if only they find that such an undesirable act is necessary to realize the loaned amount or to conduct their business in a smooth way. Hence, they are officially designated by them or by their employers as Recovery Officers, Salesmen in liquor bars, etc.

(3) ***Self-employed Goondas***: They are *goondas* or *goonda-squads* whose purpose is to make a real income by really being or becoming *goondas*. They involve in criminal acts as and when situations demand. They charge huge amounts of money for their criminal acts and now there are many such groups in many cities and, therefore, they are technically called '***Quotation Goondas***'. Every group has a leader and the *goondas* in every such squad behave as per the instructions and guidance from their leaders. Just yesterday, a leader of such a notorious *goonda squad* was killed in a *goonda* attack in Kerala—a newspaper reported. There is danger and loss of property in *goondaism*, but it brings exorbitant money for the leader and his party. No doubt, it is lucrative, though dangerous and criminal.

The *goonda* leaders have informal association and they form a network to assist mutually. They have their own transport and communication systems. They claim that they are 'Service Agencies' who render services to the demanding public at a cheaper rate than the official machinery of the Government in power, namely, the police. For example, the self-employed *goonda* squad which is actively involved in capturing the vehicles in case of the failure to repay the loan in time is called 'Vehicle Repossession Service Agency' rather than *goondas* to recapture the vehicles.

The politicians, loan sharks, business men, Abkaries, crime

syndicates, nexus crime partners, religious rackets, etc., make use of the 'services' of these gangs by frequently employing them. Though there exist 'Goonda Acts' (as the Acts are now popularly called) in many States in India, studies show that they are ineffective or having no teeth to control or reduce *goondaism* in the country.

Where there is a demand, certainly there will be the supply. The Demand-Supply theory in Economics is meaningful in Crimino-Economics too. India is a fast developing country and she is a rich market in the world. India's achievement in transport, telecommunication, software fields, human resources supply, etc., is enviable and marvellous. Richness necessitates money transactions. Many people purchase vehicles and other luxuries in life. There will be loan sharks who invest a lot of money in the vehicle market. Likewise, the liquor *Mafia*, politicians and so on make use of the *goondas*. They nurse and nurture them. During the developmental stages in any country so far in history, one notices the role of *goondas* and, therefore, some criminologists are of the view that *goondas* in small groups is a sign of development and progress. As they are criminals, and dangerously anti-social, they must be controlled and their activities checked.

Goonda Acts are enacted and a visit to a prison may show that the number of *goondas* arrested and detained under the *Goonda Acts* may be just handful. Why? There is no political or executive will to implement the Act in a serious way. If at all some *goondas* are taken into custody, they are not the source *goondas* rather are the peripheral ones. A jail visit may convince anyone that some of the detained *goondas* are physically weak and do not have the body strength to act as *goondas*. The cases registered or prosecuted or tried are weakened owing to the threats from the *goondas*. The witnesses are threatened and the policemen are attacked so much so that an atmosphere of fear persists in many cities.

The *goondas* are in demand and the principal reason is that the employment of *goondas* is cheaper than ensuring official support to get things done. The 'Input–Output' theory works strongly and in Crimino-Economics, the output in employing *goondas* is found to be more than the input. Ensuring official action necessitates expenditure and time. In spite of the money spent and the time lost, the output sometimes or often becomes zero or far away from being satisfactory. *Goondas* perform the same tasks satisfactorily well at a cheaper rate. Hence, they are in high demand. Moreover, it shows the failure of the police machinery and the criminal justice system in the country.

FROM EXTREMISM TO TERRORISM

People in India, it seems to me, are confused of (1) extremism, (2) fundamentalism, (3) fanaticism, (4) terrorism, (5) insurgency as they think that all of them are one and the same. I think that they must be made clear of the concepts—

(1) *Extremism* means a "tendency or disposition to go to the extremes. This is seen in political as well as in religious matters. Therefore, an extremist is a person who goes to extremes, especially in political or religious matters or in both. There are supporters and advocates of extreme doctrines and practices in both politics and in religion.

(2) *Fundamentalism*, though identified as a movement in American Protestantism that arose in the early part of the 20th century in reaction to modernism, it is now considered as "strict adherence to any set of ideas or beliefs which the fundamentalists hold as necessary and inevitable for the salvation of the people and society" (see Webster's). The Naxalites in India, the religious and political fundamentalists all over the country come under this category.

(3) *Fanaticism*, i.e., Fanatics, people with an extreme or uncritical enthusiasm or zeal, as in religion or in politics. They have no tolerance or they have excessive or overweening devotion to a cause or belief. In other words, an unbalanced or obsessive behaviour (see Random House College Dictionary) is noticed.

(4) *Terrorism*, as seen in Webster's is the use of violence or threats to intimidate or coerce, especially for political purposes. The terrorists resort to an activity that terrorizes or frightens the people, the purpose of which is nothing but destabilize the Government in power. They are dangerous people who, though not direct their activities to a particular person or people, keep a society under fierce

terror. In India, several such terrorists' attacks have been reported recently. In fact, *an extremist* can become a *fundamentalist* who in turn may become a *fanatic* and later to *a terrorist*. A graph can be drawn basing on the narration given above.

(5) *Insurgency* is an insurrection against an existing Government usually one's own, by a group not recognized as having the status of a belligerent (Random House College Dictionary). Hence, an insurgent is a person who rises in forcible opposition to lawful authority especially, a person who engages in armed resistance to a Government or to the execution of its laws. Here again, an extremist can become an insurgent and in India, insurgency is seen in Nagaland, Jammu and Kashmir, Bihar, Orissa and it is seen as fighting against armed forces. No doubt, insurgency is a serious situation and the insurgents are, it is suspected/confirmed, assisted, supported, encouraged or promoted by Governments outside India. Thus there exists an expression like 'Cross Border Terrorism'.

As the people are confused about the subtle differences among the terms, they use and/or misuse the words. They say *'extremism'* instead of *'terrorism 'or' fundamentalism' and 'terrorism'* instead of *'fanaticism'*. They confuse 'terrorism' with 'insurgency'. People with little or no knowledge in the subject come to T.V. platforms to say 'this and that' about this delicate topic and cause confusion among the people. The media should avoid such people to discuss on this issue. They cannot substitute experts in the topic and precisely, therefore, such type of T.V. discussions must be discouraged at any cost.

How do the people become extremists? Recruitment to extremism takes place in some parts of the country. The recruiters receive money and support lavishly from vested interests and hostile countries. They are offered jobs and are ensured high salaries. Once someone has fallen in the net he is given training and brain-washing. They live under threat and sometimes, they are forced to become terrorists or members of the suicide squads. Destabilize the government in power seems to be their motive and they cause terror in society. They bomb the railway stations, burn the railway cabins, deposit transistor bombs in passenger buses and engage in various activities that cause fear/terror in people. The insurgents attack only armed forces and thus they want to cause chaos in society.

Extremism, terrorism and insurgency, etc., are political problems and must be tackled accordingly. The crimes committed by the extremists, fundamentalists and fanatics must be dealt with as per the laws in the country by the criminal justice system. The extremists, fundamentalists and terrorists are of a special category and precisely, therefore, they must be housed in Maximum Security Prisons with extreme care and caution. Extremism may be seen not only in politics but also in religion and in my opinion, both categories ought to be counted as separate categories and thus housed separately. Vigilance against the extremist activities must be *pukka* and the intelligence unit of the State as well as Central Police ought to be activated. There is no substitute for political solutions and, therefore, concurrently with the action by the criminal justice system, political alternatives ought to be brought in to solve the issue.

SLOGAN CULTURE

"If slogans in various spheres of life and areas of activities are collected and published, we will have a slogan series publication without any hard labour"—I used to feel so often. In my view, several books can be published if slogans in India are put together. There exists a 'slogan culture' in India. India is the largest democracy in the world and precisely therefore, there are demonstrations, *dharnas, jatthas, bandhs,* and *hartals,* picketing, strikes of many descriptions such as hunger strikes, pen-down strikes, road blockades, paralyzing government functions, human chains, students' strikes, employees' strikes, strikes by vested interests of various categories and thus the list is indeed very long. All such activities need a variety of slogans and we have expert slogan writers and *'hired jattha workers'*. For, conduct of demonstrations has itself become a way of life for some. They too have a lot of ready-made slogans with them. They also sell slogans if that is necessary. Slogan shouting has become a performing art.

Little children of tender years of age play games by shouting slogans on holidays and they organize strikes in schools with 'pleasant' to hear slogans. Shouting of slogans has a psychological effect too and the more one shouts slogans, the more excited, elevated and enthused he becomes. Slogans become inspiring to some who cannot resist their impact. When they hear these slogans, they move consciously or unconsciously to shout slogans. The question here is: "Do we hear such slogan shouting in other parts of the world?" I do not think so. Even in other democracies of the world, people organize demonstrations for which they use placards containing their demands or slogans and not slogan shoutings with performing art. In India, we make use of mikes and loud speakers of any number for shouting slogans. Sound pollution is tolerated by the Indian folk or they are forced to. There is rhythm, dancing and chanting when slogans are shouted.

Just like causing physical destruction of public property during a demonstration, people utter filthy slogans and slogans containing abusive words which decent people do not want to hear or utter. This is called verbal aggression in psychology. Little children who develop their personality in such a culture are likely to have perversions. The verbal aggression transferred *via* slogan shouting is infiltrated to the developing personality of little kids and children.

Slogans may be innocent, pious, aggressive, moderate, abusive, etc., and they depend upon the persons shouting the slogans and the situations. Slogan shouting is not an offence in India, but slogan shouting followed by stone-throwing, arson or other destructive activities become offences. It becomes a law and order problem and the politicians cash it. If destruction is caused, it is justified by politicians saying that it is but natural human reactions to the emotions of the demonstrators. How unfortunate it is to see that sometimes, the police initiate actions against the destructive demonstrators only if and if only the politicians show green flag to it. Even religious leaders and spiritual men have exploited the slogan shouting to their advantages. Though slogan shouting is not an undesirable thing, it is not at all advisable to have such a slogan shouting culture developed in India. For, a culture means a culture and a culture that is developed into destructiveness cannot be encouraged at any cost in any society including democracies where demonstrations are permitted with or without control.

Not only in the streets, but also in the State Legislature and Central Parliament, one hears slogans. Shouting slogans in very high pitch has a threatening effect on people. Slogans energize the strikers. Along with the slogan shouting, sometimes, one sees effigy-burning during which time slogans are shouted with doubly surcharged energy. Though the culture of slogan shouting is seen everywhere in India, such a culture is not witnessed in many other countries/democracies. Slogan shouting is expensive, for, it needs people to shout slogans. To organize people for shouting slogans is expensive and in India, the expenses are met by vested interests. It may be the reason why *"Slogan Shouters' Associations"* are formed in some parts of the country. They render their services to anyone who demands it on payment basis. I saw a Malayalam movie recently showing the activities of such a "Slogan Shouting Association". They have experts and expertise to perform the task in a satisfactory way. Just like the hired *goondas* or quotation *goondas*, we can hire the services of slogan shouters for achieving the purpose. It is learnt that a person who goes to shout slogans presently get ₹ 500 plus 120 ml intoxicating liquor (alcohol) plus food and transport freely (during 2011). They perform well and make their services lucrative. Yes, a method to make easy money without labouring! Where are we going to with this sort of attitude and approach?

BREACH OF ELECTION PROMISES: AN OFFENCE IN A DEMOCRACY

India has a Penal Code which, as pointed out elsewhere, came into existence about 150 years ago. The Indian Penal Code, 1860 was enacted by the British during their imperialistic rule. When India became independent in 1947, the same Penal Code was accepted and the newly created democracy made some patch works in the then existed Penal Code. In fact, *'is'* was changed into *'was'* or *'has'* was changed into *'have'* and thus the Code has been in effective (?) use till date although many (I, not excluded) condemn that old museum piece in which nothing much about the contemporary or current offences are mentioned. The existing penal laws are not intended for the present Indian Democracy.

In Indian democracy, elections in some States are just declared and every political party is in the preparation of an Election Manifesto. About four decades ago, there was a humorous or joking film song in Malayalam whose English translation (as I could do it) may be—

> "Construction of an aerodrome in the vicinity of this small water canal,
> Free agricultural land for real farmers,
> Desert like barren land for the rich..."

And thus was the lavish rain of promises to the general public. Several elections were declared afterwards and for every election—no matter, it is to the Lok Sabha or to the State Legislature or to the Local Administration—every political party released their *election manifestoes.* No one bothered much about the promises, earlier promises, still earlier promises and the result has been that one and the same promises, with some changes, were repeatedly and loudly included in all manifestoes so far released. The political party leaders became the winners and the general public became the fools of the first order. Now a few questions please—

(1) Is a breach of promise during an election an offence in India? If not, why?

(2) Who makes the promises and who breaks the promises? Does the person or party making the election promises have any liability over the breach of election promises afterwards? If not, why?

(3) How to investigate the offence of the breach of election promises and who must do it and why?

(4) Is there something called the *Voters' Auditing* before every election? If not, why? What to do and how to go about?

(5) If breach of election promises is found, how should the people or the party which made the promises before election be punished?

(6) If a particular political party does not get the power to rule, it goes to the opposition. Is there any *election manifesto* for a political party in the event of it becoming a political party in opposition? If not, why not each political party bring out an *election manifesto* in case it does not get the power to rule? At present, the political parties in opposition do many destructive activities to destabilize the government in power. This is of bad taste. They should

give constructive activities and strategies even when they fail in an election.

(7) Do the voters get any victim compensation in case of the breach of election promises? If not, what to do and how to go about?

Thus the questions are many and the answers to the questions are nil. Why? The candidates to the election are not decided by the people in Indian democracy, but by vested interests and a few vocal minority leaders in every political party. The candidates who get their candidature as a gift from above, do not have any time or interest to think about their liability for the breach of promises. They will get future chances if the higher ups in the political hierarchy and vested interests favour them. It is time to deliberate over the breach of election promises and put it in the list of penal offences in the Code. Think and think—about it aloud now and right now!

Cheating a person is an offence, but cheating a nation is not! Political parties make false promises during the election without any intention to implement any one of them but with the sole motive to cheat the electorate to capture the administration. Once they come into power, they conveniently forget the promises and do not own the liability. Just like the corporate crimes, it becomes difficult to fix the *mens rea* in people responsible for it. No crime without *mens rea* is an accepted maxim and here in election promises, there is no one to own the *mens rea* and criminal liability. The law must be amended to include the violation of election promises as a crime in the Penal Code.

In frauds, say—the investment frauds, employment frauds, flat-construction frauds—criminal cases are registered and investigated. Making false promises in the *Election Manifesto* without an intention to implement them is a fraud of the first order. How can a political party ensure 10 lakhs employment positions without making a research in the field? Hence, the election promises are made without adequate research data and precisely, therefore, the promises are made without any intention to implement them. This is a real fraud.

Every political party has a duty and responsibility to convince the Election Commission that their election promises in the Manifesto are genuine. Any promises without the Election

Commission's approval must be treated as false promises to attract the electorate and thereby the political party plays unfair election practices. The Election Commission which makes controls and restrictions on anything and everything must see to it that the election frauds practiced and perpetuated by political parties down the decades are stopped forthwith. People have short memories and they are likely to forget the promises during the previous election and this weakness of the electorate must not be exploited by the political parties.

Fulfilling promises with the tax-payers' money when in power is easy. Fulfilling promises without the tax payers' money when not in power is difficult, yet desirable. Therefore, it is the urgent need of all political parties to prepare and publish the promises if they come in opposition. What is seen today is to raise objections to each and everything proposed by the ruling Government. The parties in opposition organize *Jatthas* and protest processions—even damaging and destroying public property. Why not they declare their policy, strategy and promises in case they do not come into power? Each political party ought to receive the approval of the Election Commission to such promises too and the people have a responsibility to evaluate them. In short, new and newer crimes come up in a democratic rule and the criminal justice system as well as the Election Commission must take note of them. People should get opportunities to audit the promises of the ruling party and opposition before any election is being conducted.

HOARDING OF FILES—AN OFFENCE UNDER LAW

A Chief Minister of a State Government makes accusations against the Prime Minister of a Country saying that his urgent letters were unanswered by the PMO (Prime Minister's Office) for a considerable period of time. The issue became news of great importance in the media culminating in verbal attacks and mutual accusations of the politicians belonging to the ruling front and the same of the opposition political parties. If this is what is happening at the highest realm of administration, what will be at the bottom and middle level of governmental administration? Taking notice of an issue by the media means exerting pressure or coercing the administration to act in time. Whatever that be, the question here is:

> "Hoarding of edible things, construction materials, fuels and petrol, etc., is made an offence in India. If that is so, why can't the Hoarding of Files in Government offices be made an offence?"

Every file is an essential commodity and behind each file there are human hearts, emotions, sympathies, needs, lives, concerns, considerations and what not? Each file is as important as or more important than petrol and fuel, etc., and the incredible delay in disposing the files causes irreparable damage and loss to the people at the other end. It is sometimes victimization and as per the victimological principles, the victims ought to receive victim compensation or restitution as the case may be.

What about the number of pending files or the delay in the disposal of files—a well-meaning Member of the Legislature/ Parliament may raise an occasional question in the House and often there will be a 'ready-made' answer to such a query. Neither the Member of Parliament/State Legislature who raised the query nor the concerned Minister who responded the usual question may be interested and an attitude of 'Let the dead bury the dead' is seen. The questions are:

> "If some delay takes place on the part of the citizenry to respond in time to the Government's orders, he is penalized or fined. O.K., it is fine. Then, why not the same principle is applied if undue delay is caused by the administration in the disposal of files? Why can't it be made a punishable offence? An attitude of "the head of the family can make the kitchen his toilet" is not a desirable administrative strategy."

'Who is afraid of Virginia Wolf?'—The simple answer to the question may be: 'Fishes in the Atlantic Ocean or Birds in Siberia or Stars in the sky'. Fine. They are no answers to the question. Likewise, some decisions are taken on the file and the decision taken is no decision at all. Ultimately, years and decades are taken to close the file and many who initiated the file might have died

during the long process. Nobody is responsible and no one has any liability. Government decisions take their own time is a cliché and government business is nobody's business is the approach. So long as this situation prevails, there is no salvation and the situations will go from bad to worse.

Make the *'Delay—Inordiate Delay—Extra Ordinary Delay—Excessively Inordinate Delay' offences* under law— under the caption *Hoarding of Files* with penalties proportionate to *the gravity* of the delay and the offence.

Right to Information Act has been passed, but the success is at best suspicions. In any case, it has not reached the desired level of success. The bureaucrats are able to play tricks on the Act and its effective implementation. But, something is better than nothing. In my view, if the criminal justice system takes note of the bureaucratic foul play on the effective enforcement of Right to Information Act, things will be improved to the better.

The Right to Services Act is passed in some States and the Act specifies time-limit for the disposal of files Here too, the bureaucrats can play a lot of tricks so much so that they may be successful to torpedo the effective implementation of the Act. Nevertheless, it is better to have something than nothing. Some enthusiastic or over-enthusiastic administrations hold *Adalats* or file disposal *melas* to take a final decision. Of course, they have been successful to some extent. Still, hoarding of files takes place not only in the Legislative, but also in the Executive and Judiciary. Recommendation of the Law Commission, other Commissions, Committees have been lying down for decades in the Archives of the Government even for initiating steps to make legislations. Files before the Executives are like mountains and in the Secretariat, one sees files untouched for years together. Others' files are others' files and they will remain there unattended unless someone comes to push up. The files move from one table to another and finally they are disposed of under the order of the Governor of the State or the President of the country for the citizens to make appeals after appeals. When everything is over, nothing happens. It is like a birthday gift given as a wreath on the burial day. Can this inordinate delay be made a punishable offence? What can the criminal justice system do about it? Unfortunately, the criminal justice system itself is burdened with undue delay in the disposal of cases.

What is happening in other countries? Are they having recourse to modern technology of the IT world? Why not the movement of file be made transparent? Why not the movement of file be ensured within a time frame? How can be the supervisory functions made more effective and meaningful? How should the criminal justice system respond to this aching issue of hoarding of files? Manipulations are made in the contents of a file. False or fake Government Orders are made to make the decisions favourable or unfavourable (instances have been reported that Government Orders without the Government knowing about them are made) and there is no one to question such illegal acts. What an injustice!

CRIMES RELATING TO ADVERTISEMENTS

An advertisement simply means 'a paid announcement, as of goods for sale, in newspapers or magazines, on radio or television etc.' [Webster's]. Accordingly, ***advertising*** means 'the act or practice of calling public attention to one's product, service and need, etc., especially by paid advertisements in newspapers and magazines, over radio or television, on bill boards, etc., to get more customers by advertising'[Random House College Dictionary]. Commercial means 'prepared, done or acting with sole or chief emphasis on salability, profit or success' [Webster's]. And we have a lot of commercial advertisements/advertising in all media and they become crimes in different and various ways. How?

An investment fraud called *'Teak-Goat-Mangium'* invested more than 600 crores of Indian rupees for advertisements and it amassed a lot of wealth until at last the enterprise was wound up. False employment bureaus, fake technicians and medical doctors, recruitment and Visa rackets, *Mafias* of all descriptions, white collar criminals from all professions, 'religious' frauds of many categories resort to massive advertisements. There are advertisement firms which have a lucrative business in producing films, video pictures, advertisement attractions, etc. Thus, when one views the television channels, he can see thousands and thousands of advertisements which are purposefully intended to fool or cheat the general public. The advertisements of Ayurveda medicines are without any proof to establish their claims. Sex stimulating medicines, health nourishners, energy guaranteeing medicines are plenty and they misuse the trust of the people on the media which publish such lies. Here too, ***'repeat a lie, repeat it several times... it becomes the truth'*** psychology works. The single medicine for any diseases that affect the liver, shampoo without chemicals, creams with incredible qualities, tooth pastes with dentists' certificates, detergents with unimaginable results, soaps with unthinkable benefits, gold, cloths, insurances, automobiles, fans, utensils, lotteries and other gamblings, resorts and massage centres, religious retreats and fests, relics and prayers, mobile phones and what not?—all are advertised in the print and electronic media with no liability over what they say, show or write. Neither the media nor the advertisers have any responsibility or accountability for committing frauds. People are cheated and the media make money and business by such advertisements.

What is the liability of the media to publish or publicize falsehood with an intention to cheat the public? Or do they have no liability at all? If adulterated food is sold, action is taken. If the trust is violated there is the law to initiate criminal action for breach of trust. If fake technicians are found, they are proceeded against. If false claims are made, they are caught for committing crimes. But no such actions are taken against the advertisers, advertising firms, advertising media for their cheating the public with all sorts of nefarious methods. Why? There should be laws to control advertisements and to publish only true facts under advertisement in the media.

Look at my own observation about advertisement psychology. 40 per cent of the people who see, listen or hear an advertisement will be influenced badly. Those who hear will be influenced less than those who see and hear. Those who read an advertisement will be influenced less than those who read, hear and see. Yet, 40 per cent of the people are badly influenced in varying degrees. Another 40 per cent will be influenced considerably by the advertisement. 10 per cent will be influenced marginally and 5 per cent will be less than marginally, i.e., slightly and 5 per cent will not be influenced. If the advertisement is repeated several times a day, the influence level will go up and accordingly the percentage of the people influenced will go up. If the advertisement is in colour, it has more impact. If the advertisement has background music, it is further influencing. Thus, advertisement has become a science or study of immense potentiality. Advertisement science means study to commit frauds on people. People's psychology is important and the people are cheated. On whom can the *mens rea* be fixed? When an investment fraud detected, criminal action is initiated against the culprits while those who promote the frauds by advertisement and the media are overlooked. The agents who promote the investment frauds are proceeded against while the advertisers and the media are allowed to stay in comfort zones without any criminal liability over their activities. Why do you have a double standard of approach to the agents and to the advertisers/media? There is no answer to such a question as the criminal justice system is not prepared to set the law into motion against all alike.

Presently, any one can make any advertisement in any way he likes. There is no criminal liability for him if he is committing frauds. God-men, *Avatars*, prayer-men, spiritualists and so on make false advertisements in the name of gods and the Government/laws/criminal justice system do not have any responsibility over them. In my view, every advertisement should obtain government sanction and censorship. The roads in India are contaminated with advertisement—posters, cut-outs, erotic scenes, cinema posters, photos of many political leaders or so-called leaders, religious men and what or who not? If road accidents take place as a result of such advertisements, who will be held responsible? Go to any country having good road system and vehicular traffic. One may not see as many advertisement boards as one sees in India. He may see only traffic signals and other boards that ensure safe driving and road safety. In India, advertisements are made using loud speakers on roads and vehicles. What an atrocity committed on people! Yet, the criminal justice system is blind to these injustices committed on the general public. Miserable indeed!

'PARTISM' AS AN OFFENCE IN INDIA

Humanism as seen in Webster's Dictionary is any system or mode of thought or action in which human interest, values and dignity predominate.

Humanitarianism means *having concern for or helping to improve the welfare and happiness of people and in ethics, it means the doctrine* *that humanity's obligations are concerned wholly with the welfare of the human race.*

Thus one sees many '*...isms*' and thus we take note of terrorism as well as terror causing '*...isms*' in Indian society. In simple terms, the 'terror causing *...isms*' are those behavioural patterns of people—either singly or in group—which cause terror, i.e., unsettling of human mind—in weak people that some calamity is going to take place if they do not yield to his or their vested interest/s and who show a particular behavioural pattern to achieve his or their objectives. O.K., then what is ***'Partism'***?

'Party' means a political party here and, therefore, it means a group of persons with common political opinions and purposes organized for gaining political influence and governmental control and for directing government policies [Webster's] The word ***'Partism'*** may not be seen in a dictionary in the meaning used in this discussion although there is 'party politics' given in the Webster's. It means *politics based on strict adherence to the policies and principles of a political party regardless of the public interest; partisan loyalism.*

Now—

Listen to the following attitudes and approaches of the people belonging to a political party—

(1) As individuals, the party men are not accused to be corrupt. But they accept corruption money for the party. They want party fund and, therefore, the corruption is justified and they get the full support of the party and encouragement.

(2) It is the policy of the party to excuse, justify, tolerate, encourage or promote any undesirable acts if done by party men for the benefit of the party. Therefore, any damage or destruction caused to any individual, institution, etc., is fully understandable and, therefore, happily justified. Any attack or riot or murder or arson committed is fully excused or justified, highly appreciated and encouraged/promoted. It is good for strengthening of the political party and increasing the vote bank.

(3) The party is more important than the Government in power. Therefore, anything or everything can be done for

the party although it may not be good for the Government or administration.

Of late, huge corruption cases, incredible amassing of wealth by politicians for them and their political party, collection of fund from undeclared sources and foreign agencies, clandestine depositing of black money in India and abroad, laundering of black money, participation in anti-nationalist activities are reported. Nevertheless, they get full political support and Governmental god-fathering. Resultantly, many crimes they commit become ***'No Crimes'***, rather ***'Virtues'*** for strengthening the party and for increasing the vote bank. This sort of crime is called ***'Partism'*** and it should be declared as an offence in the Penal Code. In simple terms, ***'Partism'*** means "commission or omission of crimes solely or partly for the political party to which politicians belong *to*." Unless, ***'Partism'*** is punished, India is going to have many crimes which, though crimes in law, are justified, excused, encouraged, promoted, etc. It will surely destroy the Country at last!

What is a party fund? It must be the fund raised by the party men in a legitimate way. Party fund cannot be and should not be corruption money. A party, in one way, means the top men at the helm of affairs. Party fund means the fund reaching at their hands. Many top level party 'dignitaries' are blamed for corruption and malpractices. Therefore, purifying the corruption money by saying that it goes to the party fund is nothing but sugarcoating of a bitter pill. In every sense, it is a crime and the criminal justice system ought to take it as a heinous crime.

What is the meaning of a political party or the vested interest in a political party excusing, justifying, tolerating or encouraging crimes committed by the party men? A crime is a crime, no matter who commits it. In the past and even today, party men justify the crimes and glorify them. They conduct *dharnas,* protest marches, *bandhs* and *hartals* against the criminal justice system taking action against such law breakers. A damage to a public property is a damage to the public property. Likewise a destruction to a public property is a destruction to the public property. If it is done intentionally the law violators deserve to be punished. But, the political parties, by their muscle power and strength of their supporters, show disrespect to the criminal justice system in action.

By their wrong approaches, they multiply the crimes by creating martyrs in democracy. Murder, arson, riot and many public order crimes are reported. No, this cannot be tolerated and heinous crimes should be called by their proper names whosoever may commit them.

Recently, I listened to a political leader saying in a T.V. interview that party was more important for him than the Government. What a wrong message indeed it is! A democratically elected Government is less important than a political party! Democracy means, if I say a cliché, the Government of the people, by the people and for the people. Every political party must make all endeavours to make the government to function in accordance to the Constitution of India and in a manner acceptable to the people. *'Party is more important'* and such approaches ought to be made crimes under the penal laws and such people must be proceeded against. *Partism* is and should be a heinous offence which must be dealt with by iron hands. Political criminology ought to study the subject in depth and suggest ways and means to control or reduce the crime of **Partism** in Indian democracy.

ABUSE OR MISUSE OF MEDIA

This is an era of media and media-men. In a democracy, media is the fourth estate. If anybody is afraid of something in a democracy, it is really the media and media alone. The politicians, the bureaucrats, the administrators, the ministers of the ruling government, the judges, the spiritual men, the so-named 'religious', the *Mafia*, the bandits, the crime syndicates, the white collar criminals and who not?— in fact, they are afraid of the media, for they know their limitations in a democracy. They are certainly afraid of the media if they are fake, not honest or nefarious in their activities. If one's image is lost in public, then everything is lost for him. The public image, the public trust, and the public approval—all these are important in a democracy. Precisely therefore, the media can be abused or misused to damage or destroy the public image of a person. The public image of a person is created not one day, too soon. Articles are written, cartoons are drawn, press conferences are convened, statements are produced, public addresses are made, mimicry is performed, cinemas are shot, dialogues are written, cultural programmes are organized, books are brought out, discussions are arranged and thus a variety of strategies may be adopted to caricature the true image of some personalities in public. The T.V. discussions conducted are sometimes misused by politicians to tarnish their opponents in politics. Misuse of the media or abuse of the media power—they are often blamed as the cause for the defeat of the rule by a political party after an election. Certain criminal cases are kept alive by the media and the crime which took place about many decades ago is brought to light. What about the ISRO case?—Abaya case in Kerala?—atrocities during the emergency, lock up death of Rajan at Kakkayam camp? They never die and certainly one may observe the abuse or misuse of media and media-men for catering to the parochial interests of some people and not for social welfare and community's happiness.

The advertisements in the media are another major area of media abuse or misuse. Lakhs and lakhs of people are cheated by false advertisements. In all major crimes like investment frauds, *Mafia* crimes, organized racketeering, sale of fake medicines, spurious drugs, adulterated food, sale of God's graces and prayers for healing of incurable diseases (healing ministry? as it is popularly called), etc., one sees the misuse or abuse of media power. When the crimes are sold, the media makes enormous or exorbitant profit in participating in the commission of crimes with little or no liability. Media may be misused/abused for propaganda of false news about issues, events and individuals. They publish and publicize news with views and sometimes, the views will be with vested interests or bias. The press and T.V. are owned and operated by political parties, religious men/communities, and communal interests, sectarian groups, vested interests, etc., and they make use of, misuse or abuse the media power for their advantage. There is an oft-quoted cliché—*'the pen is mightier than the sword'*—and it has been proved time and again that the saying is 100 per cent true. Now the saying is: *'The media is mightier than the bomb'* to destroy anything in public mind. The media can be print, electronic, cultural, etc. How to minimize, reduce or prevent *media crimes* is a live topic of wide discussion everywhere in these days!

Experiments have been conducted in psychological

laboratories to study the effect of media on juveniles to commit crimes. It was proved that the media did influence children by very many ways—say, by suggestion, imitation and identification, etc. Everything printed in a newspaper is believed by some and everything shown on a T.V. screen is accepted by many as true.

Can I say that the *Media* may be one of the prominent criminals in Indian democracy? In India, there is the freedom of the press/ freedom of opinion. Though the media does not have any special privileges in its freedom of opinion more than an individual does enjoy, many journalists are under the erroneous impression that they can do anything under the cover of the media or under the colour of the journalists' freedom of expression. Media ethics is not honoured by some journalists as they consider that commercialization and marketing are their only interests. I have specially noted that some media spent 70-90 per cent of their news space only for crime-reporting—as if they have nothing more or very important to report. If we go to the advertisement pages, nearly or more than 50 per cent of them contain half-truth or falsehood intended to cheat the public.

Yellow journalism is something to be abhorred. How many criminal or civil cases are filed against the media for libel, slander or defamation? How many cases end in conviction? Some journalists mix up truth and untruth in the news with their interpretations and usual tags, prefixes and suffixes to escape law and legal actions. I have asked some of my journalist friends and have asked them to enlighten me with their concept of media morality and journalists' ethics. In my view, they need to be inculcated with more information and insight in the ethics of journalism.

Some political parties have media at their disposal to publish and publicize news with their vested interests. Religious media has their vested interests. Cultural media has their interests and the truth will be seen somewhere in the interests of all of them. The question is: "Should the media be allowed to commit crimes? aid the commission of crimes?—instigate the commission of crimes? abet the instigation of crimes?—associate with the commission crimes?—conspire with the criminals for the commission of crimes? Media and crimes may be a new area for the criminologists to study and the criminal justice system to look into.

'NOQUISITORIAL' SYSTEM OF CRIMINAL JUSTICE

Many people know the accusatorial system of justice which is different from the inquisitorial model. But, no one knows much about the 'noquisitorial' system of criminal justice. Why? Such a system does not exist today or existed ever.

The accused should be presumed to be innocent—advocates the accusatorial or adversary model and India follows it.

The accused should be presumed to be guilty—says the inquisitorial system of criminal justice. Some countries, especially in the west, follow it.

Both systems are found to be defective, in my view, although the United Nations Organization accepts the principle (?) *that everybody is to be presumed innocent* until proved otherwise. My researches prove that this approach has enabled many real culprits to escape punishments.

Just consider these issues—

(1) Can you presume a person to be innocent when you know that he may have committed the offence? The slightest doubt about one's involvement in the commission of crimes will make the presumption psychologically impossible for human beings. It is *like presuming* that someone is not your brother when you know that he *may be your brother*. The pre-trial processes, namely, the arrest, remand, bail, etc., are evidence to show—not presumptions—that one is guilty. Hence, to presume that someone is innocent all on a sudden, overnight—in one minute, too soon—is psychologically impossible. The presumption itself is wrong. This is the reality behind the *accusatorial* system.

(2) Can you presume that a person is guilty when there is evidence to prove that he is innocent? Many policemen are found and proved to be not *honest, corrupt, unfair, unjust,* etc., and how can one blindly believe such people to be right always? Studies show that they register false cases, concoct evidence, manipulate records and produce tutored eye-witnesses. It is too much because there is a reality (cliché) that power and authority corrupt people

and absolute power and authority corrupt absolutely. The policemen have power and authority and precisely, therefore, they do abuse their power and misuse their authority. We have any number of instances in which we can say affirmatively that they are violators of human rights and they produce fake witnesses. My researches prove the same. Hence, to presume that the accused is always guilty is wrong and psychologically unacceptable. This is about the *inquisitorial* model.

(3) What about a *middle way*? The Latin principle is *Virtus Stat Medio* (virtue stands in the middle) is true—very true—as the real truth lies between the two extremes. The presumption of guilt against the crime-doer is at one extreme and the presumption of innocence in favour of the guilty is at the other extreme. The middle position is: The accused may or may not be innocent/guilty. Hence, the burden of proof is for the one who claims to be innocent or guilty as the case may be. This is called the "Noquisitorial System of Criminal Justice".

The word has been coined by removing 'Accusa...' and 'inquisi...' from the 'accusatorial' and 'inquisitorial' systems of criminal justice respectively. A **No** is put in their place and 'quisitorial' is suffixed. Thus the new word *'Noquisitorial'* came into being. The system has been elaborately exposed and discussed in my book *Indian Police and Equal Justice Under Law* [ISBN: 81-7648-066-5, A.P.H. Publishing Corporation, Delhi, 1999.]

No doubt, the Accusatorial System has its own Code of Procedure and the Inquisitorial model has its own Procedure Code. India is a country where accusatorial system is followed and the prosecution has the burden of proof to prove a crime against the accused. India has a Code of Criminal Procedure enacted on the basis of the accquisitorial system. Of late, some laws have been enacted by shifting the burden of proof from the prosecution to the accused. (For example, in custodial rape under the Indian Penal Code 1860 and in some other Special Laws). Although the burden of proof has been shifted, the courts in India follow the provisions of the Code of Criminal Procedure 1973 enacted on the basis of the principles followed in the accusatorial model. Resultingly, there exists conflict between the system accepted and the law followed. How far can a judge make use of the existing Code of Criminal Procedure 1973 (of India) to conduct a trial of an accused on whose shoulders the burden of proof has been shifted is a point of dispute among the criminologists and legal experts. Once the burden of proof has been shifted to the accused in a crime, the trial judge ought to make use of the Code of Procedure enacted following the principles of the inquisitorial model. There exists confusion and certainly miscarriage of justice takes place.

A situation has now emerged that those countries which follow accusatorial model want to shift to the inquisitorial model in some special cases to administer justice and they make attempts for the same. Likewise, some countries which follow inquisitorial system want to shift to accusatorial model in some special cases to administer fair justice. *Noquisitorial* model embraces two systems alike—and it does not make any presumptions in favour of or against the prosecution or the accused as the case may be. Don't believe either the prosecution or the defence. Let each one prove its worth and truth. Criminologists and legal experts are to undertake the responsibility to make the *noquisitorial system* a reality one day, too soon.

EQUAL JUSTICE SYSTEM

Equal Justice Under Law—It means that everyone must get justice. What is to God must go to Him and what is to Caesar must go to him — this is what is accepted. Equal Justice means only that and nothing more. In my book, *Indian Police and Equal Justice under Law,* I have explained and elaborated this concept as—

(1) Justice to the crime-doer/criminal;
(2) Justice to the victims/s of crime and victims of abuse of power/misuse of authority;
(3) Justice to the society; and
(4) Justice to the justice system itself.

What is the importance of these concepts? Let us see—

(1) What about the justice to the crime-doer/criminal? Evidence in hand shows that there are many who are above the law in the sense that the people have developed

a feeling that the law is or can be enforced only against the enforceable. How many politicians, higher-ups in society, the affluent or the influential, the 'religious 'god-men are punished so far? Our prisons are crowded with people who are "lesser mortals" and not with "divinities" belonging to any category enumerated above. All of them are 'hounourable men' and justice to them means just a hollow utterance or an empty word!

(2) What about the justice to the victim/s of crime or victims of abuse of power/misuse of authority?A country where victim justice is not accepted in full measure, there exist no laws which ensure victim justice, victimological compensation or restitution in the way they are given in countries where such type of justice is administered. In such a situation, there may not be any sense in talking about victim justice in India. Victims of one's crime also include his family and dependents and there is no Victim Compensation Tribunals established for giving victim compensation/restitution for the victims of crime/abuse of power/misuse of authority. As far as the justice to the victims of abuse of power or misuse of authority is concerned, there is the Protection of Human Rights Act 1993 which, it is blamed, is nothing but a teethless legislation, not enforced seriously in the country.

(3) What about the justice to society? Criminal cases registered, investigated and tried by the courts of law are acquitted in large numbers. Why? Numerous factors can be enumerated and they are not answers to the injustice/miscarriage of justice done to the society. The society invests huge amount of money and the output is nil. In some States in India, it has been observed that the conviction to the total crimes registered is just 6 per cent and after an appeal, it comes still down to 2 per cent. What is then the justice to society? A waste of money and manpower!

(4) What about the justice to the justice system itself? The police, prosecutors, defense lawyers, judges, media, people and prisons—all come under the justice system. The police are blamed for corruption and malpractices, the prosecutors for their nefarious activities, the defense lawyers for their self-interests, the judges for their

> ignorance, prejudices, partisan attitudes, corruption and qualitatively of poor performance, the media for media-wash and media trials, the people for their dishonesty and prisons for their failures in reforming the inmates. There is a growing feeling among the people that an equal justice administration is a myth-never to be seen in the present day society. What to do and how to go about?

Do the real criminals get justice? Do all criminals get proper and fair justice? If all criminals get justice, India should have more— very many more—prisons to accommodate them. India should have more—very many courts to conduct the trial in a speedier way. Do the innocent people brought before the courts of law get justice? These and similar questions are many and answers are nil. In spite of it, the system moves—continues to move administering justice to the criminals/crime-doers to an extent possible.

Do the victims of crime get justice? The question is out of question as there exists no victim fund in India. Are there laws to allow victim compensation? Yes, we have the laws, but are sterile. The barren laws are barren and, therefore, victim justice is a *tamasha* in criminal justice administration there. Many people want a victim justice system instead of a criminal justice system. Impossible indeed in India at present!

Do the society get justice *via* criminal justice system? The society should feel it. The presence should be felt and not seen. The *goonda* culture, the *Mafia* activities, production and sale of hootch and contraband items, atrocities on women and children, frauds and cheatings of all descriptions, *Hawala* money and fake notes, corruption and malpractices, adulteration, etc., are indicative of the fact that the criminal justice system and its functionings are not felt by the general public. People develop distrust on all sub-systems of the justice system. The citizenry does not get enviable dividend for the investment they make for the maintenance of the criminal justice system. For the public, the system is a white elephant. To hope that the justice system may ensure justice to the society remains to be a pious hope—never to be achieved in the near future. What a tragedy indeed! Does the justice system do justice to the system itself? The answer seems to be an emphatic no. The system experiences difficulties to convince itself that the system ensures justice to the justice system itself.

If this is the position, what is the meaning of talking about an ***Equal Justice system***? — or, a distributive system of justice? Criminologists may study the issue with more earnestness so that they can bring an equal justice system some day in the near future.

SHARKS AND ANCHOVIES OF CRIME AND THEIR PUNISHMENT

Earlier in this book, *noquisitorial* system of justice has been discussed. There, the defects in the accusatorial and inquisitorial models were brought out. Probably, those defects are the major causes of Criminal Sharks escaping punishments and the small urchins getting punished. Just consider the following—

(1) The accused should be presumed to be innocent until proved guilty. This is just not possible psychologically. The accused must be presumed to be guilty and it is also psychologically impossible. In India, the Sharks escape punishment because they are able to prove the presumption to their favour and the Anchovies are unable to do so because they are otherwise handicapped.

(2) Let one thousand criminals go unpunished; one innocent should never be punished. The Sharks are able to escape punishment along with those 'thousands' and the Anchovies are unable to exploit the principle as they are otherwise helpless. The correct principle must be that the thousand criminals should be punished and no innocent should ever be punished.

(3) When two views are possible, the view most favourable to the accused must be accepted. Why cannot the view most favourable to the administration of justice be taken in such situations? This leniency is exploited by the Sharks whereas the Anchovies are incapacitated of doing so.

(4) The accused is an individual and the prosecution is a mammoth agency having money and manpower. The individuals win and here the Sharks win because they

know how to manipulate the mammoth agency whereas the Anchovies cannot because they are handicapped otherwise.

The criminal Sharks have money, influence, power, authority, friendship with the law enforcement machinery, judiciary, politicians and the Government while the Anchovies, especially if they are poor financially, do not have them. As such, the Sharks often purchase the law, lawyers and justice. People feel that there is no law which cannot be purchased—no personnel that cannot be purchased.

The criminal Sharks have clandestine and strong friendship with the higher-ups in politics, business, judiciary and what or who not? Their cases are not investigated properly by the ordinary police men and petty (they are called so by the Sharks and some of the hierarchy) sub-inspectors. It is because, they are not allowed to conduct the investigation of cases against the Sharks in the best way. Sometimes, their cases are investigated by their own police officials.

The Anchovies do not require any hard and strong nets whereas the Sharks need it. Ordinary police men and, as said above—the petty sub-inspectors of the General Executive Branch are the investigating officials for the Sharks. The witnesses against the Sharks are killed or they commit suicide (*e.g.*, 2G spectrum case). The evidence against them is destroyed, false witnesses are created and prosecution witnesses are converted to be hostile to the prosecution by the Sharks whereas the small fries cannot do them. The Sharks may file cases after cases before various courts for 'this and that', the purpose is to delay the case until such time they get a favourable climate to torpedo the case against them. They also cause inordinate delay at every stage of the investigation, prosecution and trial by getting adjournments. Justice delayed is always justice forgotten.

The system is bad and there is no meaning in breaking the mirror just because the image is bad. Everything must be changed from the root and we must bring out a new Penal Code, a Procedure Code and an Evidence Act basing on the latest concepts and principles in administering fair justice. Both the Sharks and the Anchovies must be punished as per the law and procedure established by law.

Some of the legal theories and the jurisprudence followed till date become sometimes out of date or unusable. Psychology has developed as a science only recently and some of the principles recognized by the system of justice administration have come into being when psychology as a scientific discipline was not even born. Precisely, therefore, certain principles of jurisprudence have become obsolete and unacceptable. Changing the law is an option left with the system or accept the new psychological principles to punish the Sharks and Anchovies alike.

Why should one thousand criminals go unpunished? If they have committed crimes, they must get justice due to them. In an overenthusiasm to protect the interest of the innocent, the guilty should not be shown undue favours. Of course, the spirit of the maxim may be good, but helps many Sharks to escape punishment. Many police officers, prosecutors, defence counsels and judges are not psychologists to appreciate the dictum in 'spirit'. Hence, the principles in jurisprudence of the ancient Roman law must be subjected to further research and scrutiny with the help of recent researches in psychology and psychology of justice administration. In my view, all the thousand guilty must be punished and no innocent should ever be penalized.

An accused may or may not have committed an offence alleged. He has the status of an accused and he has no right to enjoy special privileges which the prosecution does not have. Both are equal before the judge. Precisely, therefore, when two views are possible, accept the view that ensures administration of fair and just justice. If not, Sharks will be more benefited and injustice perpetuated.

Looking to many principles of jurisprudence now followed in administration of justice from the angles of modern researches in criminology, psychology, justice science, etc., I am of the view that many of the older "principles" must be studied to make changes. These changed principles must be taught to the personnel engaged in the administration of justice. The principle followed during the period of Aristotle was that women had fewer teeth than men. Aristotle himself had two wives, but he never bothered about verifying his view by counting the teeth of his wives. Similarly, in ancient Indian law, it was believed that one man is equal to two women. In courts of law, therefore, two women had to be produced as witnesses whereas one man was enough to prove the contention. It took several centuries to correct the wrong notions and thus to stop the miscarriage of justice.

The Roman jurisprudence, if it helps to miscarry justice or to administer waste justice, must be subjected to scientific study and analysis by a team of experts—especially from the field of criminology, psychology, etc. After joining the police as the only and the first criminologist in Kerala State on the Faculty of the Police Training College, Thiruvananthapuram, I was able to convince many police officials that some of their beliefs and principles were of questionable validity. They gladly accepted and I am proud to say that administration of justice was made fairer and just by my sincere attempts.

WOUNDED JUSTICE

'Wounded Justice' is a strange and a new concept. *'Wounded Soul'*, i.e., a heart pained and which needs consolation. Justice, as said earlier, is a nebulous concept; nevertheless, everyone has his own concept about justice. For example, an innocent person who was convicted and jailed got at last an acquittal. There, one might say that he got justice. Then the question is: 'What type of justice' did he get? He got a sort of justice, but a pained justice. Firstly, get a conviction and then get an acquittal! He was innocent as well. According to the present law in India, he is not entitled to get any compensation. There is no victim justice in such cases when someone is acquitted. An acquittal may be *'an acquittal with benefit of doubt' or 'an acquittal with honour'*. In the former case, the accused might have committed the offence, but the prosecution was not able to prove the case beyond doubt. Hence, he was acquitted. Here, the question is: 'Why did the prosecution put him into trouble with insufficient or inadequate evidence? 'His acquittal is, therefore, not justice administration, but miscarriage of justice or *'wounded justice'* administration. In the latter case, the accused was totally innocent, but was charge-sheeted, put into trouble and finally got justice by an acquittal with honour. Here it is nothing but 'wounded justice' and certainly he deserves victimological compensation. But India does not have any effective law to give such victimological compensation for those who suffered wounded justice.

Mistake of fact may be a ground to wind up the proceedings,

but the question is: 'Is it not wounded justice to wind up the criminal proceedings owing to mistake of facts?' Disciplinary proceedings might be taken against innocent subordinates/ associates and after some time, it would be dropped. Is it not wounded justice to do so? The penal laws are so comprehensive that a police officer can register a case against people, put him in trouble and at last refer it as 'undetected'— so can be done by influential politicians or the ruling Government. Of late, such misuse of power or abuse of authority is seen and cases are registered against politicians with ulterior motives which may be anything other than justice. No doubt, it is wounded justice administration. The inordinate delay caused in the disposal of cases too may be wounded justice administration. Some criminal cases do not have a natural end even after ten or twelve years of delay. The accused in such cases may get an acquittal at last, but the justice he receives in such a case is nothing but wounded justice. Thus to enumerate the situations in which wounded justice is administered are many and different. Because of the extent and intensity of justice administration, one may be inclined to call 'wounded justice' administration rather than 'justice' administration or 'criminal justice' administration or 'victim justice' administration as the case may be.

I wrote a book titled *"Wounded Justice and the Story of Indian Police"*. When I studied the police closely, I could learn that the police did administer justice down the centuries since the Indian Police Act 1861, nevertheless, sometimes, they administered wounded justice or waste justice. Police to begin with was a muscle force during the British rule in India and more often than not, their muscles administered "Justice" which doubtlessly was atrocious.

Police torture prior to the Torture Commission-1855 till today exposes the extent and intensity of the muscle justice to the people. During the internal emergency in India during nineteen hundred and seventies showed the animal justice administration of the police in India. The blinding incident in a north Indian Jail is another example. The history of police in India so far is contaminated to some extent with wounded or waste justice administration.

What about the Bench and the Bar? Appeals are filed before the superior courts and every appeal proclaims to the world that something is rotten somewhere in justice administration. In appeals, convictions in the lower court get converted to acquittals or *vice versa* which again say to the justice seekers that the justice is wounded somewhere in the process. Allegations are plenty against the lawyers, prosecutors and judicial officials and they relate to corruption and susceptibility to temptations or recommendations. People lose their trust in the subsystems of justice administration which again is a manifestation of wounded justice in Indian judiciary.

Prisons are prisons, no matter their bars are made of diamonds. What is happening today? There may be custodial justice and correctional justice and many a time a convict is unable to make out the difference. People incarcerated become recidivists even after correctional treatment. Why? This is called wounded correction. If one sees the ***YouTube*** scenes of torture in prisons, he may get fainted as he cannot tolerate the intensity of the "correctional justice" administered in centres of correction or personality development as the case may be. Wounded Justice Administration by the subsystems of justice in any country is a crime in every sense and it must be checked/controlled at any cost.

MISCARRIAGE OF JUSTICE AND ABORTION OF JUSTICE ADMINISTRATION

I got my Ph.D. as early as in 1983 and at the end of my doctoral studies, I came to the conclusion that there was nothing called *Justice* and what one would see in this world was *Justice* as a *Myth* and not a *Reality*. Yes, justice was a *Myth* for me. My second daughter was born to me in 1983, and I purposefully called her *Neethie* which meant *Justice*. I wanted to see *Neethie* personified in my daughter and thus I had the personal satisfaction that I could convert a *Myth* into a *Reality*. During my research, I was able to find only 'miscarriage of justice' although I was not courageous enough to call '*Injustice*' at that time. In the name of administering justice, *Miscarriage of Justice* was administered and we claimed that everything was O.K. in the city of Denmark. "The rotten justice, the decayed justice, the wounded justice, the less justice, the perverted justice, the animal justice, the black justice, the waste justice, the delayed justice, and injustice"—the types or categories of justice administration were many and various. All of them could be put under a single word ***Miscarriage of Justice***.

Miscarriage of Justice means in Dictionary "Failure to attain the just, right or desired result" and the miscarriage is seen more in other fields than in justice administration. The word ***Miscarriage*** is used often in the medical field and it means *Abortion*. Abortion means in Dictionary the 'expulsion of a foetus before it is viable, especially, between the third and seventh month of pregnancy'. In fact, abortions take place in the area of justice administration as well. As far as the administration of justice is concerned, abortion means a failure to attain the objective or expulsion of justice without obtaining the desired result which is nothing but the truth. Just now! How many people are taken into custody or arrested without any probable causes? How many false cases are registered and investigated? How many cases are investigated in a perfunctory manner? How many false witnesses are produced? How many pieces of evidence are concocted? How many records are manipulated? How many people are harassed, arrested, tortured, humiliated, victimised and done away with? How many cases are referred to as 'Undetected'? How many innocent people are convicted? In how many cases, the investigations are wound up as found to be 'mistake of fact'? How much property is plundered during the investigation? How much corruption is seen at every stage of the progress of investigation and prosecution? How many cases are falsely prosecuted? How many innocent people are remanded? How many trials are honestly conducted? How many cases are convicted without any prick of conscience? How many cases are acquitted without any guilt feelings? How many cases are conducted without any bad influence? How many incarcerated are corrected and reformed?

For heaven's sake, I do not want to elaborate the list any more. When I wrote a book on police crimes, I did enumerate several hundreds of crimes committed by police during the course of their work and I do not want to repeat the same here. Honest answers to the questions raised above and similar questions will give more or less a clear picture of the extent and intensity of the ***Miscarriage of Justice*** or ***Abortion of Justice***. When the ***System*** cannot find a solution to the problem, then the ***System*** itself is the problem. What can be done then?

Administration of justice by various sub-systems of justice becomes the central theme in many cinemas and T.V. serials. Administration of justice becomes the topic of discussions in bus stands, railway cabins, restaurants, evening gossip meetings, parks and everywhere. In every cinema, T.V. serials, talks, discussions and chats, one listens or sees miscarriage of justice. In cinemas and T.V. serials, ultimately the *Dharma* will win over *Adharma* and the victory is through a series of miscarriage of justice. In life too, I notice miscarriage of justice more than fair and just justice. Hence, I may even venture to say that miscarriage is the normality and pure and just justice administration is an abnormality. Miscarriage of justice is the general rule and the pure and just justice is an exception. Is it true to think so?

Adam and Eve were punished and that Biblical episode is seen immediately after the creation of man by God, the Almighty. They did not get a chance to make an appeal and, therefore, the first punishments were confirmed. Confirming the punishment without giving an opportunity to make an appeal is said to be miscarriage of justice. Therefore, it is argued that miscarriage of justice is as old as humanity and will continue to be so till the consumation of the world. *Bible* teaches that Christ Jesus came to the world to save the mankind from the original sin of the first parents. Of course, the salvation history starts with the birth of Christ Jesus. Likewise, the world down the centuries makes attempt to save the man from miscarriage of justice. Thus came out the concepts of human rights justice, gender justice, juvenile justice, victim justice, social justice, etc. It continues even today just like a never ending episode. Criminologists are at it and this book is all about it.

LESS JUSTICE ADMINISTRATION

I wrote a book titled *The Justice Less Administered* and I wrote in it what was meant by Less Justice. I do not want to say that it is a sort of 'duplicate justice' or 'fake justice' or 'adulterated justice 'or 'injustice'. It is not 'wounded justice', not 'miscarriage of justice', not 'perverted justice', not 'decayed justice', not 'injustice' at all and that is all!

'Full justice 'means 100 per cent justice. Any justice less than 100 per cent justice is called rightly *Less Justice*.

Make an analysis of the following situations—

(1) Commission of crime was taken note of by the police, but they took an indifferent attitude or they closed their eyes. Pressures exerted and then a case was registered.
(2) Commission of crime was reported to police, but they took a negative attitude. Influence was exerted and then a case was registered. There was undue delay in the registration of the case.
(3) A case was registered, no further steps were taken seriously to protect the scene of crime, inspect the scene of crime and collect evidence. Political force was exerted and then necessary steps were taken.
(4) Inspection of the scene of crime was done in a perfunctory manner by unqualified or under-qualified police officials. Resultantly, contamination of evidence took place without any malicious motives.
(5) Evidence collected from the scene of crime was not sent for forensic examination; was sent but in an unscientific way. There was contamination of evidence and the test results were far away from being satisfactory.
(6) Many people were unnecessarily questioned and harassed. A few people were arrested and interrogated by unqualified or under-qualified police officials. Witnesses were interviewed in an unbecoming way by investigating officials. Third degree methods were used for getting confessions and torture was resorted to for getting information.
(7) Search was conducted at odd hours even by intruding into the privacies of people, seizures were made in an untrustworthy manner, property plundered and not included in the search list, false witnesses were produced.
(8) Overenthusiasm and perverted-sense of justice made the police to concoct evidence, to produce tutored witnesses and manipulate records.
(9) The prosecutors conducted the case in an indifferent way or with overenthusiasm and extra-interest or with false witnesses or with fake evidence etc.
(10) The judges were said to be partial, prejudiced, parochial and unjust with preconceived theories, bias and

prejudices. They had a defective development of personality and perverted attitudes and outlook. They wrote the judgments bringing out only half truths.

(11) The prisons were punitive institutions and thus one sees administration of 'something' which is' less than justice' and one may call it ***Anything*** but not justice proper ! This is called ***Less Justice***.

A criminal justice system works in every democracy, but to set the law into motion is indeed difficult, time consuming, laborious and expensive. How many people will be able to afford such troubles and tribulations to get justice? People in general find it very difficult to get justice owing to the inertia, indifference, lack of interest, apathy, overwork, too much of political pressure, corruption, favouritism, affinities, blood relations, recommendations, introductions, 'ologies' 'isms' of the investigating, prosecuting or adjudicating personnel in justice administration. In spite of all, ultimately, justice may be administered and the allegation is that it will be "less justice" and not justice proper. People sometimes say that they receive 40 per cent or 50 per cent or 60 per cent or 70 per cent justice and seem to be dissatisfied by the system. Some people say that they receive justice from the court ultimately, but to reach up to the court, is indeed very hard. Putting everything together, they feel that what they receive is only "less justice".

Sometimes, the police may be just, but the prosecutor may not be. Why? There may be many intervening factors that cause less justice administration. Lack of knowledge and expertise in the law, science of investigation, procedure, etc., may work as factors responsible for less justice or waste justice administration Money has its influence in many litigations. The appearance of veteran lawyers may be another factor. The personality traits, outlook, philosophy and attitude of the presiding officers may have their impact on less justice or waste justice administration. Inadequate laws and antiquated laws of evidence may further act as a cause of less justice.

"Less justice" may be a subjective concept and varies from individual to individual. Accepting the subjectivity in evaluating justice as 'less justice', yet in that subjectivity there may be a lot of truth. Media publicity may be yet another reason for less justice and a judge, like others, will be influenced by the media. Instances are not rare that media trials exerting influence on decisions making. "Less justice" administration does not mean that justice is totally denied. It means that the customer does not get the justice expected by him. He has expectations and the justice system has the obligations. Something happened in between the obligation and expectation which resulted in less justice administration.

I do not think that the Indian criminologists are of the view that 'less justice administration' is a crime. At the same time they want more perfection in the system. Whether or not the expectation of the criminologists will be fulfilled is a matter to be seen in future.

SCALE TO AWARD PUNISHMENTS

What is the scale to award a punishment? Bentham and Beccaaria suggested that the severity of punishments should be proportionate to the gravity of the offence committed. Perhaps, this idea had its origin in St. Thomas Aquinas, a Catholic theologian who proposed a similar scale for the award of punishment to the sinners after their death and it was done during the 13th century or so. Accordingly, those who committed mortal sins were entitled to get ***'Hell'*** after death and those who committed venial sins would receive ***'purgatory'*** after their death. The days which must be spent in purgatory for purification of the soul after death depended on the gravity of the venial sin committed. The classification of crimes as cognizable and non-cognizable under the Indian law had its roots in the classification of sins by St. Thomas Aquinas. Non-cognizable crimes are of less serious nature than the cognizable crimes like the venial sins and mortal sins in Catholic theology.

When Bentham and Beccaria suggested the scale basing on the hedonistic calculus, the objective of punishment was not even 'incapacitating' as seen in the Indian Penal Code 1860. When Macaulay framed the Indian Penal Code, he prescribed imprisonment for almost all crimes and the imprisonment was, as said elsewhere, punitive in nature. Of course, it changed into peno-correctional and later to correctional and still later to correction, reformation, rehabilitation, resocialization and reintegration to society back. The latest approach is 'to the development of human personality in an upright way in the right direction' The questions that arise now are—

(1) Are the Thomist and Benthan-Beccaaria scales relevant today to award punishments?
(2) What is the criterion by virtue of which the gravity of crime is decided by the Judge?
(3) What is the purpose of punishment? If the objective is to develop human personality in an upright way in the right direction, then how must a Judge decide the severity of punishment?
(4) If the crime doer has not developed his personality in an upright way in the right direction during his jail life, what is the liability of the Judge awarding the punishment? What is the responsibility of the prison staff for the failure of their mission?
(5) Are the Judges and the jail staff competent enough and qualitatively up to date to award the punishment and to attain the objective of the punishment? If not, what are the factors responsible for the failure?

Questions are many and the answers are nil. In fact, there exists no scientific criterion or scale to award punishments to crime doers. There exists no diagnosis of the crime and the crime-doer. And what is done today is a sort of *Adhochism* or *Avanavanism* (i.e., arbitrarily deciding the punishment as the Judge feels or likes) in administration of justice. It needs discussion today extensively.

What is the scale employed by the Legislators (law-makers) to fix the punishment and its intensity/duration of imprisonment when they draft the provisions of law? Common sense? Arbitrary decision? Any scientific criteria? No one knows. Again, how do the judges take a decision on the quantum of punishment to the offenders when they convict them after a trial? Some judges award harder punishments whereas some others give a lighter punishment for one and the same offence. How? The judges are given the discretion to do so. The law always says "Shall be punished with imprisonment of either description which may extend to....years". A judge who is very harsh to sex offenders is not found to be that harsh to thieves or pickpockets. Why? His attitude to the offence matters a lot here. Psychologists may argue that his personality is the deciding factor. In fact, there exists no scientific criterion to decide on the quantum of punishment. If the objective of incarceration is the development of the inmate's personality in an upright way in the right direction, the judges should see to it that the purpose of imprisonment is materialized. The prison officials must see to it that the objective of incarceration is actualized. It seems to me that no one is bothered about such finer points during incarceration. The verdicts come from the courts in a ritualistic way after the trial for the media to report and the people to forget (?) The criminal justice system does not seem to be concerned with the fulfilment of the objectives of incarceration. Just like a mental patient is forgotten when he is admitted in a mental hospital, a convict is ignored generally by the public when he is incarcerated. Who wants him?/who needs him? No auditing is done to understand the success of incarceration or other types of punishment. No studies or researches worth mentioning come out of jails. Sometimes, recidivists come out and at some other times, hardened criminals come out. Theoretically, the criminal justice system is a nice concept, i.e., a system or a process by which a law breaker is converted to a law observer. But what happens? No conversion, but only hardening. Should we still retain imprisonment as a method of punishment for the judicial functionaries to award it arbitrarily without any purpose? Can we say that punishing an offender is a sort of misuse of power or abuse of authority or a human rights violation? No one answers the question; yet the system continues. For what? Why should an offender be punished? What should be the punishment? How should one be punished? What is the scale to award punishment? We do not move an inch forward. We remain at the same spot from where the journey started.... A meaningless ritualism or a process without any purpose!

QUALITY OF JUDGES

'Once a Judge, always a Judge'; ***'Once a Judge, always a Just man'***—people say so or better believe so. Yes, it is only a belief which means "having confidence in the truth, the existence or the reliability of something, although without absolute proof that one is right in doing so"[Webster's]. It is a question of faith in somebody

or something. Faith means belief that is not based on proof. Judges are human beings—every sense, mortals and precisely, therefore, the unquestioned belief or faith in Judges has been without sufficient empirical evidence. The empirical evidence proves that a Judge is not always just and the merit of a Judge is decided by the quality of his judgements and the quality is decided not by the Judge by himself but by the people in a democracy.

India had, till recently, no test to enroll oneself as a lawyer. Once, a person is enrolled as an Advocate, he becomes eligible to become a Judge if he is selected or appointed. The selection process presently does not have any objective test to assess the personality or aptitude of those entering into judicial positions as magistrates, munsiffs or judges. Allegations are plenty—open and otherwise—that people who are not suitably qualified have entered into the judicial service—even to the higher levels. Of late, there have been many allegations of corruption and malpractices against judges of the higher and highest judiciary in India. Some of the judges and judicial functionaries of lower service have been detected as people of little or no integrity and their judgments have been found to be qualitatively inferior or containing injustice or miscarriage of justice.

In USA, once a study was conducted to know the justness of white judges to the black. The result of the study has been shocking or far away from being satisfactory. In India, no such serious studies have been conducted to know the quality of judges and the same of the judgements pronounced by them. Nevertheless, the judges of the superior courts, Supreme Court of India, retired judges/Chief Justices and so on from time and again, speak loudly that a specified percentage of the judges (One Chief Justice of the Supreme Court of India said, as pointed out earlier, that 20 per cent of the judicial officials were corrupt in a public address at Kollam in Kerala State) are corrupt, are people of questionable integrity, honesty, fairness and justness. Why do they become so? The reasons are many and various. Some of them are—

(1) They become susceptible to the influence and recommendations.
(2) They become a spatula of politicians who offer them positions and postings.
(3) They become corrupt and people of no moral values.

(4) They become the nexus partners of crime syndicates and white collar criminals.
(5) They become friendly with corrupt lawyers and other affluent/influential people.
(6) They suffer from lack of knowledge in law and other sciences.
(7) They suffer from psychological problems, affinities, prejudices, pre-conceived ideas and parochial loyalties.

The list can be very long. Now attempts are made to rectify the defects, but it takes time.

Advertisements on the T.V. screens, newspapers and other media are seen about the quality of gold—.916 **Gold**. There may be objective tests to decide on the quality of gold. In spite of the advertisements repeatedly people are not inclined to have trust on the jewelleries. The sellers of gold want to create public trust on the quality and purity of the gold. Again, advertisements are seen in the media about the quality of treatments given in hospitals, about the quality of education offered in colleges, about the quality of automobiles sold in the market, about the quality of medicines, quality of prayers, quality of services, etc. What about the quality of services rendered by the sub-systems in justice administration? Studies on police performance, reports of various committees/ commissions on police, people's daily observations on police activities, media reports, etc., tell loudly about the quality of the police service in justice administration. What about the quality of prosecutors' services?—of the defence lawyers' services? What about the quality of services of the judicial officers? No research studies, no advertisements, no transparency, no ways to know it. In the present set-up, what to do and how to go about? Can we subscribe to the view that all our judicial functionaries are qualitatively fine? In order to decide on the quality of the judiciary, the character, attitude, values, personality traits, morality, conscience, approaches, maturity, skill, knowledge, etc. of the judges ought to be subjected to tests. We do not have any such objective tests to decide upon the quality of judges. Should we not think about such tests to objectively measure the quality of judges to create public trust and confidence on the judiciary? If the response is "*Yes*" to the question, do it here and now. We have no time to waste...

PSYCHOLOGY OF JUDGES

'Offences against women should be tried by women judges'— this is a demand often raised by some of the Women's Organizations in India. According to them, women-judges are psychologically better than men-judges to administer proper and just justice to offenders who commit crimes against women. In one study in India, it was found that women-judges who tried rapists were seen to have awarded lesser punishments to rapists than men-judges. Why? Judges who had very poor relations with their life partners (husbands or wives as the case might be) were more inclined to grant divorces whereas those who had good relations with their family simply refused to give divorces. They made every attempt to see that rupture did not take place in family life.

Judges are not divinities. They have their weaknesses or frailties which all human beings do have. They have a past, a developmental period, a personality, an outlook, an attitude, a vision, drives, motives, emotions, education, etc., and they have their influence on the psychology of judges and their behavioural dynamics. If a member of the suppressed religious community in India behaves in a particular manner to a member of the upper community, he may have visible or invisible reasons for it. A judge is not an exception and he cannot be so. There are no bias-free judges as everyone has his prejudices and preconceived notions about issues, events and individuals. People are superstitious and some have fake beliefs.

A judge is born into a community, brought up in a community and precisely, therefore, he has his mental script written accordingly. The gown of the judges does not and cannot transfer him totally from that earthly existence to a supernatural existence. He is a man— a human being after all and he behaves exactly like other human beings. His philosophy, affinities, "... ologies", "... isms", likes and dislikes affect him a lot to be a judge, to function as a judge. Certainly, his judgments will reflect all those things over which he has little or no control. There is a story about Galileo and the story is as follows. He said: "the earth rounds the sun". The Holy Church was against his observations as it was different from what the *Bible* taught. Therefore, he was taken to the Inquisition and the clergy said that he would be pardoned if he just said: "Excuse me, it is the Sun that rounds the earth and not the earth that rounds the Sun as I said earlier".

Galileo was assured of a pardon. Galileo agreed everything and said kneeling before the Inquisition that the Sun rounds the earth and then stood up and faced the people and said: "Yes, it is the earth that rounds the Sun". Of course he was awarded death as a consequence. Likewise, the conviction in a man or the evidence in his hand has an influence upon his decisions and judgements. The judicial judges are no exceptions to this general rule. Any number of instances are quoted by lawyers to say how a judge would behave if he were to take a decision, nevertheless, they too are amenable or susceptible to influences, introductions and recommendations. The stories of corruption and malpractices among the judicial functionaries are coming out in battalions and, therefore, the psychology of judges too is exactly like the psychology of other human beings with strengths and weaknesses. Modifications in their psychology take place just like they take place in other human beings. They are mortals and nothing more and nothing less.

This is a dialogue from a Malayalam drama.

The Judge to the convict: "What is your last wish?" (this question is asked to a convict who stands at the foot of the gallows just before the execution).

The convict to the Judge: "I want to kiss your wife".

Hearing this, the judge became wild and ordered: ***"Hang him immediately".***

The convict said to the Judge (smiling): "Your Honour, when I say that I want to kiss your wife remaining at the foot of the gallows under your custody, you become furious and order to hang me immediately. Your Honour, please answer me. What should I do with a man when I see him in a compromising position with my wife?"

The question was to all and it tells everyone that the psychology and the psychic forces working in a judge are not different. Yes, the **Push Factors** in judges are the same as they are in other human beings. Look at the *Egogrammes* drawn by judges and the same by others in different walks of life. There will not be much differences. I have subjected judicial officers, police officers and college students to some experimental tests (psychological) in my classes and I could learn that there were no much differences in the test results among them. The conclusion is that the psychology of judges is not very much different from the same in others. **Push-Pull-Ego Factor** Theory works with them exactly like it works with others in different professions/walks of life.

A Judge has *'conscious, subconscious, unconscious'* layers in his mind. A Judge has his *'Parent-Adult-Child-Ego States'* in him. A Judge employs *Ego* defence mechanisms to establish his homeostasis when he is in conflicts or when he experiences frustrations. A Judge has emotions, likes, dislikes, values, etc. A Judge has gender feelings, tender feelings, ego feelings, etc. Hence, in what way the Judges are different from other human beings? Certainly, they are no way different—they are no way different from other human beings.

Understanding human behaviour is what the Judges do when they administer justice in a court of law. Criminal behaviour is a human behaviour and very much a social fact. If so, the Judges may hate the crime and not the criminal. For, if the Judges too hate the criminal just like many others do in society, administration of justice will be in disarray. Hence, make a Judge psychologically fit to administer justice before he assumes the position of a Judge. He should be given instructions in criminology, understanding human behaviour, etc. immediately after his recruitment to the post of a judicial officer. Besides the induction training, each one should be exposed to various in-service training courses to improve the administration of justice.

CRIMINAL JUSTICE ADMINISTRATION JUST LIKE GOVERNMENT BUSINESS

Government Business, Everybody's Business

'Government business, nobody's business'—They are probably the words or felt impressions of the common man and they cannot be without any basis. Government business takes its own time and its own course. The general public develop such feelings and make such expressions as a result of their felt experiences in transacting business with the Government. The questions here are—

Q. How much is the delay between the registration of a case and the completion of investigation or trial, etc.?

Ans. The answer will be shocking to human conscience to admit that the delay can be/may be several years–even decades!

Q. What is the delay in the investigation of criminal cases alone?

Ans. Presently, criminal cases are investigated by qualified, unqualified or under-qualified officials; are investigated in a perfunctory manner; are done in a ritualistic way. Investigations are done by several officials one after another, one agency after another agency, one set of officials after another set so much so that there are criminal cases whose investigations are going on for decades together even for fifteen or sixteen years of long delay. The expenditure incurred will be something which only human imagination can conceive of.

Q. What about the nature of investigation?

Ans. The nature may be from total negativity to excessive positivity, from extreme benevolence to extreme atrocity; from extreme indifference to extreme enthusiasm and all depends upon the persons involved and the situations demanding. The Government is said to be a headless entity and precisely, therefore, the officials transacting business can do it in "this way or that way" as they decide. Though many say that the law will take its course, the experience proves that any law will take its course depending upon the officials enforcing the law. Even big rivers change their course as some people want them to and if so, the Government business is as the Government wants—as nobody wants and precisely, therefore, as the vested interests want it. This may be applicable not only during investigation but also during prosecution, trial, adjudication and incarceration.

Q. Who is that much interested to administer proper criminal justice?

Ans. People who are entrusted with the administration of criminal justice look 'up, down, above, below, beyond, amidst and in between' to ensure that they are in a safe position and in comfort zones. Accordingly, they manage and manipulate things while they transact business for the Government. Today's ruling political party becomes tomorrow's opposition and today's opposition becomes tomorrow's ruling political party. Hence, the officials are like a pendulum swinging left and right while they transact business for the Government in power. Instances are plenty to show that many officials who transact business for today's Government are put into extreme trouble and peril by the next Government which comes into power. There are cases of many civil servants being shut in prisons for transacting business for the Government. Thus one sees abuse of power or misuse of authority for self-interest and for the vested interests while the business is transacted for the Government.

This sort of behaviour as explained above is seen in all areas of legislative, administrative and judicial functions. Hence, transacting business for the Government can or will include commission of several types of crimes in all descriptions. Thus, in one way, the Government in power becomes **the biggest criminal**! Is it true to think so?

What happens in the field of justice administration? Justice administration is time consuming, taxing and highly expensive. A patient who died of cancer recently told me once that he did not want any more any treatment; rather he preferred to die. Why? Cancer treatment is time-consuming, taxing and highly expensive. There exist uncertainties at the end of which the cancer patient always dies. In a similar way, there exist uncertainties in criminal justice administration and no one can say with certainty the end result. There may be a vague hope or a hope against hope until the case is finally disposed of. An affluent minister of the Government once said in a T.V. interview that anyone in his position would have committed suicide. For, the troubles he had to undergo were unthinkable and beyond human tolerance. According to him, criminal justice administration too is just like any other government business. Some die during the process while some survive 'dead'. Is it a crime to cause undue delay in administration of justice? If it is not a crime, then what it is? Let the criminologists answer the question.

GENDER JUSTICE ADMINISTRATION—A VOCABULARY

Sex— either the male or female division of a species, especially as differentiated with reference to the reproductive functions.

Male— a person bearing an *X* and *Y* chromosome pair in the cell nuclei and normally having a penis, scrotum, and testicles and developing hair on the face at adolescence; a boy or man.

Female— a person having two X chromosomes in the cell nuclei and normally having a vagina, a uterus and ovaris, and developing at puberty a relatively rounded body and enlarged breasts, and retaining a beardless face; a girl or a woman.

Eunuch— a castrtated man especially one formerly employed by oriental rulers as a *harem* guard or palace official (1350-1400)

Gender identiy— a person's inner sense of being male or female, usually developed during early childhood as a result of parental rearing practices and societal influences and strengthened during puberty by harmonal changes

Masculine— pertaining to or characteristic of a man or men.

Feminine— pertaining to or characteristic of a woman or women

Gender role— the public image of being male or female that a person presents to others

Gender specific— for characteristic of or limited to either male or female.

What is gender-justice? What is sex-justice? There is a view that the sex is purely biological and the gender is socio-cultural. Sex-wise, woman is biologically weaker than man; but socio-culturally man and woman can be theoretically equal, yet practically unequal. For there is something called the 'Gender Role' which is explained above. There is another thing called the 'Gender Status' and accordingly father, brother, husband and so on have their status; mother, sister, daughter-in-law have their status. There is yet another thing called 'Gender Specific' and its meaning is given above.

Taking everything together there is something called 'Sex-Justice' and not 'Gender-Justice'. Accordingly, no one shall be discriminated under law on the basis of *sex* alone. Justice should be done taking into account sex-inequality and sex-difference. As the women is weaker in many aspects, she should be given more protection and security by passing special laws and by enforcing them. Gender Justice—the expression is more applicable in other areas of justice administration like 'labour, wages, education, industry, etc.', and not in the field like criminal justice administration where a crime is a crime, no matter, whoever commits it.

INTERPRETED JUSTICE

Let us think that the Justice is objective. Nevertheless in reality?

Justice is Subjective?	Justice is just and fair?
Justice is objective?	Justice is equitable?
Justice is objectively relative?	Justice is nebulous?
Justice is cultural?	Justice is transparent?
Justice is socio-cultural?	Justice is accountable?
Justice is legal?	Justice is visible?
Justice is moral?	Justice is viable?
Justice is total?	Justice is eternal?
Justice is wholistic?	Justice is full?
Justice is equal?	Justice is impartial?

There is–

Criminal Justice	Communal Justice
Victim Justice	Political Justice
Crimino–Victim Justice	Popular Justice
Gender Justice	Democratic Justice
Social Justice	Jungle law Justice
Administrative Justice	Hard Justice
Domestic Justice	Correctional Justice
Natural Justice	Fake Justice
Gender Justice	Reformative Justice
Equal Justice	Sex Justice
Moral Justice	Environmental Justice
Juvenile Justice	Open Justice
Human Rights Justice	Earthly Justice
Accountable Justice	Cruel Justice
Cosmic Justice	Transparent Justice
Parochial Justice	Distributive Justice
Religious Justice	Animal Justice
Divine Justice	Caste Justice
Racial Justice	Linguistic Justice
	International Justice

Justice to be done to—

The aged and the infirm
To the socially handicapped
To the economically handicapped
To the mentally challenged
To the lunatic and those who suffer from mental disorders
To the suppressed community
To the workers and the working people
To the organized working class/disorganized working class.
To the sick, to the disabled
To the physically handicapped
To the tortured and the victimized
To the incorrigible and the uncontrolled
To those who need special care and protection
To the educationally backward
To the downtrodden and the repressed
To the women and girls

Thus, one wants justice in many areas. But, the reality is: Justice, Justice, everywhere; but no justice anywhere! This is the reason why there arise conflicts among the individuals, groups, communities, races, regions, states, countries throughout the world down the millennia.

There is—

Miscarriage of Justice	Marginal Justice
Less Justice	No Justice
Part Justice	Waste Justice
Wounded Justice	Perverted Justice
Injustice	Prejudiced Justice

What to do? How to go about? Let us think aloud. And the problem will continue until the consummation of the world! Crimes, justice and criminology are the same, no matter, they are written in India or in America. America (U.S.A) being a richer nation than India today, certainly they invest a lot of fund for criminological studies and researches. Criminology as an academic discipline is taught in universities both in America and in India. Nevertheless, one doubts seriously whether not the subject has received its due importance in India as it has in U.S.A. I am of the firm view that the criminology must be introduced in more universities at the graduate, post-graduate, M.Phil. and Ph.D. levels. There must be post-doctoral researches as the discipline is getting more and more importance in these days and the days to come. A crime centred world is certainly dangerous as people want to live in peace and not in war and not at all amidst crimes and criminals.

Bibliography

AUTHORITATIVE AND AUTHENTIC BOOKS AUTHORED BY DR. JAMES VADACKUMCHERY

Acquittals in Administration of Justice, Ph.D. Thesis, Kerala University, (mimeo), Thiruvananthapuram, 1983

Activism, Accountability and Justice (ISBN: 81-7341-4324-X), Indian Publishers' Distributors, Delhi, 2004.

Appachanum Ammayum: Inganeum oru Dampathikal (Malayalam), *(ISBN: 81-9097-300-2)* Paridhi Publications, Thiruvananthapuram, 2014.

Bankers' Safety: Methods and Techniques, (ISBN: 81-7022-937-5), (Second edition), Concept Publishing Company, Delhi, 2002.

Child Labour (Malayalam), State Literacy Mission, Thiruvananthapuram, 2000.

Crime and Society: Current Issues and Trends, (ISBN: 81-7648-024-X), A.P.H. Publishing Corporation, Delhi, 1999.

Crime, Law and Police Science, (ISBN: 81-7022-995-2), (Second edition), Concept Publishing Company, Delhi, 2003.

Crime, Police and Correction, (ISBN: 81-7024-939-2), A.P.H. Publishing Corporation, Delhi, 1998.

Criminology and Penology, Kairali Books International, Trivandrum, 1983.

Departmental Inquiries and Injustice, (ISBN: 81-7024-899-X), A.P.H. Publishing Corporation, Delhi, 1997.

Goodbye Police: Memoirs of a Criminologist, (ISBN: 81-7341-390-8), Indian Publishers' Distributors, Delhi, 2005.

Human Behaviour and Law Enforcement, (ISBN: 81-7024-688-1), Ashish Publishing House, Delhi, 1995.

Human Relations in Banking: How to get along Better with People?, Santha Publishing House, Cochin, 1988.

Human Rights and the Police in India, (ISBN: 81-7024-722-5), A.P.H. Publishing Corporation, Delhi, 1996.

Human Rights Friendly Police: A Myth or Reality?, (ISBN: 81-7648-150-5), A.P.H. Publishing Corporation, Delhi, 2000.

Human Values and Police Behaviour, Bureau of Police Research and Development, Ministry of Home Affairs, Government of India, 2000.

India's Supreme Court and Police: Consensus and Conflicts, (ISBN: 81-7341-301-0), Indian Publishers' Distributors, Delhi, 2003.

Indian Police 2001: What Went Wrong Here? (ISBN: 81-7024-967-8), A.P.H. Publishing Corporation, Delhi, 1998.

Indian Police and Equal Justice Under Law, (ISBN: 81-7648-066-5), A.P.H. Publishing Corporation, Delhi, 1999.

Indian Police and Miscarriage of Justice, (ISBN: 81-7024-792-6), A.P.H. Publishing Corporation, Delhi, 1997.

Indian Police and Nexus Crime, (ISBN: 81-7835-037-8), Kalpaz Publications, Delhi, 2002.

Judiciary and Juvenile Justice, (ISBN: 81-7341-389-4), Indian Publishers' Distributors, Delhi, 2005.

Juvenile Delinquency (Malayalam), State Literacy Mission, Thiruvananthapuram, 2000.

Management Thoughts for Justice Administration, (ISBN: 978-81-7268-233-0 (HB)] Logos Press, New Delhi, 2013.

Management Thoughts on Police Administration, (ISBN: 81-7024-914-7), A.P.H. Publishing Corporation, Delhi, 1998.

Misguiding Philosophies and Millennium Police, (ISBN: 81-7341-278-2), Indian Publishers' Distributors, Delhi, 2003.

National Police Commission: Issues for Rethinking, (ISBN: 81-7024-826-4), A.P.H. Publishing Corporation, Delhi, 1998.

Police and the Society, Kairali Books International, Trivandrum, 1985.

Police and Human Rights, (ed.), Kerala Police Officers' Association, Thiruvananthapuram, 1994.

Police and the People (Translation of the title: Public Relations at the Cutting Edge Level: Case- study materials by Prof. C.K. Muhammed Ummer), The State Institute of Language, Kerala, Thiruvananthapuram, 2000.

Police Criminology and Crimes, (ISBN: 81-7835-091-7) Kalpaz Publications, Delhi, 2002.

Police Enforcement Crimes and Injustice, (ISBN: 81-212-0471-5), Gyan Publishing House, Delhi, 2001.

Police Interrogation: DOs which the police do not DO, (ISBN: 81-7024-974-0), A.P.H. Publishing Corporation, Delhi, 1998.

Police Leadership: The Inside Story, (ISBN: 81-7648-120-3), A.P.H. Publishing Corporation, Delhi, 1999.

Police Morality, (ISBN: 81-7835-038-6), Kalpaz Publications, Delhi, 2001.

Police, Victim and Victim Justice, (ISBN: 81-7479-043-8), Kaveri Books, Delhi, 2001.

Police, Women and Gender Justice, (ISBN: 81-7648-137-8), A.P.H. Publishing Corporation, Delhi, 2000.

Policing the Largest Democracy: 50 Years and After, (ISBN: 81-7024-979-1), A.P.H. Publishing Corporation, Delhi, 1998.

Policing the Police: A Nation's Cry, (ISBN: 81-7479-060-81), Kaveri Books, Delhi, 2003.

Professional Police Witness Interviewing, (ISBN: 81-7648-061-4), A.P.H. Publishing Corporation, Delhi, 1999.

Public Relations at the Cutting Edge Level: Case-study Materials, National, Delhi, 1985.

Road Users' Guide (Malayalam), Assistant Motor Vehicle Inspectors' Association, Ernakulam, 1997.

Society, Police and Crimes: Tasks and Challenges, (ISBN: 81-7341-266-0), Indian Publishers' Distributors, Delhi, 2002.

Sociology of Policing India: 2000 and Beyond, (ISBN: 81-7341-279-0), Indian Publishers' Distributors, Delhi, 2003.

The Complete Reference Methodology of Research in Criminology Law Justice and Correction (Vol. I), (ISBN: 81-7341-414-8), Indian Publishers' Distributors, Delhi, 2007.

The Complete Reference Methodology of Research in Criminology Law Justice and Correction (Vol. II), (ISBN: 81-7341-448-0), Indian Publishers' Distributors, Delhi, 2010.

The Complete Reference Methodology of Research in Criminology Law Justice and Correction (Vol. III), (ISBN: 81-7341-449-7), Indian Publishers' Distributors, Delhi, 2010.

The Justice Less Administered, (ISBN: 81-7341-380-0), Indian Publishers' Distributors, Delhi, 2005.

The Police and Delinquency in India, (ISBN: 81-7024-725-X), A.P.H. Publishing Corporation, Delhi, 1996.

The Police, The Accused and Criminal Injustice, (ISBN: 91-7024-806-X), A.P.H. Publishing Corporation, Delhi, 1997.

The Police, the Court and Injustice, (ISBN: 81-7024-806-X), A.P.H. Publishing Corporation, Delhi, 1997.

The Police, The People and Criminal Justice, (ISBN: 81-7024-862-9), A.P.H. Publishing Corporation, Delhi, 1999.

The Unseen Phases of Crimes, (Malayalam), *(ISBN: 81-909360-1-8)*, H&C Publishing House, Trissur, 2009.

Index

mind. Such people do not have peace of mind. As a pious seminarian, I had closely watched dying people suffering from the fear of death. It may be a phobic reaction or irrational fear, yet people have it. Praying to God for pardoning sins, craving for mercy for absolving of the wrongs committed, confession to priests, fear of hell, purgatory, rebirth, saying excuse me, pardon me—there are many such things and practices in daily life and all of them indicate the existence of guilt feelings. In the development of penology and prison system, an objective of punishment was said to be atonement, expiation in prisons. The presumption was that the crime-doers had a conscience and consequent feeling of guilt.

Conscience in an Upright Way: How?

When an infant is born, the neonate has a mind where nothing is written. It is a *Tabula Rasa* which means a mind not yet affected by any experiences, impressions etc. It is a plain blackboard where nothing is written. No doubt, a blackboard is for writing or drawing on it with pencil or chalk. Here, everything is written or drawn by many and the most important person at the birth and immediately after the birth of an infant is the mother. The home is the first conscience formation centre and the mother is the first teacher there.

Conscience formation means the act or process of forming the conscience and there is a formative period for every new born. Formative period means a period during which the conscience is given a form or shape. It is a period of moulding human conscience and the conscience must be formed in an upright way in the right direction.

Yes, the mother writes, the father writes—the family writes—the neighbourhood writes—the community writes—the school writes—the society writes—the media writes—the literature writes—the friends write—the religion writes and thus those who form the conscience of a developing child are many and various. Broken homes, lack of love, alcohol at home, lack of intelligent parental control, easy money making at home, defective moral and family conditioning at home, slum life, life in affluence, obscene literature, family disorganization, divorce and separation, desertion, orphanhood, overcrowding at home, quarrels at home,